Air Warfare

Air Warfare

✦ FROM WORLD WAR I TO THE PRESENT DAY ✦

GENERAL EDITOR: THOMAS NEWDICK

THUNDER BAY
P · R · E · S · S

San Diego, California

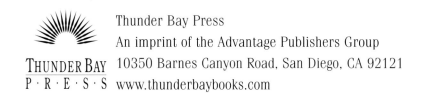

Thunder Bay Press
An imprint of the Advantage Publishers Group
10350 Barnes Canyon Road, San Diego, CA 92121
www.thunderbaybooks.com

Amber Books Ltd
Bradley's Close
74–77 White Lion Street
London N1 9PF, UK
www.amberbooks.co.uk

Library of Congress Cataloging-in-Publication Data

Air warfare : from World War I to the present day / general editor, Thomas Newdick.
     p. cm.
 Includes index.
 ISBN-13: 978-1-59223-825-5
 ISBN-10: 1-59223-825-4
 1. Air warfare--History. I. Newdick, Thomas.
 UG625.A57 2008
 358.4--dc22
                        2008011141

Printed in Thailand

1 2 3 4 5 12 11 10 09 08

Project Editor: James Bennett
Design: Brian Rust
Picture Research: Terry Forshaw

Contents

Introduction   6

Early Air Wars   8
1794–1939

World War II: War in the West   38
1939–1945

World War II: Africa and the Mediterranean   70
1940–1945

World War II: The Eastern Front   90
1939–1945

World War II: The Pacific   112
1941–1945

World War II: Strategic Bombing   144
1939–1945

Air Wars in the Insurgency Era   164
1948–1988

The Air War in Vietnam   200
1964–1973

Middle East Wars   232
1945–1973

The Falklands and Lebanon   252
1982

Desert Storm and the Balkans   268
1990–1999

The Global War on Terror   306
2001–Present

Index   316

Introduction

Since the beginning of the industrial age, it has been a truism that warfare has driven technological progress. But nowhere, perhaps, has the pace of technical change been as rapid as in the field of air warfare.

SUCCESSIVE DEVELOPMENTS

In the space of less than a century, successive conflicts have witnessed the first aviators take to the air over the trenches of the Western Front in their flimsy constructions, while today, network-centric warfare and GPS-guided weaponry are among the buzzwords in the Global War on Terror, in which multi-million-dollar aircraft play arguably a more important role than ever before. On the way, aircraft have been a key feature of another truly global conflict – World War II – in which many concepts of aerial warfare finally reached maturity, and the aircraft's lingering critics were forever silenced.

At the outbreak of World War I in 1914, aircraft were yet to carry armament; by 1939, the aerial fighting machine had evolved to include concepts such as the monoplane wing, stressed-metal construction, heavy-caliber weaponry, retractable undercarriage and enclosed cockpits. By the end of that war, the value of the combat aircraft had been put beyond all doubt, not just as a platform for carrying guns or bombs, but as a transport, reconnaissance or maritime asset. Indeed, the aircraft had proven itself not just capable of turning the course of a battle, but as a war-winner in its own right. This latter fact was demonstrated on an unparalleled scale with the nuclear destruction of the

The naval war in the Pacific demonstrated just how far air power had come, as bomb- and torpedo-carrying aircraft flying from carrier decks rendered the big-gun battleships of the previous era obsolescent.

Japanese cities of Hiroshima and Nagasaki in 1945.

HIGH STAKES

The end of World War II had brought with it the nuclear age and, at the same time, initiated the Cold War that would define the latter half of the 20th century. By now, however, the global stakes were so high – and the capacity for nuclear destruction so enormous – that the Cold War itself would see warplanes put to use not in direct confrontations between the

superpowers of the US and USSR (with a few exceptions), but in smaller-scale conflicts. These colonial confrontations, flashpoints and 'bush wars' demanded a whole new method of waging war from the air, but the pace of technological advance never slowed.

After the Korean War saw jet combat come of age, Vietnam would demonstrate once and for all the value of the helicopter and the emerging potential of guided weaponry. On the other hand, the fighting in Southeast Asia brought to light the limitations of technology, with air-to-air missiles (AAMs), for instance, falling well short of expectations. Nevertheless, the value of this same technology would begin to be realized in various conflicts that afflicted the Middle East during the Cold War period, in which the superpowers tested their own concepts in a crucible of 'hot war'.

TECHNOLOGICAL ADVANCES

At the start of the 1980s, air wars fought over the Falklands and Lebanon may not have led to any great shift in the strategic – or even local – balance, but they would see long hoped-for technological advances such as 'fire and forget' AAMs and unmanned aerial vehicles finally prove themselves. After the end of the Cold War in the early 1990s, defence budgets have shrunk, while the cost of technology has skyrocketed, but successive conflicts in Iraq and Afghanistan have only confirmed that air power – whether manned or unmanned – will continue to play a vital role throughout the 21st century.

Thomas Newdick
Berlin, March 2008

The final years of the superpower stand-off saw unprecedented technological development, and yet these examples of the final generation of Cold War warplanes – a US F-16 and Russian Su-27 – have not met in battle – at least not yet. Instead, the end of the Cold War heralded a new age of conflict: the Global War on Terror.

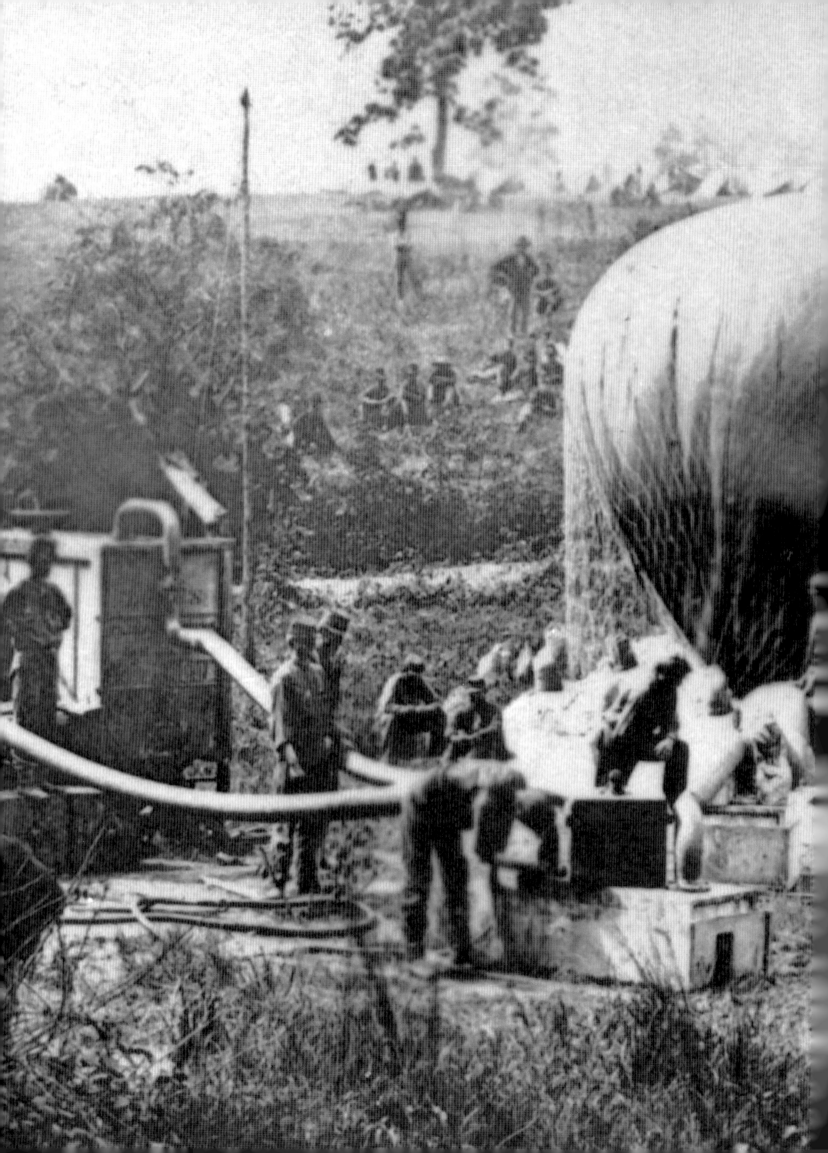

Early Air Wars
1794–1939

The world's first flying machines were the tethered kites used in ancient China where, it is believed, the manned kite saw limited use in warfare for the gathering of intelligence on enemy forces' dispositions, and possibly also as an aerial communications relay facility. A primitive form of hot-air balloon was also developed in China, in the second and third centuries of the current era, and early examples were also used for military communications. In the Western world, the first flight was made by the Montgolfier brothers' hot-air balloon in 1783, but this primitive type was soon overtaken by hydrogen-filled balloons. These early balloons also saw limited military use, the first known example being a French balloon for tethered observation in the Battle of Fleurus (1794).

During the US Civil War (1861-65), the balloon was operated by both the Union and Confederate sides for sometimes effective battlefield observation. The first US balloon intended for use by the military, named *Union*, was prepared for action by the Union side in August 1861. The Confederacy had more significant problems, not least because the blockade of Confederate ports prevented the arrival of balloon silk. The Confederacy therefore used dress-making silk for the envelopes of its balloons, and even then there was often no gas with which to fill them. Both sides had abandoned the use of balloons by 1863.

The balloon saw limited use for observation in the US Civil War, notably by the Union side, but its early potential fell foul of political in-fighting. Seen here is a phase in the process of inflating a balloon of the Union forces.

Eugene Ely makes history on 14 November 1910 as his Curtiss biplane departs from a ramp over the bow of the light cruiser USS *Birmingham*. Still just short of flying speed, the aircraft would shortly accelerate out of its downward trajectory to reach the nearby shore.

The first powered heavier-than-air flight was achieved by the Wright brothers in the US during December 1903, but controlled and sustained flight started to become accepted as a reality only from a time in 1908.

Nevertheless, while important steps in the creation of effective military aviation were made in the first decade of the 20th century, it was in the period between 1910 and the outbreak of World War I in August 1914 that the practical origins of military aviation can be found.

On 7 January 1911 the first live bombing trials were flown at San Francisco, California, by Lieutenant Myron S. Crissy and Philip O. Parmalee in a Wright Type B biplane. On 18 January Eugene B. Ely, in a Curtiss Golden Flyer, landed on a platform specially built over the stern of the cruiser USS *Pennsylvania* at anchor in San Francisco Bay. On 1 February Glenn H. Curtiss made two successful flights from the water at San Diego, with a single main float in place of the triple floats used in earlier tests.

On 1 April 1911 the British formalized their move into military aviation with the establishment of the Air Battalion of the Royal Engineers with two companies, namely Nos 1 (Airship, Balloon and Kite) and No. 2 (Aeroplanes). On 1 July Curtiss demonstrated the A-1 floatplane, the first aircraft built for the US Navy, operating from Lake Keuka.

NORTH AMERICAN PIONEERS

The aircraft's possible role in war was presaged on several occasions during 1910. On 19 January Lieutenant Paul Beck dropped sandbags, representing bombs, over Los Angeles, California, from an aircraft flown by Louis Paulhan, and on 30 June Glenn H. Curtiss dropped dummy bombs from a height of 15m (50ft) onto a buoyed area representing the shape of a battleship on Lake Keuka, New York. On 27 August James McCurdy, a Canadian, sent and received messages from a Curtiss Golden Flyer biplane via a wireless set at Sheepshead Bay, so starting the era of aerial wireless telegraphy. On 14 November Eugene B. Ely became the first man to lift off from a ship, his Curtiss Golden Flyer taking-off from a platform built over the bow of the cruiser USS *Birmingham*. Weeks later, Ely would effect the first successful aircraft landing on a warship.

After it had declared war on Turkey on 20 September 1911, Italy sent an expeditionary force to Tripolitania, where on 22 October Capitano Carlo Piazza carried out a reconnaissance of Turkish positions between Tripoli and Azizzia in a Blériot Type XI. This flight marked the first use of a heavier-than-air craft in war. In the course of North African operations, on 10 March 1912 two Italian airships completed a reconnaissance of Turkish positions, their crews dropping several grenades without inflicting any damage.

On 13 April 1912 the British created the Royal Flying Corps (RFC), and this came into existence one month later when the Air Battalion and the Naval Air Organisation became its Military and Naval Wings. During June the German navy created a naval airship division. The first US trials with an aircraft carrying a machine-gun began on 2 June 1912. The machine was a Wright Type B flown by Lieutenant Thomas de Witt Milling, and the Lewis light machine-gun was operated by Captain Charles de Forest Chandler.

In the course of the First Balkan War (1912-13), the Bulgarian air arm bombed Turkish positions at Adrianople. One of the first air-

> On or about 30 November 1913, the world's first air combat took place when Phillip Rader and Dean I. Lamb, flying in support of rival Mexican factions, fired revolvers at each other without achieving any hits.

dropped bombs was developed by Captain Simeon Petrov of the Bulgarian air arm during this time, and was widely used during this war, including the first night bombing on 7 November 1912.

THE AEROPLANE GOES TO WAR
On 10 May 1913 Didier Masson, a supporter of the revolutionary General Alvarado Obregon, became the first airman to drop bombs on a warship when he attacked Mexican government gunships. On or about 30 November the world's first air combat took place when Phillip Rader and Dean I. Lamb, each flying in support of a rival Mexican faction, fired their revolvers at each other without achieving any hits. On 20 April a US Navy detachment left Pensacola on board the USS *Birmingham* to join elements of the US

Atlantic Fleet operating off Tampico during the Mexican crisis, another detachment from Pensacola joining the USS *Mississippi* before she too steamed for Mexican waters to assist in military operations at Veracruz. An AB-3 flying-boat and an AH-3 floatplane were later used to photograph the harbour at Veracruz and search for mines. On 2 May the first mission in direct support of ground troops was flown as men of the US Marine Corps near Tejar reported that they were under attack and requested the aviation unit at Veracruz to report the position of their attackers.

On 1 July 1914 the Naval Wing of the Royal Flying Corps was re-created as the Royal Naval Air Service (RNAS) under Admiralty control, and on 28 July a Short seaplane air-dropped a 356mm (14in) torpedo weighing 367kg (810lb).

BLÉRIOT XI MONOPLANE

Type: monoplane

Powerplant: 16.5–19kW (22–25hp) Anzani three-cylinder fan-type

Maximum speed: 75.6km/h (47mph)

Weights: 230kg (507lb)

Dimensions: span 7.79m (25ft 7in)
length 7.62m (25ft)
height 2.69m (8ft 10in)
wing area 14m² (150sq ft)

293

The Vickers F.B.5, nicknamed the 'Gunbus', was one of the world's first true warplanes. Designed before World War I, it had a 7.7mm (0.303in) Lewis machine-gun on a trainable mounting in the front of the central nacelle, ahead of the pilot's cockpit and pusher engine.

On the outbreak of World War I in August 1914, the importance of military aviation to the various combatants can be gauged by the numbers of aircraft each fielded. Germany had 246, Russia 244, France 138 and the UK 113. Right from the start of the war, the theatres in which aircraft found their primary importance were the Western and Eastern Fronts. The initial German offensive through Belgium and into northeastern France was supported by less than 12 *Feldfliegerabteilungen* (field aviation detachments) equipped with

about 60 Taube monoplanes, and Albatros and Aviatik biplanes. On the opposing side were 21 French *escadrilles* (squadrons) of Blériot, Breguet, Caudron, Deperdussin, Farman, Nieuport and Voisin aircraft, and the British created a force of 63 aircraft (Avro Type 504, Blériot Type XI, Farman, Royal Aircraft Factory B.E.2 and RAF B.E.8 aircraft) in the hands of four squadrons which moved to France during August.

The units in France were scattered over a large operational area, and opposing aircraft only occasionally encountered each other. Even so, the success of earlier tactical reconnaissance efforts soon convinced each side that it would be useful to deny such a capability to the enemy, and as a result rifles, carbines, shotguns, pistols and even

extemporized weapons such as grappling hooks on the ends of ropes soon made their inadequate appearance. The best weapon would be the machine-gun, but this was heavy, unwieldy and difficult to install in a tactically useful manner, especially as the observer in all two-seat aircraft was at the time installed in the front seat and therefore surrounded by struts and bracing wires. Another difficulty was the propeller of all tractor aircraft, for this rotated directly ahead of the optimum position for any fixed gun on the upper side of the fuselage, ahead of the pilot who would have to aim and fire the weapon in any single-seater.

What was needed was the means to synchronize the firing of the machine-gun with the rotation of the propeller

What was needed was the means to synchronize the firing of the machine-gun with the rotation of the propeller so that there was no blade ahead of the muzzle as the gun was fired.

so that there was no blade ahead of the muzzle as the gun was fired. There were no such synchronizing equipments in service, although several had been trialled before the war. Thus the first aircraft specifically designed to carry a forward-firing machine-gun was the Vickers F.B.5 'Gunbus', a 'pusher' design and as such fitted with an engine and propeller behind the pilot and observer in a central nacelle. This layout demanded that the tail unit was

carried by booms converging from the trailing edges of the upper and lower wings outboard of the disc swept by the propeller. This added drag, so decreasing performance, and also presented difficulties in rigging and maintaining the aircraft.

FRENCH BREAKTHROUGH
The French had been experimenting with the synchronization of a forward-firing gun since 1913, using steel plates on the backs of the propeller blades to

deflect any bullets that might strike them. However, the first German aircraft to be shot down by a machine-gun in an opposing aircraft was an Aviatik two-seater reconnaissance machine shot down on 5 October 1914 by Sergeant Frantz and Caporal Quénault, the latter simply resting his Hotchkiss machine-gun on the side of his cockpit in a Voisin biplane and firing a burst into the German aircraft. It was not until Lieutenant Roland Garros, in a Morane-Saulnier Type L parasol-wing monoplane, destroyed three German aircraft in April 1915 that the era of the forward-firing gun began in earnest. Garros had been involved in the problematical pre-war synchronizer gear experiments, and was now flying an aircraft not fitted with such gear but retaining deflectors. This allowed the rapid evolution of the basic air fighting tactic of flying directly at the opposing aircraft and aiming the

The Breguet company of France produced many types of warplane in the first stages of World War I, this being one of the several Bre.4 variants which were used as bombers and general-purpose aircraft.

fixed forward-firing gun along the flight path. After achieving five aerial victories, and thereby becoming the world's first 'ace', Garros was forced down behind German lines on 19 April, and taken prisoner.

The Germans had already come to the sensible conclusion that deflector plates were only an interim solution, and that the real solution to the problems posed by a fixed forward-firing gun lay with an effective synchronizer arrangement. Anthony

Early fixed forward-firing armament was based on a machine-gun (here an 8mm/0.315in Hotchkiss weapon) firing through the disc of a propeller whose blades were protected in their rear edges by wedge-shaped steel deflectors.

Fokker, a Dutch pioneer now building aircraft for the Germans, entrusted the task to his company's engineers, who quickly designed an effective mechanical system. This was installed in a development of the Fokker M.5k monoplane to create the E.I, which thus became the world's first effective fighter with a mechanism that synchronized the firing of the gun with the position of the propeller blades. The E.I entered service in June 1915, and aircraft of this type were then delivered in small numbers for allocation to reconnaissance units, with the object of providing the vulnerable two-seaters with a measure of protection as they went about their increasingly important tactical tasks.

The E.I was soon complemented and then replaced by improved *Eindecker* (monoplane) fighters from Fokker and a few other manufacturers.

The British possessed no gun interrupter gear, so it had to make do with a pusher type, the single-seat Airco D.H.2, with which No. 24 Squadron was equipped as the first RFC 'fighter' unit. No. 24 Squadron reached France early in 1916 and soon proved its worth with aircraft carrying a fixed forward-firing Lewis gun. The French were technically and tactically more advanced at this time, and by the end of 1915 had started to introduce aircraft such as Morane-Saulnier Type LA and Nieuport Nie.10 two-seaters, and then the classic Nie.11 'Bébé' and

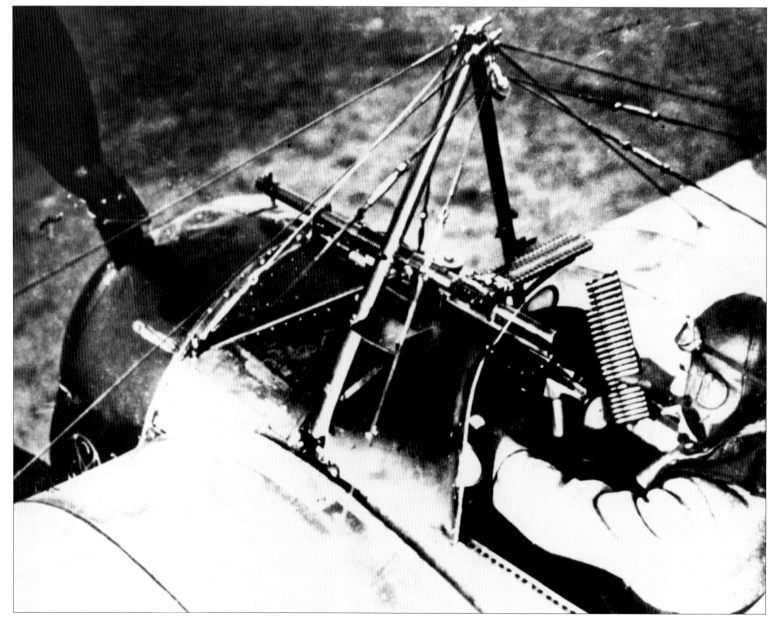

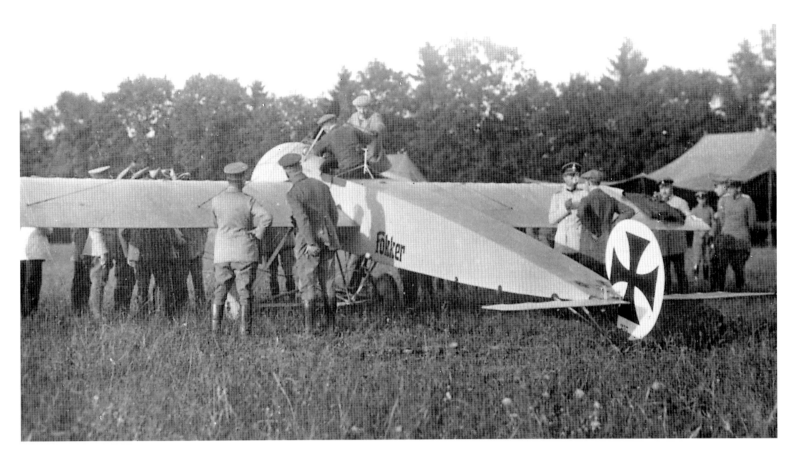

following Nie.17 single-seater fighting 'scouts', as they were called at the time. These were armed with a fixed forward-firing gun above the parasol wing of the Morane-Saulnier or the upper wing of the Nieuport sesquiplanes to fire over the propeller disc, and started the process of eroding the Germans' air superiority.

FIRST FIGHTING SCOUT

Even as the D.H.2 pilots of the RFC were developing and disseminating the skills of the newborn art of air combat, the British were perfecting their first effective synchronizer equipment as the Sopwith-Kauper interrupter gear, and the Admiralty contracted for the first true British fighting scout, the Sopwith Pup, for the RNAS's fighter squadrons. The Pup was delivered from the late summer of 1916, and began to build its reputation as a great fighter from September of that year in combat over the coasts of northeastern France and Belgium. Homogeneous equipment was still not wholly accepted, and

among the squadrons of the RNAS the celebrated No. 8 Squadron was formed during October 1916 with a mix of Pup and Nieuport single-seaters and Sopwith 1½-Strutter two-seaters. In the unit's first two months of service, No. 8 Squadron's pilots destroyed 20 German aircraft. All three of the aircraft were thought excellent in their different ways, the 1½-Strutter being the world's first genuinely effective multi-role warplane, but it was the Pup which received the greatest plaudits for its

In Germany the Fokker company took the air armament process one step further with the *Eindecker* monoplane armed with the world's first true synchronizing system to ensure that the gun did not fire when there was a blade in the gun's line of fire.

combination of good performance, considerable agility and perfect handling characteristics.

Though somewhat surprised by the speed with which the Allies had been able to respond to and then overcome the *Eindecker* fighters by the late spring

THE 'FOKKER SCOURGE'

It was inevitable that more far-sighted German pilots, such as Oswald Boelcke and Max Immelmann (the 'Eagle of Lille'), would soon see that the fighter should not be reserved for defensive escort, but employed offensively to take the air war to the Allies. With Boelcke in the lead, the Germans swiftly created offensive fighter tactics, often using cloud to stalk their unwitting opponents before closing and delivering a decisive burst from a blind spot, either from below or out of the sun. This was the start of the period of German air superiority over the Western Front known as the 'Fokker scourge', a phase of the air war in which the Allies could offer no real challenge.

of 1916, the Germans responded quickly with a new generation of fighter biplanes such as the Albatros D.I and D.II, Fokker D.I and Halberstadt D.II. As a result of their biplane configurations, these were sturdier than the somewhat flimsy E-type monoplanes, and could therefore be thrown around the sky more aggressively. With greater power from their water-cooled six-cylinder inline engines, they also offered better all-round performance than the E-type fighters with their air-cooled rotary engines. Most important of the series, however, were the two Albatros fighters, which introduced a fixed forward-firing armament doubled to two machine-guns.

Another celebrated fighter that made its debut before the end of 1916 marked another approach to the task of creating a fighting scout, combining good climb as a result of its low wing

The first true British fighter was the Airco D.H.2 designed by Geoffrey de Havilland. This was a neat and agile type with good performance and provision for one gun in the nose. Lack of a synchronizer gear meant that de Havilland adopted a pusher layout for his warplane.

loading and a high level of agility as a result of its compact overall dimensions. This was the Sopwith Triplane, which was a simple evolution of the Pup, and therefore armed with only one gun, with the required wing area packed into three wings of small overall dimensions to ensure that agility was not adversely affected. The lightly loaded Triplane was preferred by the RNAS, while the RFC preferred the French solution to the next-generation fighter, namely the SPAD S.VII. This also retained the now obsolescent armament of just one machine-gun, but was a comparative brute of a machine with 50 per cent more power from its Hispano-Suiza

'BLOODY APRIL'

Desperate to attain the land advantage over the Germans, the Allies launched a series of major offensives under the cover of large numbers of obsolescent two-seaters flown increasingly by novice pilots rushed to the front to replace more experienced men lost with their ineffective two-seaters. The Sopwith Triplane was the Allied fighter that proved most successful in challenging the German air superiority of spring 1917, the period known to the British as 'Bloody April'. The Triplane was flown only by naval squadrons, but so dire was this period for the British in the air that naval units were subordinated to the RFC.

water-cooled V-8 engine than was available from the Triplane's air-cooled rotary engine. The S.VII was thus very strongly built and possessed good outright performance, but lacked the manoeuvrability of the Sopwith Triplane.

The German air arm, the Luftstreitkräfte, had been radically reorganized since the end of 1915, starting with the creation of the *Fliegerabteilungen-Infanterie* (FlAbt-Inf, or infantry contact patrol detachments) to provide their ground forces with tactical support. These units had quickly proved their worth but suffered heavy losses. The FlAbt-Inf units clearly needed their own air support, and thought was therefore given during the summer of 1916 to the creation of a dedicated fighter arm. Largely the conceptual child of Oswald Boelcke, who was killed on 28 October 1916 after scoring 40 aerial victories, a fighter arm of 37 *Jagdstaffeln* (*Jasta*, or fighter

The Sopwith Pup was a viceless and very popular fighter with beautifully harmonized controls. The type was also used in early experiments in landing on the platform of a moving ship. Here Squadron Commander E.H. Dunning prepares to land on HMS *Furious* with the aid of clutching hands.

squadrons) was built by April 1917. Most of the new units flew the excellent Albatros D.III, an improved version of the D.II with a sesquiplane rather than biplane wing cellule.

RICHTHOFEN'S CIRCUS
Despite escort by new fighters including the Sopwith Triplane single-seater and Bristol F.2B Fighter two-seater, which were available only in small numbers, the number and rate

> The SPAD S.VII was very strongly built and possessed good outright performance, but lacked the manoeuvrability of the Triplane.

Possibly the best two-seat fighter of World War I was the Bristol F.2B Fighter, which was fast, sturdy and agile, and had a trainable machine-gun in the rear cockpit to augment the fixed forward-firing gun in the front of the fuselage.

of Allied losses rose appallingly as the German fighter arm grew in capability under the leadership of new fighter leaders such as the redoubtable *Rittmeister* Manfred Freiherr von Richthofen, eventually the leading ace of World War I with 80 victories.

During 'Bloody April' the RFC lost no fewer than 316 pilots and observer/gunners. New aircraft could be supplied quickly, but the training of airmen was slow and inadequate, and men with only a few hours of flying experience were rushed to France in the dismal hope of plugging the manpower gap, only themselves to become ready victims.

Yet fine fighting aircraft, exemplified by the RAF S.E.5, Sopwith Camel, SPAD S.VII and S.XIII, and F.2B Fighter were either entering or were on the verge of entering full service. Thus from the late spring of 1917 the pendulum of the air war would swing back in the other direction as the re-equipped fighter squadrons of the RFC, RNAS and French Aviation Militaire regained an air superiority which they were not to lose for the rest of the war.

GERMAN 'FIRE BRIGADES'
The success of the dedicated *Jasta* was so great that the Germans came to the conclusion that while they might not be able to compete with the Allies in terms of the number of aircraft and units they could deploy, they could create mobile 'fire brigade' units of major aces for deployment to important sectors of the front as and when required to provide local air superiority. This was the origin of the *Jagdgeschwader* (fighter wing), known to the Allies as a 'flying circus' and comprising some 30 or more fighters.

The first of these, formed on 24 June 1917 under the command of

> The US had joined the war on the Allied side in April 1917, but was at the time very poorly equipped to fight a modern war as her armed forces were small and her weapons both few and technically obsolete.

von Richthofen, was Jagdgeschwader 1 and comprising Jastas 4, 6, 10 and 11. By the end of 1917 it was clear that air fighting had changed permanently.

The US had joined the war on the Allied side in April 1917, but was at the time very poorly equipped to fight a modern war as her armed forces were small and her weapons both few and technically obsolete. This was especially true of the US Army's air

arm, and the US 1st Aero Squadron did not reach France until September 1917. The 94th and 95th Aero Squadrons did not arrive until a time early in 1918 and first saw combat only on 14 April. For lack of adequate US warplanes, the air units of the American Expeditionary Force in France flew mainly British and French aircraft. Even so, the Germans appreciated that it was only a matter

of time before large and well-equipped American land and air formations became available for service in France, effectively destroying the military balance that had lasted from 1915 and which had been epitomized by the stalemate of trench warfare. Germany therefore decided on a last-ditch series of five offensives to gain victory while this was still possible. The first of these swept west on 21 March 1918, by which time the German fighter squadrons were operating a mix of the obsolete

A fighter flown by many of the great German aces of World War I was the Albatros D.V, which could be produced in large numbers and was armed with two fixed forward-firing machine-guns, but which lacked the outright performance of later Allied fighters and was structurally suspect in its lower wing.

S.E.5A

Type: single-seat fighter

Powerplant: one 149kW (200hp) Hispano-Suiza
V-8 piston engine

Maximum speed: 218km/h (135mph)

Service ceiling: 6705m (22,000ft)

Weights: empty 635kg (1397lb); maximum take-off
weight 887kg (1951lb)

Armament: one forward-firing synchronized
7.7mm (.303cal.) Vickers machine-gun and one
7.7mm (.303cal.) Lewis gun over centre section of
upper wing, plus up to four 18.6kg (40lb) bombs

Dimensions: span   8.12m (26ft 7in)
            length   6.38m (20ft 11in)
            height   2.90m (9ft 6in)
            wing area 22.67m² (244sq ft)

Fokker Dr.I triplane inspired directly by the Sopwith Triplane, the well proven but now obsolescent Albatros D.V biplanes, and the new Siemens-Schuckert D.III biplane.

Covered by these, the primary German two-seaters for the reconnaissance and artillery observation roles were the AEG C.IV, Albatros C.X and C.XII, DFW C.V, LVG C.V and C.VI, and Rumpler C.V and C.II, while more specialized two-seaters for the close support and attack roles included the Halberstadt CL.II and CL.IV, and the Hannover CL.II and CL.III. A new departure was represented by the Junkers J.I, which was an armoured biplane for the close support and attack roles, and as such the precursor of the dedicated attack aircraft which were so important in World War II.

By this time, though, the British and French had the aircraft, the

Seen in front of a Fokker Dr.I triplane are Germany's greatest ace of World War I, *Rittmeister* Manfred Freiherr von Richthofen (right) who achieved 80 'kills', and his brother Lothar, who was killed after achieving 40 victories in a remarkably short time and might otherwise have rivalled or excelled his brother.

> By spring 1918, the British and French had the aircraft, the numbers and the training to maintain their air superiority.

numbers and the training to maintain their air superiority, and not even the late appearance of great fighters such as the Fokker D.VII could alter this fact, especially as the Sopwith Snipe was just as good.

By the time the German offensives had been checked, the British were pouring new fighter squadrons into France at the rate of one per week with Camel, F.2B and S.E.5a aircraft. With the German offensives halted by 17 June 1918, the Allies now went over to the offensive, the British launching the decisive effort on 8 August. The ground forces operated under an umbrella of air power, which now included seven squadrons of Camel fighters tasked with the 'trench fighting' or close support role.

The Germans had lost many of their great aces during the period of the five 'final offensives', and their capabilities were now further eroded by the loss of more invaluable airmen

at a time when replacements were only poorly trained, and flying became ever more difficult for lack of essentials such as fuel.

STRATEGIC BOMBING CAMPAIGN
At the start of World War I, the only nation that possessed any capability to project strategic air power by means of heavier-than-air bombers was Russia, which had a small number of Sikorsky Ilya Muromets four-engined bombers.

The first mission flown by these limited but nonetheless pioneering 'heavy' bombers was on 15 February 1915. The aircraft operated with impunity but to little real effect, largely at night, and it is believed that only 73 Ilya Muromets bombers had been built before the Bolshevik revolution of November 1917 ended production.

German bombing capability at the beginning of the war was vested solely in the airships of the German army and navy, but the German leadership would not commit these behemoths to long-range attacks for fear that the Allied powers would gain a propaganda victory from German attacks which would inevitably kill civilians. Thus the airships of the Germany navy – which had a force that was both larger and more modern in its equipment than the German army – logged many hours in the air and miles over the sea and land, the latter mainly of England, as they tried to find and attack purely military targets. It was an impossible task, and given the almost non-existent bombing accuracy of the day, the airship attacks inevitably caused casualties among the civilian population.

A conceptual descendant of the Pup, the Sopwith Camel was the most successful fighter of World War I. This fighter was armed with two or sometimes three fixed forward-firing machine-guns, had good performance and agility, but was considered tricky to fly.

> After Allied aircraft had bombed Karlsruhe in western Germany, Kaiser Wilhelm II finally authorized the bombing of London.

TARGET: LONDON

By mid-1915 the German army had joined the offensive. After Allied aircraft had bombed Karlsruhe in western Germany, Kaiser Wilhelm II finally authorized the bombing of London. The airships flew many missions over the UK, sometimes carrying what were for the time very large bombs. The British defence was essentially incapable of intercepting and destroying the raiders, and it was only during the night of 2/3 September 1916 that the first airship was brought down over the UK by an aircraft. Although the airship continued to be supported, especially by the German navy, almost until the end of the war, the use of these

capable but highly flammable machines was cut back strongly and finally halted later in 1918 as British defences had been much strengthened in response to raids.

The bombing role had been pioneered in operational terms during 1914-15 by 'B' and 'C' category unarmed and armed two-seaters of the so-called *Brieftauben-Abteilungen* (carrier pigeon detachments) and *Kampfstaffeln* (battle squadrons), the latter flying the AEG G.I. These then gave way to the *Kampfgeschwadern* (battle wings) each with some 36 air-craft: KG 1 was located initially on the Eastern Front and later on the Western Front, KG 3 at Ghent for raids on England, and KG 4 on the

Impressed by the good climb rate and agility of the Sopwith Triplane, the Germans produced a number of triplane fighters. The most successful of these was the Fokker Dr.I, but this was obsolescent even as it entered service and was employed mainly for defensive fighter tasks.

Italian Front. The plan to deploy bomber aircraft against targets in southern England had been proposed during October 1914 at a time when a German army advance along a considerable portion of the French north coast seemed likely. In the event the advance along the coast ended at Ostend in Belgium as the German armies swung south towards Paris, and the initial bomber effort involved only the small single-engined aircraft of the Brieftauben-Abteilung Ostende, which could barely reach Dover.

It was not until 1916 that the more formidable twin-engined Gotha and Friedrichshafen bombers reached service, but short-term demands forced their initial commitment to the Verdun and Somme campaigns. In the circumstances, therefore, it was the spring of 1917 before KG 3 was finally in the position to bomb English targets from its Belgian bases. KG 3 carried out a daylight raid on 25 May with 23 Gotha G.IV bombers. Weather conditions prevented the bombers from approaching London, so they roamed over Kent and dropped bombs on targets such as Gravesend, Maidstone, Ashford and Folkestone. The last was the worst affected, six bombs killing 95 persons and injuring 260 more.

There were other raids in the period up to the end of August. The most notable of these was that of 13 June, when some 20 G.IV bombers attacked the East End and City of London, killing 162 persons

GERMAN BOMBER DEVELOPMENT

With the potential of the large bomber revealed by Russian efforts on the Eastern Front during the early months of the war, a number of German designs started to make their appearance in 1915, beginning with the Siemens Forssmann and then proceeding via a series of Zeppelin-Staaken aircraft. Originally known as *Kampfflugzeuge* (battle aircraft), these were later categorized as 'G' type twin-engined aircraft from the Gotha stable, starting with the G.II, of which a small number was built in 1916.

FOKKER D.VII

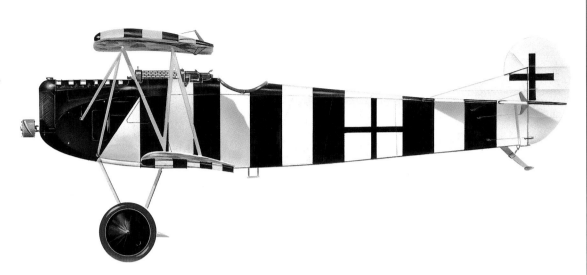

Type: monoplane

Powerplant: one 138kW (185hp) B.M.W III six-cylinder inline piston

Maximum speed: 200km/h (124mph)

Endurance: 1 hour 30 minutes

Weights: empty 735kg (1620lb); maximum take-off weight 880kg (1940lb)

Armament: two fixed forward-firing 7.92mm LMG 08/15 machine guns

Dimensions: span 6.95m (22ft 9in)
length 8.9m (29ft 2in)
height 2.75m (9ft)
wing area 20.5m² (221sq ft)

> On the German side, it had become clear that the rising rate of losses was not being matched by any significant rise in the damage being inflicted on England.

(including 16 children in a school) and injuring 432 more. The shock to the British public was enormous, the more so as the defences were clearly incapable of deterring or destroying the attackers. The outcry led to the establishment of a commission to make recommendations about the way in which the defences could be improved. The commission's most ambitious and far-sighted recommendation was that the RFC and RNAS should be combined into the world's first fully autonomous air force, which would be better able to coordinate an effective air defence. As a result, the Royal Air Force (RAF) came into existence on 1 April 1918.

On the German side, it had become clear that the rising rate of losses was not being matched by any significant rise in the damage being inflicted on England. Thus the attacks were switched to the night, which offered the probability of reduced losses. KG 3 flew its first night attack on 3/4 September 1917. One 50kg (110lb) bomb hit a naval barracks in Chatham, killing 131 men and injuring 90 others in the worst single bomb incident of World War I.

NOCTURNAL RAIDERS
Germany already had plans more ambitious than those which could be realized by the twin-engined bombers, and in 1916 had established the Reisenflugzeugabteilungen (Rfa, or giant aircraft squadrons) 501 and 502 for service on the Eastern Front with a very mixed assortment of large bombers. The best of these was the 10-man Zeppelin-Staaken R.VI, a four-engined machine spanning 42.20m (138ft 5.63in) and able to carry bombs of up to 1000kg (2205lb) as well as four defensive machine-guns. In September 1917 Rfa 501 reached Belgium, and by the end of the same month had become

operational on night attacks on southeast England. The accuracy of the bombing was still poor, but the British civilian losses actually decreased even though a greater weight of bombs was being dropped.

The effort of the German bombers was maintained on a sporadic basis during the winter of 1917-18, when a few airships raids were also flown. The British were now being altogether more active in strengthening their defences with belts of anti-aircraft (AA) guns, more searchlights, barrages of tethered balloons, and a greater number of modern fighters, including the Camel and F.2B, offering an improved chance of effecting an interception. The last major German raid was made on 19/20 May 1918, when 38 Gotha and three R-category aircraft, and at least two airships, departed for England. Here they ran into a determined AA and fighter defence, which each downed three Gotha bombers. This marked the effective end of the German bombing of England.

The British and French did not initially have the same overall faith in strategic bombing as the Russians and Germans. Even so, the RNAS revealed clear thinking and considerable ingenuity in a few small-scale but

The world's first four-engined heavy bomber was a Russian type, the Sikorsky Ilya Muromets built by the Russo-Baltic Wagon Works. The type had poor performance except in range, was bedevilled by engine supply and reliability problems, and was eventually built in only modest numbers.

notably effective attacks. As early as 8 October 1914, and after the failure of an earlier attempt, a pair of Sopwith Tabloid single-engined aircraft of the Eastchurch Squadron, based at Antwerp, bombed the airship hangars at Düsseldorf. One pilot hit the designated target and destroyed the new Zeppelin Z.IX, and the other bombed the railway station at Cologne. However, it was not until 19 August 1915, when Colonel Hugh Trenchard took over command of the RFC in France, that a single squadron was allocated to each army for bombing. In the same month the British began work on their first genuine heavy bomber design, the twin-engined Handley Page Type

O/100, which entered service in November 1916.

Meanwhile the British and French limited themselves to tactical bombing of German targets on and behind the Western Front using a miscellany of aircraft types carrying bombs massing no more than 50kg (112lb) until June 1917, when the British introduced a 153kg (336lb) weapon.

Only in October 1917 did the RFC form the 41st Wing to bomb industrial targets in Germany with types including

Germany's most important bombers of World War I were the twin-engined Gotha G.III and G.IV. These types flew over the Western Front, but were also notable for their daylight, and later their night, attacks on targets in the southern part of the UK.

ZEPPELIN-STAAKEN R.IV

Type: seven-crew heavy bomber

Powerplant: two 119kW (160hp) Mercedes D.III
and four 164kW (220hp) Benz Bz.IV inline
piston engines

Maximum speed: 125km/h (78mph)

Service ceiling: 3700m (12,150ft)

Weights: empty 8772kg (19,298lb); maximum
take-off 13,035kg (28,677lb)

Armament: up to seven 7.92mm machine guns,
plus bombload of 2123kg (4670lb)

Dimensions: span   42.20m (138ft 5in)
             length   23.20m (76ft 1in)
             height   6.80m (22ft 4in)
             wing area   332m² (3572sq ft)

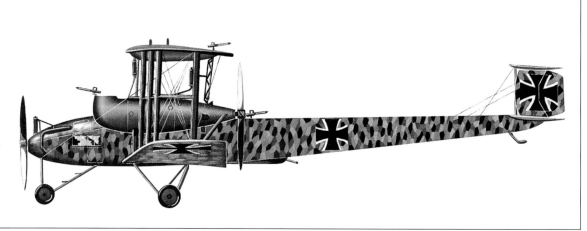

the RAF F.E.2b and Airco (de Havilland) D.H.4 single-engined machines and, as the contribution of the RNAS's 'A' Squadron, the twin-engined O/100 aircraft.

BRITAIN ON THE OFFENSIVE

The 41st Wing delivered its initial daylight attack, using eight D.H.4 bombers, against a factory near Saarbrücken on 17 October, and its first night attack against the same target on 24/25 October by nine O/100 bombers. The offensive continued through the winter of 1917-18, and by June 1918 the 41st Wing of four RFC and one RNAS squadrons had undertaken 142 raids, 57 of them on targets within Germany.

Trenchard pressed constantly for an enlarged British effort, wholly independent of army supervision in

> The 41st Wing delivered its initial daylight attack, using eight D.H.4 bombers, against a factory near Saarbrücken on 17 October 1917, and its first night attack against the same target on 24/25 October.

France, and in June 1918 approval was given for the creation of the so-called Independent Force (IF), under Trenchard's command, with three squadrons of the 41st Wing re-equipped with the D.H.9 and two squadrons of the 83rd Wing.

More strength was assigned to the IF in August with the arrival of three squadrons equipped with the new and improved O/400 twin-engined

bomber, and one with the improved D.H.9a. One of the squadrons already in France also converted from the wholly obsolete F.E.2b to the O/400.

The greater offensive capability of the IF is reflected in the fact that, in the six months to the Armistice which ended World War I on 11 November 1918, its squadrons dropped 550 tons of bombs including weapons up to a weight of 748kg (1650lb), mostly on German airfields and towns, for the loss of 109 aircraft and 264 men killed or missing.

September 1918 witnessed the creation of No. 27 Group (the 86th and 87th Wings) for planned addition to the IF. The equipment for the new

FIRST RAID FOR BRITAIN'S 'HEAVIES'

A major change was signalled in the British concept of strategic bombing in August 1916, when several RFC squadrons were allocated to a separate command dedicated to strategic bombing rather than tactical support bombing. It was a move in the right direction, but the British still lacked a bomber able to translate their intentions into any form of reality over any distance beyond the German rear areas behind the Western Front. However, on 16/17 March 1917, the RNAS's 3rd Wing undertook the first British attack by a heavy bomber when a single Type O/100 bombed Moulin-les-Metz railway station.

In the early days of aerial warfare, the methods of bomb carriage, aiming and release were decidedly rudimentary, and the power of the lightweight bombs essentially negligible. Developments during the war were rapid and major.

Germany also developed several types of long-range heavy bombers with four-, five- or even six-engined powerplants. The best known and most capable of these were the Zeppelin (Staaken) warplanes, here epitomized by the R.VI with two tractor and two pusher engines.

formation was to be the new Handley Page V/1500 four-engined heavy bomber capable of carrying 30 113kg (250lb) bombs or one 1497kg (3300lb) bomb. As it happened, only three examples of the V/1500 had been delivered by the time of the Armistice, and among the tasks considered for this powerful new bomber was the bombing of Berlin.

The IF was disbanded early in 1919, but by that time it had paved the foundations for the development of strategic bombing as a cornerstone of modern warfare, as confirmed in World War II.

AIR WAR AT SEA

Both the British and German naval air arms were full of activity right from the start of the war, the German service's airships being employed for raiding over the UK as well as scouting over the North Sea and Baltic Sea, and the aircraft of the RNAS attacking targets in Belgium and Germany as well as being

employed as torpedo-bombers in the Dardanelles.

Once the war was fully into its stride, the German navy's air operations were undertaken by two branches of the service, namely the Marine Luftschiffabteilung controlling the airships, and the Marine Fliegerabteilung responsible for heavier-than-air craft. Formally established only in December 1914, the latter already had seaplane bases at Heligoland, Kiel, Pützig and Wilhelmshafen. The first seaplanes were posted to bases along the coast of occupied Belgium in December 1914, and by the closing stages of the war the

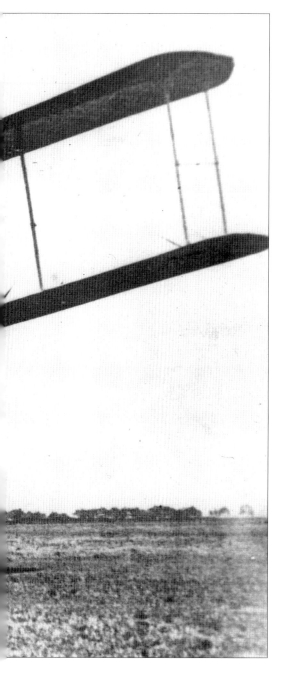

Marine Fliegerabteilung had expanded to several hundreds of aircraft located at no fewer than 32 bases along the coasts of the North Sea, Baltic Sea, the western side of the Black Sea and Turkey's Black Sea and Aegean Sea littorals. The primary concentration was along the coast of Belgium, and from here Friedrichshafen and Hansa-Brandenburg seaplanes were operated

The UK developed several ways to counter the airship and bomber, including the type of balloon barrage seen here. Connected laterally by cables carrying long trailing cables, the balloons were tethered in the likely flightpaths of incoming bombers.

The best British-designed light/medium bombers of World War I were the Airco D.H.4 and successor D.H.9 series. These were sturdy and possessed sufficient performance to tangle successfully with fighters, and carried a useful bomb load.

in some numbers and with considerable success over the southern reaches of the North Sea, later fighting a number of extended air-to-air combats with Felixstowe F.2 flying-boats of the RNAS operating from bases in East Anglia.

On 11 August 1916, a notable day in aviation history, a Sopwith Camel fighter lifted off a barge being towed at speed to intercept and shoot down the airship *L.53* over the North Sea, and on the same day a force of 14 Hansa-Brandenburg W.29 floatplanes located six British coastal motor boats and sank three of them with machine-gun fire.

The British made considerable use of aircraft for a number of coastal and maritime tasks, and also pioneered the development and then the limited use of the aircraft carrier.

Seen here dwarfing an S.E.5a fighter, the Handley Page V/1500 was the largest British bomber to enter production in World War I. It was just too late to see active service in the war.

Developments of the Airco D.H.9 series served the British and US air forces with great distinction and longevity right into the later part of the 1920s and even the early 1930s.

BIRTH OF CARRIER AIR POWER

The process which led to the true aircraft carrier started with the launching of aircraft from platforms constructed on the turrets of capital ships, via towed lighters, to specially constructed decks on converted vessels such as the light battlecruiser HMS *Furious*. This was in effect the first real aircraft carrier, as opposed to earlier extemporizations and interim measures such as seaplane tenders, which merely transported aircraft that were craned out onto the sea for operations.

While small non-rigid airships and large Felixstowe flying-boats patrolled the UK's coast during the latter part of the war, searching for the German submarines which had become so grave a threat to the UK's maritime lines of communications, the seaplane squadrons of the RNAS and later the RAF operated in significant numbers in the Mediterranean.

In World War I's other great theatre, on the Eastern Front, both the German and Russian air arms operated with

some vigour right from the beginning of the war, the Russians concentrating their efforts in eastern Poland, and especially the province of Galicia. The Russians produced only small numbers of indigenous designs, most notably the Ilya Muromets, and up to the time of her exit from the war after the Bolshevik revolution, flew aircraft mainly of British and French origins. The Germans flew basically the same aircraft as they did over the Western

Front, but in smaller numbers and with a slightly later entry to service. From the spring of 1917, however, the quality of Russian air units declined as a result of the political, social and economic unrest which led finally to the Bolshevik Revolution and Russia's exit from the war as a member of the Allied powers.

Much farther to the south, Turkey joined the war on the side of the Central Powers in November 1914, and at the suggestion of Winston Churchill, the First Lord of the

The O/400 was the most important British heavy bomber of the period late in World War I, and was the type which provided the basis on which the V/1500 was created. The O/400 could carry 907kg (2000lb) of bombs, and carried three to five 7.7mm (0.303in) defensive machine-guns.

Admiralty, the Allies planned to force the Dardanelles from the Aegean Sea and take Constantinople, so compelling the Turks to sue for peace and opening a maritime route through which supplies and weapons could be delivered to Black Sea ports for the use of the struggling Russians.

The initial naval offensive failed in March 1915, and was followed by a series of ultimately failed amphibious assaults on the Gallipoli peninsula by

The Turks held their own on the ground, and by the later stages of 1915 the Allies decided that no decisive success could be achieved, and started to withdraw.

Commonwealth forces with British naval support and aircraft of the RNAS. Among the latter were Short Type 184 floatplanes, and these achieved the world's first successes with air-launched torpedoes, sinking several small Turkish vessels.

GERMAN REINFORCEMENTS

Turkey lacked an effective air arm, and Germany came to her assistance from April 1915 with a small detachment of aircraft and crews. The Turks held their own on the ground, and by the later stages of 1915 the Allies decided that no decisive success could be achieved, and started to withdraw in December 1915.

The British and their Empire allies were also fighting the Turks in Palestine and Mesopotamia. Here again the Turks could put only token numbers of aircraft into the air, and again the Germans came to their assistance, but in overall terms the British possessed and kept the upper hand. The same basic pattern of development was evident in Mesopotamia, where limited German air support for the Turks was overwhelmed by the British air strength. The air campaign against the Turkish ground forces in Mesopotamia also helped establish the concept and practice of British

For attacks on German and Turkish shipping, and for the protection of the sea lanes round the UK, the British made extensive use of floatplanes such as these Short Type 184 machines, which could carry one small air-launched torpedo or bombs.

'imperial policing' from the air during the 1920s and early 1930s in areas such as North Africa, the Middle East and India. Here aircraft could bring their capabilities to bear rapidly and effectively in areas difficult to reach by land, so allowing uprisings to be nipped in the bud before they could grow to major proportions.

THE ITALIAN FRONT

The Austro-Hungarian air arms also grew in capability during the same period, and towards the end of 1916

there appeared much more capable fighters such as the Aviatik D.I and Brandenburg D.I. By the late summer of 1917 the Italian air and land forces began to face a greater threat as Germany moved ground forces into the theatre in an attempt to stave off Austro-Hungarian defeat.

The Italians suffered a crushing defeat in the 12th Battle of the Isonzo, or Caporetto, and the arrival of British and French forces was needed to help stabilize the front early in 1918. The Germans then pulled out their forces

The Short Type 184 floatplane operated from the water after being craned out from a seaplane carrier, and was recovered by the reversal of the process. The torpedo was carried between the struts bracing the side-by-side pair of floats.

for use in the last five offensives on the Western Front, and static warfare once more became the norm until the last great Italian offensive in October 1918 led to Austro-Hungarian clamour for an armistice early in November.

Between the end of World War I in 1918 and the start of World War II in

One of the key developments of World War I was the creation of the world's first aircraft carriers. These first carried only individual take-off and landing platforms, but the full-length flight deck was in the final stages of development late in the war.

The air campaign in Mesopotamia helped establish the concept and practice of British 'imperial policing' from the air.

ITALIAN AIR ARMS AT WAR

Italy entered World War I on the Allied side in May 1915, opening a new front against Austria-Hungary in northern Italy. By this time the Aeronautica del Regio Esercito had a useful strength of about 12 squadrons, equipped mostly with aircraft of Blériot, Farman and Nieuport design, while the naval air arm in the Adriatic Sea possessed a miscellany of seaplanes. Opposing these Italian assets was the Austro-Hungarian Luftfahrttruppen, a force already heavily committed on the Eastern Front and therefore able to offer only limited opposition to the Italian air forces. The campaign on the Italian front largely mirrored that on the Western Front. An aspect of air warfare in which the Italians excelled, however, was long-range flight for reconnaissance and bombing, and as Italian aircraft began to probe ever deeper into Austria-Hungary after crossing the Alps, the Germans were again faced with the need to bolster an ally. This took the initial form of deliveries of modern aircraft, but despite a number of difficulties, the Italian air arms grew steadily in basic strength and overall capability, and as a result the attacks by Caproni multi-engined bombers continued without serious interference. By the middle of 1916 the Italian air arms totalled 32 squadrons.

Many experiments with the installation and use of heavier weapons were made in World War I, but the standard weapon remained the rifle-calibre machine-gun on a fixed or trainable mounting.

1939, the technology of aviation advanced very rapidly after being stalled for the first few years after World War I. In 1918 most aircraft were biplanes based on a wire-braced wooden structure covered largely with fabric, with fixed tailskid landing gear, wire rigging, an open cockpit and an engine delivering something in the order of 186.5kW (250hp).

During the 1920s the major changes were the adoption of steadily more powerful engines and the replacement of wood by steel and then aluminium alloy as the primary structural medium,

The Martin B-10 was the US Army's first all-metal bomber, introduced in 1932. Interwar aircraft design proceeded so rapidly, however, that by the outbreak of World War II the type was obsolete, having been superseded by the Boeing B-17 Flying Fortress.

and aircraft of this type were used right into the middle of the 1930s, seeing operational service in conflicts such as the Russian Civil War (1918-21), the Russo-Polish War (1919-20), the Chaco War (1932-35) of South America, the first stages of the Sino-Japanese War from 1932, the Italian conquest of Abyssinia (1935-36) and even the earlier stages of the Spanish Civil War (1936-39). In this last the Nationalist side received significant aid from the involvement of German and Italian forces, while the Republican side received Soviet material support.

INTERWAR DEVELOPMENTS

By the mid-1930s a major change was evident, initially as a result of the development in the US of the 'modern' aircraft of metal stressed-skin construction, a cantilever monoplane wing with trailing-edge flaps, landing gear with retractable main units, enclosed accommodation, and engines of greater power and reliability driving variable-pitch propellers. This technical change then spread to military aircraft, starting with bombers. This change meant greater performance and the ability to carry heavier offensive and defensive armament, and when fighters of a comparable 'modern' type started to appear they introduced heavier fixed forward-firing armament. By 1939 maximum speeds had tripled, service ceilings doubled (with oxygen masks now standard), and the range and warload of bombers had increased enormously.

Most of the combatants in World War I produced their own warplane types, and Austria-Hungary was no exception, with fighters such as the Aviatik D.I, which was at first structurally suspect and armed with two 8mm (0.315in) Schwarzlose machine-guns.

World War II: War in the West 1939–1945

Having taken the Saarland and Rhineland regions (both placed under Allied control by the Treaty of Versailles drawn up at the end of World War I), Austria, and Czechoslovakia without hindrance from the Western powers, Adolf Hitler, Chancellor of Germany, turned his attentions towards Poland. Hitler's military planners favoured a new type of campaign for the invasion of Poland, in which fast-moving ground forces acted swiftly against a series of objectives. Key to this 'lightning warfare' – *Blitzkrieg* – was close support from the air.

Germany had successfully circumvented the restrictions of the Treaty of Versailles on its production of military aircraft, through the manufacture of military types for export and the development of a series of advanced commercial aircraft. On the eve of the invasion the Luftwaffe was therefore able to field some of the finest aircraft in the world, including He 111 and Do 17 bombers, Ju 87 dive-bombers, Bf 110 heavy fighters – known as *Zestörer*, or destroyers – Bf 109 single-engined fighters, Hs 123 close-support and Hs 126 reconnaissance aircraft, and a fleet of Ju 52/3m transports. When *Fall Weiss* (Plan White), the attack on Poland, began at 0426 on 1 September 1939, these types were pitched into battle with a primary objective of destroying the Polish air force, before providing support to the army.

Poland's most potent fighter, the PZL P.11c was hopelessly outclassed by the Bf 109, although able to combat the Bf 110 in a turning fight. Perhaps the most capable Polish aircraft was the PZL P.37 Los, but just

The indigenous PZL P.11 was the best fighter the Poles could muster in the face of the German onslaught. It was very agile, but too lightly armed to be really effective.

PZL P.11

Type: single-seat fighter

Powerplant: one 470kW (630hp) Bristol Mercury V
S2 piston engine

Maximum speed: 375km/h (233mph)

Service ceiling: 8000m (26,246ft)

Weights: maximum take-off weight 1650kg
(3638lb); empty 1147kg (2529lb)

Armament: 2 or 4 x 7.92mm (0.312in)
machine-guns

Dimensions: span   10.7m (35ft 2in)
           length   7.5m (24ft 9in)
           height   2.85m (9ft 4in)
           wing area 17.9m² (192sq ft)

36 of these advanced bombers were in service at the time of the invasion.

The first Luftwaffe aircraft into action were the Ju 87B-1 Stukas of Stukageschwader 1 (StG 1), and Do 17Z-2 bombers of KG 3, attacking bridges, airfields and other military targets. Warsaw and Krakow were also raided, while He 111s were in action along the Baltic coast, attacking naval installations.

The *Zerstörergruppen* flew their Bf 110s as escorts to the bombers, their crews soon adopting dive and climb tactics to defeat the nimble PZL fighters. After a major air battle over Warsaw on 3 September the game was largely over for the Polish fighter pilots and the Luftwaffe re-tasked its Bf 110s with strafing missions. When the Soviet Union invaded on 17 September Poland was effectively lost, but Warsaw did not surrender until 27 September, after 1,150 Luftwaffe bomber missions had pounded the city three days earlier. Poland fell on 6 October 1939.

Norway was absolutely vital to Hitler's ambition for European and, ultimately, world domination. Only by securing the country could he guarantee the supply of Swedish iron ore so vital to his war industries. Norway also had important military value, in furnishing ports from which the Kriegsmarine (German navy) could operate in the North Sea and bases from which the Luftwaffe's bombers could strike the UK.

NORWAY CAMPAIGN
In the UK, First Sea Lord Winston Churchill had been pushing for German iron ore ships traversing Norwegian sea lanes to be interdicted, and for the mining of Norwegian waters. His suggestions were ignored, even as Hitler was making plans for an invasion. In the event, a German ship moving British prisoners of war was boarded by a Royal Navy party in Norwegian waters on 16 February 1940. Regardless of the legality of the boarding, Hitler took it as an excuse

for his invasion. He also considered it inevitable that Denmark should be taken, since the Luftwaffe needed the major airfield complex at Aalborg for its assault against Norway.

Just after 0500 on 9 April 1940, troops simultaneously marched across the border into Denmark and landed by sea. They were followed by another of the Luftwaffe's weapons, the *Fallschirmjäger*, or parachute troops, which were used for the first time to take the Aalborg airfields. Such was their impact that within 20 minutes Ju 52/3ms were landing on the airfields to disgorge troops and equipment. By evening Copenhagen had fallen and Denmark was in German hands.

Norway had also come under attack on the morning of 9 April. The initial attacks were by seaborne forces, the invasion coming as a shock to British and Norwegian forces even though an RAF Sunderland had spotted German ships off the Trondheim coast during the afternoon of 8 April. With troops coming ashore, Bf 110s began strafing targets and quickly destroyed Norway's meagre force of Gladiator Mk II biplanes. Bombing attacks on military installations were followed by the arrival of *Fallschirmjäger*, which

> Just after 0500 on 9 April 1940, German troops simultaneously marched across the border into Denmark and landed by sea.

quickly took the country's major airfields. Nevertheless, on 11 April the Royal Navy staged a brave comeback, with eight Skuas of No. 803 Naval Air Squadron (NAS) adding *Königsberg* to the list of German vessels sunk or crippled in a series of actions. Indeed, as poor weather kept the Luftwaffe from interfering, British troops were able to land at Harstad on 15 April, then at Namsos on the 16th and Andalsnes on the 18th. However, the threat had been recognized and the Luftwaffe turned its bombers against these landings and other pockets of Norwegian and British resistance.

A squadron of RAF Gladiators was flown off HMS *Glorious* on 23 April in a vain attempt to counter Luftwaffe attacks. Flying from the frozen Lake Lesjaskog the biplanes proved difficult to operate and by the evening of 25 April, 11 of No. 263 Sqn's aircraft were unserviceable. By 26 April their fight was over and the surviving crews evacuated as nearby Andalsnes was

> Narvik remained under Allied control, but by early June 1940 German forces were sweeping through France and there was no option but for the UK to withdraw its forces from Norway.

destroyed by the Luftwaffe.

The final Allied stronghold in Norway was now Narvik. As April turned into May, the Luftwaffe increased its forces in Norway the better to take Narvik. Allied aerial support came only from the Gladiators of the luckless No. 263 Sqn and the Hurricane Mk Is of No. 46 Sqn, RAF. The former had once again flown off *Glorious*, this time to Bardufoss on 26 May, where it was joined by the Hurricanes. Narvik remained under Allied control, but by early June German forces were

sweeping through France and there was no option but for the UK to withdraw its forces from Norway.

TOWARDS THE BIG PRIZE
The biggest prize that Europe had to offer Hitler was the UK. Even as his forces were engaged in Poland he was planning an invasion through

French *Chasseurs Alpines* look on as a British Blackburn Skua fighter is prepared for take-off on a frozen Norwegian lake. The arrival of these aircraft came too late to prevent Allied defeat in Norway.

Above: The RAF's Hurricane destroyed more enemy aircraft than all other defences combined during the Battle of Britain. No. 56 Sqn's aircraft were scrambling from North Weald during the campaign.

The invasion of Western Europe became a reality on 10 May 1940. German troops swarmed into Holland and Belgium, passing through Luxembourg, following audacious airborne assaults by gliderborne troops and *Fallschirmjäger* in Belgium and Holland.

Belgium and the Netherlands, into France and to the Channel ports that would allow him to amass an invasion fleet for the attack on the UK. *Fall Gelb*, Plan Yellow, the invasion of Western Europe, became a reality on 10 May 1940. German troops swarmed into Holland and Belgium, passing through Luxembourg, following audacious airborne assaults by

Left: Narvik became the focus of concentrated German attention. Bombing destroyed many ships in the harbour, as this April 1940 image graphically testifies.

gliderborne troops and *Fallschirmjäger* in Belgium and Holland.

DUTCH COLLAPSE
As early as 0300 on the 10th, German bombers were in action, KG 4 in particular attacking the airfield at Waalhaven-Rotterdam, which was

accepting Ju 52/3ms just a few hours later. There was little aerial resistance from the Dutch, whose Fokker D.XXI fighters represented a meagre challenge to the Luftwaffe's Bf 109E and Bf 110 fighters.

As part of an Anglo-French alliance, the British Expeditionary

Force had been established in France with a large number of troops and two air components. Of these, the British Air Forces France (BAFF) formation was tasked with the support of BEF troops and included Lysander, Blenheim and Hurricane squadrons. The second component, the Advanced Air Striking Force (AASF), was put in place to compensate for the

For the Allied soldiers trapped around Dunkirk the wait was tireless and bloody. They saw little evidence of support from the air, as weather conditions hampered flying.

woeful lack of a modern French bomber force. As such it consisted of Battle and Blenheim bombers, and further Hurricane fighters.

IN DEFENCE OF FRANCE

The AASF, under French command, was first committed to attacks against German units in Luxembourg at noon on 10 May. Three Battles out of eight despatched were lost on the initial raid, with follow-up raids wreaking an equally heavy toll on the Battle units. By 12 May the Anglo-French alliance was focusing its attentions on denying

access to the bridges over the Albert Canal at Maastricht. Again Battles and Blenheims were committed, with terrible losses, while Flying Officer D. E. Garland and Sergeant T. Gray received the Victoria Cross for pressing home their attack with some success, although they and their Battle were lost. Their wireless operator, Leading Aircraftman L. R. Reynolds, was not honoured. Now the BEF was focused on the defence of France.

On 13 May the Germans crossed the River Meuse into France to

These No. 610 Sqn, RAF, Spitfire Mk I pilots were re-enacting a scramble for the camera. Scenes like this were typical of British fighter airfields during the long summer of 1940.

establish a bridgehead at Sedan. The Allies attacked with Battle, Blenheim, LeO 451 and Amiot 354 bombers, but the Allied bomber force had all but ceased to exist by 14 May. Even with the French D.520, MS.406, Bloch 152 and Hawk 75 fighters adding their strength to those of the RAF, the German advance in the air and on the

FALL OF THE LOW COUNTRIES

The BAFF was unable to assist the Belgians during the 10 May 1940 onslaught. Instead both RAF Fighter and Bomber Commands sent a handful of Blenheims against Belgian targets, although fighter sorties were made by the BAFF. On 11 May Fighter Command sent UK-based Hurricanes over Belgium and Holland, while AASF Hurricanes attacked Ju 52/3m transports on the ground and Ju 87s in the air. Fighter Command was in action again on 13 May, sending Spitfire Mk I and turret-armed Defiant fighters into combat. Of the six Defiants sent out by No. 264 Sqn, only one returned. On the ground the struggle continued, but a huge raid by the He 111H-1 bombers of KG 54 during the afternoon of 14 May saw a large area of Rotterdam destroyed and signalled the Dutch capitulation.

EVACUATION FROM DUNKIRK

In the UK, Churchill had taken over as prime minister after the resignation of Neville Chamberlain, and his decision it was, on 20 May 1940, to evacuate British forces from the Continent. So swift had been the German advance that the *Wehrmacht*'s lines of communication were now becoming over-stretched and as Allied troops began to form up in the Dunkirk-Ostend area ready for evacuation, Hitler called a stop to the armoured offensive. His commanders wanted to press on to wipe out the massive Allied troop concentration stranded on the coast, but instead the task was left primarily to the Luftwaffe. Since 15 May Air Chief Marshall Sir Hugh Dowding had been resisting moves to send fighter reinforcements to France. He believed that they should be held in reserve for the forthcoming defence of the UK, and while the pull-out from France vindicated his position, it meant that air cover for the Dunkirk evacuation would have to be provided from bases in the UK. Defiants, Spitfires and Hurricanes joined a renewed air support campaign. Fortunately for the Allies, the Luftwaffe's Bf 109s and Ju 87s were at the limits of their range over the evacuation beaches. Nevertheless, the remaining Allied fortifications and flotilla of craft assembled for the evacuation were still under constant bomber threat.

The evacuation began on 26 May and was severely hampered by the Luftwaffe. Poor weather on the morning of 29 May kept the Germans on the ground, but with improving weather in the afternoon the RAF patrolled in greater force than ever before. The weather once again favoured the Allies on 30 May, 58,823 troops being evacuated. Next day, 68,014 got away as fog further hampered air operations. The morning of 1 June saw Ju 87s attacking shipping through a window in the weather, but conditions closed down again and allowed the evacuation to continue until 4 June, by which time 338,226 Allied troops had left France.

ground was unstoppable. By 19 May BAFF and AASF survivors were pulling back to the west.

The Armée de l'Air (French air force) fought on with its motley collection of fighters, bravely

defending Paris as the bad weather continued, but with German ground forces as far south as Lyon, an armistice was signed by French leaders on 22 June 1940.

THE BATTLE OF BRITAIN

'The Battle of France … ,' announced Churchill, late in June 1940, ' … is over. The Battle of Britain is about to begin.' The *Blitzkrieg* type of campaign could not work against the islands of the UK. Three possibilities therefore presented themselves: maritime blockade might starve the UK into submission, a massive bombing campaign might bring it to its knees, or an invasion might be possible if air superiority could be established over southern England. History records that the latter was the chosen option.

The first raid against the UK saw Ju 88A-1 and He 111H-1 bombers attacking the airfield at Mildenhall on the night of 5 June. Another raid was flown on the 6th, before attacks began again on 18 June. The targets were airfields and the raids were initially flown in response to the first of Bomber Command's strategic missions, which was flown against the Ruhr on 15/16 May. This strike in itself was flown as a reprisal for the attack on Rotterdam. German

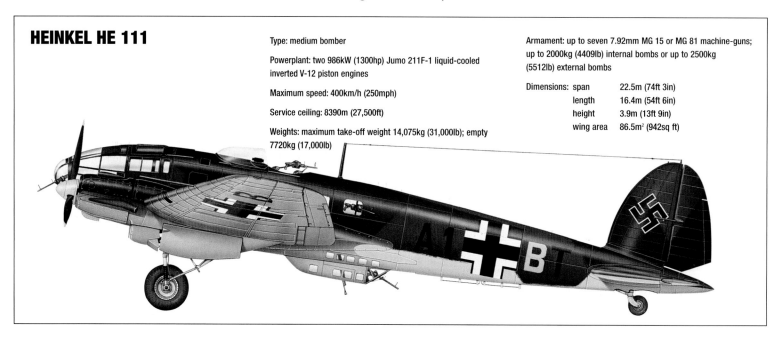

HEINKEL HE 111

Type: medium bomber

Powerplant: two 986kW (1300hp) Jumo 211F-1 liquid-cooled inverted V-12 piston engines

Maximum speed: 400km/h (250mph)

Service ceiling: 8390m (27,500ft)

Weights: maximum take-off weight 14,075kg (31,000lb); empty 7720kg (17,000lb)

Armament: up to seven 7.92mm MG 15 or MG 81 machine-guns; up to 2000kg (4409lb) internal bombs or up to 2500kg (5512lb) external bombs

Dimensions:	span	22.5m (74ft 3in)
	length	16.4m (54ft 6in)
	height	3.9m (13ft 9in)
	wing area	86.5m² (942sq ft)

'The Battle of France … ,' announced Churchill, late in June 1940, ' … is over. The Battle of Britain is about to begin.'

For fascinated watchers on the ground the only evidence of a Battle of Britain dogfight might be the swirling contrails created at high altitude by the fighters' exhausts.

nocturnal operations over the UK now continued more or less constantly, as did Bomber Command sorties to Germany. Now the first stage of the Battle of Britain began, with the Luftwaffe attempting to gain air superiority over the English Channel, while at the same time closing it to British shipping. Bf 109Es flew *frei Jagd* (free chase) missions over the Channel in order to tempt the RAF

into combat, while Do 17Zs, Ju 88s, He 111s and Ju 87s attacked airfields, shipping and coastal targets. On 10 July the Luftwaffe upped its game with a large raid against a shipping convoy. Battle was joined by the Hurricanes and Spitfires, which engaged the Do 17Zs and their Bf 110C escorts, with up to 100 aircraft embroiled in the dogfight that resulted. Now regarded as the first day

of the Battle of Britain, the actions of 10 July preceded the issue on 11 July of orders from Luftwaffe high command for intensive air operations against the UK.

The UK had built up a network of Chain Home radar stations and these, combined with a system of fighter control and a well-trained Observer Corps, frequently allowed the RAF to overcome the Luftwaffe's advantage in having surprise and altitude over the defenders. So it was that after

weather permitted, with the exception of 25 July, when a massive force of Bf 109Es overwhelmed the RAF interceptors. From 8 August the weather improved and the fighting escalated. It was time for Fighter Command to concentrate its resources on countering the bomber hordes.

EAGLE DAY

Now the Luftwaffe laid plans for *Adlerangriff* (Attack of Eagles), its major effort of the campaign, which was to start on *Adlertag*, Eagle Day. To be actioned as soon as the weather allowed, *Adlertag* was originally scheduled for 10 August, but was delayed to the 13th. Luftwaffe intelligence, notoriously unreliable, considered that Fighter Command had received a crippling blow on the 8th, a conclusion that would serve the high command badly. However, it also realized the importance of radar to the RAF's defence and tactics were rapidly adopted to counter the system. The Luftwaffe had also come to accept that the Bf 110 had met its match, but the big Messerschmitt had been earmarked for long-range fighter-bomber – *Jagdbomber*, or *Jabo* – missions into the UK. The needs of *Adlerangriff* prevailed and as early as the evening of 12 August, British fighter bases once more came under concerted attack, while a daring low-level raid by the Bf 110C-6 *Jabos* of Erprobungsgruppe 210 struck radar stations on the coast.

The morning of 13 August began in confusion. Reichsmarschall Göring, Commander-in-Chief Luftwaffe, ordered the cancellation of *Adlerangriff* in light of forecast poor weather. The message was not received by all of the units already in

successful raids early in the morning of 11 July, timely warning was received of a Stuka raid approaching Portland. The bombers were escorted by Bf 110Cs, but the four squadrons of RAF fighters sent to intercept were well placed. They made short work of the Ju 87s while their escorts found themselves unable to turn with the

defenders. Four were shot down and the combat represented the beginning of the end for both types in daylight operations in the West. Bad weather now kept flying to a minimum until the cloud lifted on 19 July to reveal a number of convoys in the Channel.

The Luftwaffe's campaign continued at a similar intensity as

MESSERSCHMITT BF 110

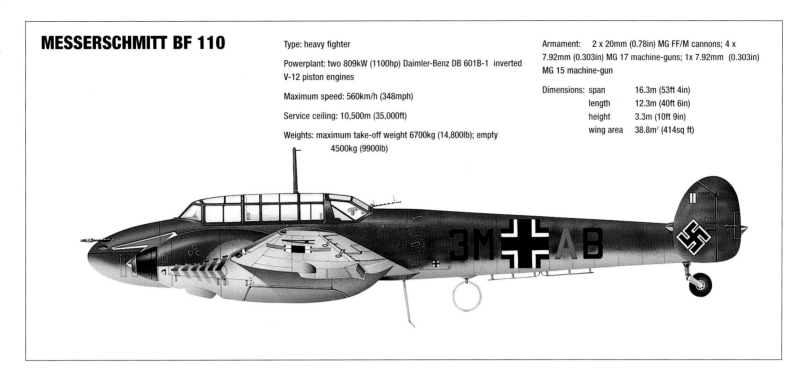

Type: heavy fighter

Powerplant: two 809kW (1100hp) Daimler-Benz DB 601B-1 inverted
V-12 piston engines

Maximum speed: 560km/h (348mph)

Service ceiling: 10,500m (35,000ft)

Weights: maximum take-off weight 6700kg (14,800lb); empty
        4500kg (9900lb)

Armament: 2 x 20mm (0.78in) MG FF/M cannons; 4 x
7.92mm (0.303in) MG 17 machine-guns; 1x 7.92mm (0.303in)
MG 15 machine-gun

Dimensions: span   16.3m (53ft 4in)
            length   12.3m (40ft 6in)
            height   3.3m (10ft 9in)
            wing area   38.8m² (414sq ft)

the air, resulting in KG 2's Do 17Z-2s arriving over the UK without their fighter escort, while a *frei Jagd* sortie by the Bf 110s of I./JG 2, scheduled to coincide with a raid by KG 54, saw the fighters in place but no bombers. Not until later in the afternoon, in poor weather, did full-scale raids get under way. The bombing continued after dark and at the end of the day the Luftwaffe could count 45 aircraft lost, while 13 Fighter Command machines had gone down. The weather played a decisive role in the fighting of 14 August, keeping raids to a minimum, but on 15 August a vicious battle saw the RAF's Nos 41, 72, 73, 79, 605 and

616 Sqns engaging the He 111H-1s of KG 26 and their Bf 110D-0 escorts, as well as the Ju 88A-1s of KG 30. For the day, Luftwaffe losses were 79, against 34 for the RAF.

A CHANGE IN TACTICS

It was clear that the Luftwaffe's tactics were failing. No longer could bombers be sent over enemy territory in daylight without close fighter escort. The RAF had begun to ignore the *frei Jagd* machines to concentrate on the bombers beneath, and with the toll on bombers and crews rising, the decision was taken to keep the fighters close to their charges. These

new tactics were noted by RAF pilots on 16 August, when Bf 109Es were seen flying at the same level as the bombers, alongside and ahead of them, weaving to keep their speed down and maintain formation. The campaign proper was again slowed by weather, but on 18 August the Stuka was once more committed in force, this time to suffer terrible losses. The battles were intense and continued throughout the day for the loss of 71 German aircraft against 27 of the RAF's.

One of the hardest days of the Battle was over, but the RAF was becoming desperately short of combat-ready pilots for its plentiful supply of new and repaired aircraft. As exhausted, but experienced men needed to be rested, so the demand for their skills became greater. Fighter Command was forced to maintain a cadre of experienced men and to bolster them with pilots fresh out of training, from where many of their instructors had already been taken for service on the front line, and from Battle and Lysander squadrons. Fighter Command was at its lowest ebb and could not maintain the pace of operations.

THE ILL-FATED DEFIANT

On 19 July 1940 the RAF received early warning of raids building up over the French coast, although Ju 87B-2s were able to strike at ships in Dover harbour without challenge. Reacting to the Dover raid, Fighter Command launched Hurricanes and Defiants, the latter being tasked with a low-level patrol off the French coast. No. 111 Sqn's Hurricanes saw Bf 109Es moving in to attack the Defiants of No. 141 Sqn, but were unable to attack the German aircraft in numbers owing to radio failure. The Defiants were savaged by the Messerschmitts, whose pilots knew well that the Defiants' turrets could not be brought to bear in countering an attack from behind and below. Out of nine Defiants only three returned and the type was immediately withdrawn from the day-fighter role.

British were mounting attacks against the Channel ports where forces were building for the forthcoming invasion. The *Jagdgeschwader* were now forced to

Below: Tower Bridge dominates the foreground while London burns after another Luftwaffe raid. Massed raids against the capital became common as the Battle of Britain continued.

BATTLE LOST?

The Luftwaffe maintained its pressure on the RAF's airfields, the devastation of the so-called sector airfields, which were vital links in the fighter-control communications chain, being especially worrying. Orders now went out to direct the minimum of resources at incoming fighters, avoiding costly fighter-versus-fighter combat. Meanwhile, Göring's consideration that the Luftwaffe should concentrate on destroying the enemy's fighters by bombing saw him tying his Messerschmitts even more closely to the bomber formations. He was also under pressure to attack Bomber Command bases since the

Fighter Command was at its lowest ebb and could not maintain the pace of operations.

engage the enemy from a position where they were 'low and slow'; the opportunity to destroy Fighter Command in the air had been lost. Still though, Fighter Command was suffering grievous losses in fighter pilots killed and could not sustain its defence of the UK. But then, on the night of 25 August, Bomber Command struck at Berlin for the first time. Hitler was incensed and Göring embarrassed. A decision was made that would change the course of the war. Six of seven sector stations were

> The *Jagdgeschwader* were now forced to engage the enemy from a position where they were 'low and slow'; the opportunity to destroy RAF Fighter Command in the air had been lost.

out of action and irreplaceable pilots were still being lost at an appalling rate when, on 7 September, the Luftwaffe changed tactics. In reprisal for the raid on Berlin it had been assigned a new objective: London.

THE BLITZ BEGINS

The first raid against London on 7 September 1940 involved a mixed fleet of 348 bombers, with 617 Bf 109 and Bf 110 fighters in close attendance. Fighter Command responded in force, downing 41 for the loss of 28 of its own. Raids continued until 15 September, when a series of attacks was met by determined fighter opposition. By the end of the day 60 German aircraft had been lost in return for 26. RAF Fighter Command had won a remarkable victory against all odds. It led to yet another change in Luftwaffe tactics in which low-level daytime *Jabo* raids and night-time bombing attacks on London became the norm. It also led directly to Hitler's decision to postpone *Seelöwe* (Sealion), the invasion of the UK.

By 17 September, with his mind already on the campaign against the Soviet Union, the *Führer* had made his proclamation. The UK could wait, while Luftwaffe bombers hammered London. The city's inhabitants would suffer nightly terror as the RAF struggled to tackle an elusive enemy, but Fighter Command, and the country at large, had been saved.

The Luftwaffe had invested heavily in navigational aids and training for nocturnal bombing operations and now this policy would pay dividends in the campaign against London. On the contrary, the RAF had done little work towards finding schemes to combat bombers at night, so while the Luftwaffe was able to bomb with reasonable accuracy, the defenders were left blind.

NIGHT BLITZ

As Britain struggled to install the nascent AI Mk III airborne radar into a suitable airframe for night-fighting work, Italian fighter and bomber forces joined their Luftwaffe allies to take part in the 'final destruction' of the RAF. The Italians proved to have little capability, however, and although Italian forces arrived in France during September, not until 11 November were they committed. In their attack on Harwich six BR.20M bombers and three fighters – likely a mix of CR.42 biplanes and G.50bis monoplanes – were shot down by Hurricanes, which lost none of their number. The Italians were not tasked on a major raid again. British laboratories had now begun developing equipment for the detection of enemy bombers. Radar was finally making its way into Blenheim and, soon, early Beaufighter

Early in 1941 the Bf 109F arrived, so preventing the Spitfire Mk V from gaining the upper hand. This Bf 109F-2 served with JG 2.

aircraft, while devices that homed on German navigation signals were also developed. A system of

Ground Controlled Interception radars was erected, able to control RAF night-fighters and bring them to within range of their onboard radar sets.

In October new orders were issued which took the so-called night Blitz into a new phase. London remained the primary target, but now industry and other city targets were nominated. Massive, destructive raids ensued, especially against Coventry, which was all but destroyed on the night of 14/15 November, but the defenders achieved their first real step forwards on 19/20 November 1940, when

If the Bf 109F made life difficult for the RAF, then the Fw 190A came as a very nasty shock indeed. An entirely new Spitfire variant – the Mk IX – had to be developed to counter it.

Flight Lieutenant Cunningham and Sergeant Phillipson downed a Ju 88 in their AI Mk IV-equipped Beaufighter. As the night-fighter and anti-aircraft defences improved, so the RAF also began jamming the Luftwaffe's navigation signals. It was at this point that the Luftwaffe again changed tactics. Through January and into February 1941 the weather again precluded sustained operations, but

A system of Ground Controlled Interception radars was erected, able to control RAF night-fighters.

RAF night-fighter successes were mounting and Luftwaffe bomber assets were badly needed in other theatres.

The Dieppe landings were ill conceived and received only badly managed support from the air. The RAF's fighter screen successfully protected the Royal Navy's ships, however, only two being damaged.

on 19/20 February the Luftwaffe began a new series of attacks that also targeted shipping. The raids continued into May, but night-fighter successes were mounting and Luftwaffe bomber assets were badly needed in other theatres. Soon the *Kampfgeschwader* began withdrawing and the Blitz came to a halt. The Battle of Britain was over.

Fighter Command had been left combating nightly raids and unwilling to release aircraft to other theatres: the threat of invasion had diminished but not entirely gone. Thus a large number of day-fighter units was based in the UK with little to do, since the threat of the Luftwaffe by day had all but disappeared. Then, on

20 December 1940, a flight of two No. 66 Sqn Spitfires entered enemy airspace at low level near Dieppe. They penetrated inland before strafing electricity installations, troop accommodation and vehicles. Fighter Command was going on the offensive.

FIGHTER OFFENSIVE

The new leader of Fighter Command's No. 11 Group, Air Vice Marshall Leigh-Mallory, considered that German forces on the French and Belgian coasts were having an easy life. They suffered no offensive action and could operate at will. He had advocated the use of 'Big Wing' tactics – not dissimilar to the Luftwaffe's *frei Jagd* – throughout the Battle of

Britain, and now he pushed to use these large fighter formations on offensive sweeps over occupied territory. In the event, while such tactics remained at the core of these operations, a number of different types of mission evolved, each with a codename. Initially known as Mosquitos and later designated as Rhubarbs, low-level sweeps by pairs of fighters or sections, became commonplace. Intruder operations also began, where Blenheims and, later, Douglas DB-7s or Havocs, lurked over German bomber bases in hope of causing mayhem as the bombers went about their nocturnal business. The first fighter sweep was flown on 9 January 1941, the Luftwaffe refusing to engage, just as the RAF had eventually avoided reacting to the Luftwaffe's *frei Jagd* efforts. Clearly bombers needed to be involved as bait to draw up the Messerschmitts for attack by the Hurricanes and Spitfires. No. 2 Group drew the short straw for most of this work and when the first of the so-called Circus missions was flown on 10 January it included six Blenheims, and Spitfires and Hurricanes from six squadrons. The Hurricanes provided close escort to the Blenheims, while the Spitfires

Below: Badly outclassed by the Luftwaffe's fighters, as well as being very vulnerable to flak, the Blenheim was among the key BEF types in 1940. These Blenheim Mk IVs served with No. 139 Sqn in France.

The first fighter sweep was flown on 9 January 1941, the Luftwaffe refusing to engage, just as the RAF had avoided reacting to the Luftwaffe's *frei Jagd* efforts.

remained behind at higher altitudes ready to pounce on any defending force. The raid went well and a few Bf 109Es were tempted into combat. One Hurricane was lost, but the remaining fighters went down to tree-top height to strafe targets of opportunity and seek out recovering or launching Luftwaffe fighters, as the bombers made good their escape at

low level. The aggression shown by these RAF pilots in taking the fight to the enemy at low level augured well for the future, but high command considered it best to proceed more carefully, lest losses should begin to accumulate. No further low-altitude tactics were used until late in 1943. This effectively allowed German fighters to engage the enemy well

Union. Stepping up the offensive now became a priority as Luftwaffe fighter units were posted east, leaving just two complete *Geschwader* – JG 2 and JG 26 – in France. These two units contained a core of *Experten* (elite pilots), however, while the RAF was struggling to find targets within the Spitfire's range that the Luftwaffe considered worth defending. The RAF also found that its losses consistently achieved very little, and opposition to the Circuses began to grow from within the ranks of Fighter Command. Nevertheless, they continued, along with other operations including the Roadstead, tasked against shipping, and the Ramrod, involving a large force of bombers or fighter-bombers despatched to destroy a specific target. Then, on 31 August 1941, a Hurricane was lost to a new type of fighter. The Fw 190 had entered service and immediately even the best of the Allied machines, the Spitfire Mk V, was outclassed.

within their own range and to land and take-off – operations during which they were most vulnerable – with impunity.

The pattern of Circuses continued through 1941, with the presence of *Scharnhorst* and *Gneisenau* at Brest adding to the Luftwaffe's defensive burden. On the plus side the service received the much improved Bf 109F and an early-warning radar chain was constructed along the coastlines facing enemy territory. By mid-June 1941 Circus operations had proved about equal in losses for both sides and then, on 22 June 1941, with the full knowledge of the British, who had long been intercepting and decoding top-secret German communications, the *Wehrmacht* attacked the Soviet

DIEPPE DISASTER
In March 1942 the RAF once again took up the offensive on the Continent, having slackened the pace of operations late in 1941. For this renewed effort, which included Rodeo fighter-only sweeps, the Boston led the bombing effort. By April, however, it was clear that the RAF was losing more aircraft than the Luftwaffe and the offensive was stopped, to be restarted in July in a manner that strove to avoid any

THE CHANNEL DASH

Long moored at Brest and the subject of multiple bombing attacks, the battlecruisers *Scharnhorst* and *Gneisenau*, and the heavy cruiser *Prinz Eugen* finally attempted to break out late on 11 February 1942. A massive Luftwaffe effort was arranged to cover their movement, but the British failed to respond until Lieutenant Commander Eugene Esmonde launched the Swordfish of No. 825 NAS on the following morning. The attack was a bloodbath, Fw 190s engaging the Swordfish and their Spitfire escorts. All of the torpedo-bombers were lost, with just five of their 18 crew surviving. Esmonde was awarded a posthumous Victoria Cross.

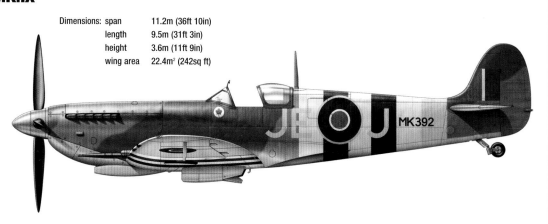

SUPERMARINE SPITFIRE MK.IX

Type: single-seat fighter

Powerplant: one 1129kW (1515hp) V-12 Rolls-Royce
Merlin 61 piston engine

Maximum speed: 657km/h (408mph)

Service ceiling: 12,192m (40,000ft)

Weights: maximum take-off weight 3402kg (7500lb);
empty 2545kg (5610lb)

Armament: Two Hispano 20mm (0.78in) cannon and
either four 7.92mm (0.303in) machine-guns or two
12.7mm (0.50in) machine-guns; 454kg (1000lb) of
bombs

Dimensions: span   11.2m (36ft 10in)
length   9.5m (31ft 3in)
height   3.6m (11ft 9in)
wing area 22.4m² (242sq ft)

contact with fighters, especially the Fw 190.

Within this period of technological disadvantage the Allies, in concert with the newly involved Americans, began plans for an invasion of Europe. It was considered that a major assault might take place in spring 1943 and as such a reconnaissance was needed to assess German resistance. On 19 August 1942 Allied forces were therefore landed at Dieppe. The first of the RAF's Spitfire Mk IXs, which could at last match the Fw 190, were in action, as well as the new Typhoon Mk IB and the Mustang Mk I. The fighters performed well in defence of the fleet, but casualties were high as the Fw 190s were flown with skill and aggression. On the ground the troops fared badly, and the operation could be considered nothing but a bloody failure. For its lessons learned Dieppe was notable, but it also marked the first involvement of the United States Army Air Force (USAAF) in a Circus operation, with B-17E Flying Fortress

bombers attacking the Luftwaffe's JG 26 base at Abbeville.

BOMBERS ENTER THE FRAY

The B-17 raids initially proved difficult for the Germans to counter. The Fw 190 and new, high-altitude Bf 109G-1 struggled to penetrate the bombers' defensive fire. The Luftwaffe was forced to develop tactics to defeat the B-17s and, later, B-24 Liberators, while the USAAF eventually had to admit that its bombers could not defend themselves and that a fighter escort must be provided to ensure their success. By October preparations were underway for the Allied invasion of North Africa and by 8 November 1942, fighter units were being pulled back from France to counter the Allied threat. The offensive in the West continued unabated, however, and on 23 November the Fw 190s of III./JG 2 used head-on attacks against the B-17s for the first time. The Achilles' heel of the big bombers had been discovered.

Since late 1940 *Jabos* had been in operation over the UK, flying fast, low-level 'tip and run' attacks against all manner of targets. The Bf 109 and, especially, Fw 190 fighter-bombers involved in this work had been very difficult to counter until the Typhoon Mk IB and Griffon-engined Spitfire Mk XII became available. The latter came into play from April 1943, by which time the demands of other theatres were already depleting the *Jabo* effort. By June of the same year just one unit remained on *Jabo* duties, its pilots a rag-tag group of freshmen and ex-*Zerstörer* crew whose performance was generally poor – several became lost and landed in the UK by mistake.

Elsewhere, the Spitfire LF.Mk IX had appeared in March 1943, able to out-fly the Fw 190. Earlier still, the P-47C Thunderbolt had become operational with the USAAF's 4th Fighter Group and at last represented an aircraft that could catch a speeding Fw 190 or Bf 109G in the dive. With US forces now pouring into the UK, Fw 190s in demand in the Mediterranean and the East, and the strain on German fighter pilots beginning to show, Luftwaffe casualties began to increase. Then the V-weapons appeared.

During August 1943 Allied photo-reconnaissance aircraft began

> The Luftwaffe was forced to develop tactics to defeat the B-17 and B-24, while the USAAF had to admit that its bombers could not defend themselves.

This photograph shows a tiny fragment of the build up to Operation Overlord. Crated supplies and Waco Hadrian gliders, in various states of re-assembly, litter the area.

bringing back images of construction sites in northern France. The Allies were already aware of Hitler's V-weapon programmes and identified these as launch sites for the V-1 flying-bomb terror weapon. The first strike against a V-1 site was flown on

With US forces now pouring into the UK, Fw 190s in demand in the Mediterranean and the East, and the strain on German fighter pilots beginning to show, Luftwaffe casualties began to increase. Then the V-weapons appeared.

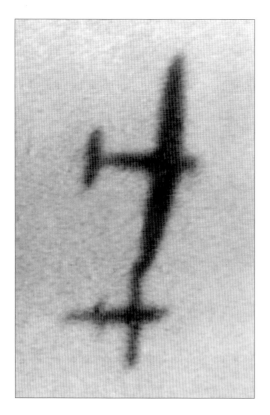

The Merlin-engined P-51 Mustang emerged as one of the great fighters of the war.

27 August by B-17s and thereafter followed an intensive campaign of attacks by heavy bombers, medium bombers and fighter-bombers.

The year 1943 was also notable for the introduction of key US fighter types: the P-51B Mustang and P-38 Lightning. The P-38 never really adapted well to the European theatre, but the Merlin-engined P-51 emerged as one of the great fighters of the war.

The invasion of Europe finally arrived on 6 June 1944, with the Allied landings in France – D-Day. In preparation for the landings Fighter

Left: Fighter pilots sometimes used wing-tipping to destroy V-1 flying-bombs. This involved placing the fighter's wingtip under that of the missile and forcing it up to send the weapon out of control.

Below: Officers of the British 6th Airborne Division synchronize watches prior to boarding their aircraft for Normandy. The machine in the background is an Armstrong Whitworth Albermarle.

Above: Dakotas acted as tugs for innumerable Horsa gliders during the D-Day landings. These aircraft were part of the second wave in support of the 6th Airborne Division.

Command had been dissolved in November 1943, the new Allied Expeditionary Air Force (AEAF) being composed of US and British forces and earmarked for forward deployment in the wake of the invasion, and Air Defence Great Britain (ADGB) staying 'home' to defend the UK.

D-DAY TRANSPORTS

A massive fleet of transport aircraft, gliders and glider tugs was assembled by the Allies in the UK for the initial assault of Operation Overlord, the invasion of northwest Europe. C-47 Skytrain and Dakota transports towed gliders and delivered paratroops and supplies, RAF Albermarles and converted Stirling bombers also towed gliders, while the gliderborne troops travelled to battle in their Hadrian, Hamilcar and Horsa gliders. Overhead RAF and USAAF bombers and fighters continued pounding German targets, including French transport infrastructure. With the initial assault a precursor for the primary amphibious landings, by the evening of 6 June 1944 beachheads had been firmly established. There followed bitter fighting through the hedgerows and lanes of Normandy.

OPERATION MARKET GARDEN

On the Continent, German forces had withdrawn to their defences in Holland and General Montgomery devised a plan to avoid confronting these positions. He aimed to have airborne forces land behind the German lines at Arnhem, in a two-part operation called Market and Garden. The joint operation began on 17 September 1944. It progressed badly, however, and by 21 September the survivors of the British force around Arnhem were escaping as best they could. Market Garden was but a costly setback for the Allies, however, and the march to the Rhine continued.

Right: The first sortie by the Meteor Mk I was flown by No. 616 Sqn, RAF, on 27 July 1944. On 4 August a V-1 became the jet's first victim, being brought down by wing-tipping.

Below: Hitler's revenge weapons were indiscriminate, being launched in the general direction of a city-sized target. The damage to this Guildford, Surrey, street was caused by a V-2 in March 1945.

Offensive operations were now aimed almost entirely at 'softening up' targets and attacking communications ahead of the invasion. By now German fighter defences were concentrated on combating the bombers of the US 8th Air Force and new aircraft, including the superlative Mosquito, were in widespread service and had

only to worry about the fearsome flak over enemy territory.

'CAB RANK' SORTIES

The combat in the wake of D-Day was particularly difficult because of the region's narrow roads, along which armour could travel while evading enemy forces. Soon the Typhoon, now armed with rocket projectiles, became

the weapon of choice against such armour. Orbiting Typhoons, flying 'cab rank' patrols, waited to be called onto targets by ground controllers. The toll taken of enemy armour and road traffic in Normandy was horrific.

On 13 June 1944 the menace of the V-weapons became all too real when a V-1 came down on Swanscombe, on the north Kent coast.

Now ADGB began tasking its Spitfire Mk XIV, Mustang Mk III, Mosquito NF.Mk XIII and all-new Tempest Mk V fighters against the weapons. These Diver patrols, which aimed to shoot down the unmanned missiles, were joined from 2 August by the RAF's first jet fighter, the Meteor Mk I, as part of an increasingly complex and effective defensive screen.

The slow progress towards Germany continued into the winter of 1944, with failed counteroffensives through the Ardennes in December and from the air on 1 January 1945. The latter, Operation *Bodenplatte* (Baseplate) was an ill-conceived attempt to use tactical air power in wiping out the Allied air

Above: Horsas litter a landing zone as paratroopers stream from Dakotas overhead. The Arnhem landings led their participants directly into trouble and resulted in a resounding defeat for the British.

forces on their forward bases. It succeeded primarily in taking many of the remaining Luftwaffe veterans out of the fight – Allied losses in aircraft and crews were easily replenished from reserves. The Germans also lost many of their latest aircraft, including several of the Fw 190D-9s and Me 262 jets, as well as burning valuable

Finally, on 7 March 1945, US troops crossed the Rhine, followed on the 24th by an airborne operation that saw US and British forces landed east of the Rhine around Wesel.

aviation fuel for little return. Finally, on 7 March 1945, US troops crossed the Rhine, followed on the 24th by an airborne operation that saw US and British forces landed east of the Rhine around Wesel.

Now the Luftwaffe began last-ditch operations in defence of Berlin. Me 262s began entering the battle in numbers, although never more than

Below: The Anson Mk I – as here – was the cornerstone of RAF Coastal Command at the outbreak of war. Nine squadrons flew the type, while one other flew the Hudson Mk I and another flew the Vildebeest Mk IV biplane.

'SCOURGE OF THE ATLANTIC'

The Luftwaffe had shown its proficiency in anti-shipping strikes early on in the conflict and while it remained lethal in littoral zones, it was over 'blue water' that its aircraft really began to have an effect. Dubbed 'scourge of the Atlantic' by Churchill, the long-range Fw 200 Condor was able to prosecute targets far out into the Atlantic, as well as providing details of their positions to other aircraft and, when the Luftwaffe and Kriegsmarine were cooperating efficiently, U-boats. Together the Condor and U-boat came to threaten Britain's very survival.

50 in a single operation, and the latest Bf 109K, and the Ta 152 derivative of the Fw 190, became more widespread. Nevertheless, there was no longer any hope and with the Soviets closing on Berlin from the east unconditional surrender became inevitable.

The struggle against the U-boat received its first boost with the introduction of ASV Mk II radar, which allowed RAF Coastal Command Hudsons, Wellingtons, Catalina flying-boats and Liberators to detect surfaced submarines. The reach of such aircraft was limited, however, leaving a U-boat hunting ground in the mid-Atlantic where neither US nor RAF aircraft could reach. Other technology, including the Leigh Light, which illuminated targets for night-time attack by patrolling aircraft, was also employed, but still the aircraft could not accompany the convoys over the entire route across the Atlantic.

Although Hitler had discounted the possibility of defeating the UK by maritime conflict alone, the debilitating effect of preventing the country's resupply from the US and Canada by sea was key to his strategy.

In September 1939 some 26 ships \were lost to U-boat attack, including the aircraft carrier HMS *Courageous*. Against the submarine menace RAF Coastal Command could only field the Anson and rather more capable Sunderland, both ill-equipped for

such combat. Indeed, not until 30 January 1940 would Coastal Command claim a sinking – of *U-55* by a Sunderland – although the boat had already been damaged by the Royal Navy.

ANTI-SHIPPING STRIKES

The war against the U-boat was to be a war of technology and means, while that against surface units was pursued with some success from the outset. Among the major contributions of Allied air power in defeating the German navy was the disabling of *Bismarck*'s steering gear by Swordfish out of HMS *Ark Royal* on 26 May 1941. The crippled battleship was then destroyed by Royal Navy vessels, to mark the end of Germany's capital ship sorties. Elsewhere the Beauforts, Beaufighters and, latterly, Mosquitos, of Coastal Command attacked

As early as November 1939 the first Fw 200 maritime reconnaissance unit was forming. With the fall of France in 1940 the Condors, as well as the U-boats, began operating from French bases.

surface units throughout the war, while the Fleet Air Arm and Bomber Command variously contributed to the campaign against Germany's other great ships, among them, *Scharnhorst*, *Gneisenau*, *Prinz Eugen* and *Tirpitz*.

ESCORT CARRIERS

The major breakthrough came with the commissioning of HMS *Audacity*, a converted war prize which embarked eight Martlet (F4F Wildcat) fighters for its initial operation on a Gibraltar–England convoy in December 1941. Although the ship was lost on 21/22 December, its Martlets destroyed two Condors and proved the effectiveness of this type of vessel. The way for escorts armed with fighters and anti-submarine aircraft had been paved, although more needless losses had to be sustained before their use became widespread.

Convoy PQ-16 to the Soviet Union became the first to experience greater Luftwaffe anti-shipping efforts during

Bismarck was a prime target for the Allies, but it defended itself well against air and naval attack. The ship was finally sunk by naval gunfire on 27 May 1941, after its steering gear had been disabled by a Swordfish torpedo-bomber.

May 1942. Over five days it was attacked by Ju 88s for the loss of seven ships. Hitler was displeased, having wanted all 35 ships destroyed. PQ-17 was therefore targeted in a maximum effort by around 264 aircraft. It sailed from Iceland on 27 June and was attacked almost constantly through to 4 July. Twenty-three out of 33 ships were lost and air defences became essential for all future sailings. PQ-18 included HMS *Avenger* with its Sea Hurricane Mk IB and Swordfish aircraft, and the catapult-armed merchantman *Empire Morn* with its Sea Hurricane Mk IA. During its sailing five bombers were shot down and 21 damaged, for the loss of four Sea Hurricanes and 13 ships. Large-scale attacks in the Arctic could no longer

Left: Already forced to the surface, this Type VII U-boat is suffering under depth-charge attack. Hunting and killing submarines from the air was a difficult task, even with the latest technologies available to the Allies.

By 1944 the Liberator GR.Mk IV was in Coastal Command service. Based on the Consolidated B-24J and equipped with retractable search radar in its lower rear fuselage, it was a formidable maritime aircraft.

attacks in the Arctic could no longer be sustained by the Luftwaffe, but in the Atlantic the war against the U-boat was far from over.

Increasing supplies of very long range aircraft from the US, particularly the Liberator, allowed Coastal Command to take its radar-aided war on the U-boat further out to sea and ASV (Airborne Surface Vessel) radar equipment was now available to almost all of its aircraft. But the key to defeating the U-boat menace lay in the escort carrier. Six

new ships entered service with Martlet and Swordfish complements during 1943, while the US Navy introduced six larger vessels supporting Grumman Wildcat fighters and Avenger anti-submarine aircraft. At last the Atlantic gap between the coverage of North America-based aircraft and those of Coastal Command could be covered. U-boat losses began to mount and their attacks became less effective as evading Allied aircraft became a primary concern.

THE U-BOAT MENACE

Meanwhile, Coastal Command, bolstered by Liberator and Catalina units from the US, began a vicious campaign against boats transiting

between their French ports and the Atlantic killing grounds. For the U-boat it represented the beginning of the end. At the close of 1941 there was a very real possibility that the UK could not survive the U-boat scourge.

By the end of May 1943 Admiral Doenitz, the brilliant mastermind of Germany's U-boat campaign, was ordering his boats out of the Atlantic after the sinking of five submarines in five days, for the loss of not a single Allied ship. The U-boats would regroup and renew their offensive, but the escort carriers, and land-based anti-submarine aircraft with their improving technology, would never again allow them to become a threat of war-winning potential.

> U-boat losses began to mount and their attacks became less effective as evading Allied aircraft became a primary concern.

World War II: Africa and the Mediterranean 1940–1945

On 10 June 1940, Benito Mussolini declared war on the UK and France. By 28 October his forces were in Greece and heading for a rout, but his belligerence threw the whole Mediterranean theatre into conflict. In particular the island of Malta took on great importance as a naval base, especially with the loss to the Allies of the French fleet at the signing of the Armistice. Malta would also act as an 'unsinkable aircraft carrier' for the basing of aircraft that could strike at Italian shipping and land targets, but had no permanent RAF squadrons and only meagre anti-aircraft defences.

Realizing the threat that Italy now posed, Commodore F.H.M. Maynard, Commander Air Headquarters RAF Mediterranean Command, based on the island, ordered the assembly of three Fleet Air Arm (FAA) Sea Gladiator Mk I fighters from the components of four stored on the island. This was a prophetic move for, in the early hours of 11 June 1940, Regia Aeronautica (Italian air force) SM.79 bombers began operations against the island. Two Sea Gladiators reacted and the constant attentions of the biplanes during the eight raids of the day saw to it that future attacks were flown under the protection of CR.42 and MC.200 fighters. Malta gained an offensive capability on 24 June when four No. 767 Naval Air Squadron (NAS) Swordfish arrived to become No. 830 NAS. Fighter reinforcement also arrived, initially as 12 Hurricane Mk Is flown off HMS *Argus*.

Undoubtedly the best of the Italian bombers to serve during World War II, the Savoia-Marchetti SM.79 went on to shine as a torpedo-bomber over the Mediterranean.

These Macchi MC.200 fighters were operated by 22° Gruppo, 52° Stormo, in the defence of Rome during 1940. Italian pilots initially resisted the fitting of canopies to their fighters' cockpits.

Mussolini's adventures in Greece were going spectacularly awry and German involvement, not only in Greece, but also in the wider Mediterranean and North African theatres, was an inevitable result. The Italians were also faring badly in North Africa and in order to keep Axis interests in the region alive, Hitler began moving Luftwaffe units into Italy. Attacks began on a Malta supply convoy on 13 January 1941, Italian Z.1007bis, SM.79 and Ju 87B-2 aircraft working with German Ju 88A-1s. On the 14th HMS *Illustrious* came under accurate attack by 30 German Stukas. It was badly damaged, but made port in Malta where it became the subject of attacks, until making good its escape to Alexandria on 23 January. X Fliegerkorps, the parent unit of the Luftwaffe units in Italy, was having an immediate effect.

He 111H-3s began making regular anti-shipping reconnaissance sorties and mining operations over the sea, while Ju 88 and Ju 87 bombers attacked Malta's airfields. Soon the fighter forces were improved, with 7./JG 26 taking up station on Sicily with its Bf 109E-7s. Now the Luftwaffe began *frei Jagd* operations and even though British radar was in operation, the airfields on Sicily were so close that little warning of attack could be provided. German reinforcements continued arriving and air supremacy was gained over Malta.

MALTA'S REPRIEVE

Continued attacks cost 96 Axis aircraft between June 1940 and the end of February 1941, but Malta was running out of skilled fighter pilots. Fortune would have it that X Fliegerkorps assets were now tasked with supporting the fighting in North Africa, and additional effort was also required in Yugoslavia, Greece and Crete, with the result that Malta now drew only the attention of the Regia Aeronautica.

With Italy having declared war on the UK, Air Commodore R. Collishaw, in command of No. 202 Group in

ATTACK ON TARANTO

During the latter half of 1940 and into spring 1941, the Royal Navy was at large in the Mediterranean. The aircraft of HMS *Eagle* struck at Vichy targets in North Africa and then became involved in supply sorties to Malta. HMS *Illustrious* arrived in the theatre during August, along with the new Fulmar Mk I fighter. Its Fulmars and Swordfish wreaked havoc before the Swordfish flew a daring and devastating raid against the Italian fleet moored at Taranto. A masterful plan of attack worked brilliantly, with the loss of just two Swordfish and one crew for at least three battleships and two destroyers badly damaged. Flushed with the success of Taranto, the British rampage continued, with HMS *Ark Royal* joining in and *Argus* embarking Swordfish for anti-submarine work.

North Africa, ordered his Blenheims against the Italian airfield at El Adem. The aircraft attacked on 10 June 1940 with total surprise – Italian high command had failed to inform its units in Africa of the declaration of war. Fighter combat was joined for the first time on 29 June, three RAF Gladiators facing a similar number of CR.42s for the loss of two of the Fiats.

The pattern for British-Italian encounters in the air had been set. The Italians were no match for the RAF, even given the poor state of its equipment in the region – resources were jealously guarded back home as German aggression increased in the prelude to the Battle of Britain. Even so, Wellington Mk IC bombers began arriving to mark an increase in the

The Italians were no match for the RAF, even given the poor state of its equipment in the region.

RAF's bombing capabilities, while Hurricane Mk Is began replacing Gladiator biplane fighters.

GERMAN INVOLVEMENT

General Sir Archibald Wavell, commander of Commonwealth troops in North Africa, now began a bold offensive aimed at capturing Libya and Cyrenaica. Air power played an important part in the campaign and again the pattern of British air supremacy was evident. Wavell led his

forces deep into Libya, before halting the advance for fear of breaking lines of communication. At this point Allied resources began to be diverted to Greece, while X Fliegerkorps was instructed to begin operations against Allied forces in Libya and Egypt, as well as in the Mediterranean. More

Shown here in 1939 shortly after it was commissioned, HMS *Ark Royal*, along with its embarked Swordfish, enjoyed a period of great success, before being sunk late in 1941.

> Hitler was keen to hold Rommel back until the Afrika Korps had been built into a strong force, but it was clear to the Generalleutnant that Commonwealth forces were over-extended and weak.

ominously, Generalleutnant Erwin Rommel arrived in Tripoli on 12 February 1941 to take charge of the meagre German forces already in place to support the Italians. The Afrika Korps had arrived in North Africa and a supply effort began by sea and air to bring the Korps up to strength. Bf 110s began strafing attacks on British forces on 10 February, while Ju 88s attacked

Benghazi and shipping.

Hitler was keen to hold Rommel back until the Afrika Korps had been built into a strong force, but it was clear to the Generalleutnant that Commonwealth forces were over-

The Gladiator was flown by both RAF and South African Air Force (SAAF) squadrons in the Mediterranean theatre. It initially fared well against inferior Italian opposition.

extended and weak. He decided that a series of light armoured thrusts could inflict telling damage and in the face of the first of these, on 31 March, the Allies began to withdraw.

ROMMEL ON THE OFFENSIVE
Skirmishes soon began in the air as RAF and Royal Australian Air Force (RAAF) fighter units countered the Luftwaffe's Bf 110s and long-range Ju 87R-1 dive-bombers with some success. By 4 April

Above: Although it became outclassed in the air-to-air arena by the latest variants of the Bf 109, the Hurricane performed vital work in the ground-attack and anti-armour roles.

Benghazi had fallen to Rommel and as German forces moved into Greece and Yugoslavia it was decided to preserve the RAF's assets by withdrawing to Egypt. Nevertheless, attacks and defensive operations continued. The Hurricanes were in action, combating a large force of Ju 87, Bf 110 and G.50 aircraft, on 14 April, while the Afrika Korps complained of a lack of fighter cover.

This deficiency was made up on 15 April when the Bf 109E-4/N fighters of JG 27 began moving into Ain-el-Gazala for action from the 19th. The Messerschmitts were based just 105km (65 miles) from the port of Tobruk, which was coming under severe German pressure and would remain with the Allies, under a state of siege, behind German lines.

Rommel struck at Tobruk on 30 April, but once again its mainly Australian garrison held out. He was forced to withdraw as lines of supply became over-stretched. Then the arrival of the Tiger convoy brought tanks and 53 Hurricane Mk I fighters,

HAWKER HURRICANE MK.II

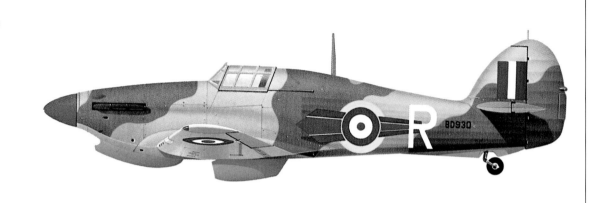

Type: single-seat fighter

Powerplant: one 883kW (1185hp) Rolls-Royce
Merlin XX V-12 piston engine

Maximum speed: 547km/h (340mph)

Service ceiling: 10,970m (36,000ft)

Weights: maximum take-off weight 3950kg
(8710lb); empty 2605kg (5745lb)

Armament: four 20mm (0.78in) Hispano Mk II
cannon

Dimensions: span   12.19m (40ft)
            length 6.3m (20ft 8in)
            height 4m (13ft 1in)
            wing area 23.92m² (257sq ft)

> The Allies briefly held air superiority over the battlefield, but the advantage was soon lost and another ignominious withdrawal was inevitable.

which, in part, allowed the Allies to embark on Operation Brevity, a counteroffensive to capture the Halfaya Pass, on 15 May. With the Pass secured, Operation Battleaxe would push on to Tobruk to relieve the Australians. Halfaya was initially taken, but the Germans managed to scrape together enough fuel to get some of their tanks rolling.

With only limited air cover the Allies fared badly in the ensuing fight and the Pass was back in German hands by 27 May. Battleaxe went ahead regardless on 14 June, only to stall on the 17th following a counterattack. The Allies briefly held air superiority over the battlefield, but the advantage was soon lost and another ignominious withdrawal was inevitable.

BATTLE OVER CRETE

By agreement with the Greek government, British personnel began establishing a base on the strategically

important island of Crete in November 1940. The base was minimally defended with AAA and just a single squadron of fighters was allocated, No. 805 NAS being equipped with Fulmar Mk Is, Sea Gladiators and a reserve of F2A Buffalos. Sunderlands were forward-based in Suda Bay, and radar was installed around the island.

In April 1941, the RAF Air Staff declared that the air defence of Crete was impossible and it therefore became only a useful forward base for aircraft tasked with convoy protection duties in the Mediterranean. Among the motley selection of machines assembled for this vital duty was a handful of Bombays, Blenheim Mk IFs, Hurricanes and Gladiators, the latter three types frequently encountering German Bf 109Es.

From 14 May these encounters turned into a sustained campaign against the island as the first in a week-long series of level and dive-

bombing attacks hit home. Ten Hurricanes came in from Egypt to reinforce the air defences, but by 19 May only three Hurricanes and three Gladiators could be mustered. Any serviceable aircraft were withdrawn with immediate effect. Hitler had finalized his plans for Operation *Merkur* (Mercury) – a bold plan using a mix of gliderborne, parachute and seaborne troops to take the island.

Almost 500 Ju 52/3m transports were assembled in southern Greece for the assault on 20 May. Even before the transports took off the Germans had made two key errors. First, they had misunderstood the terrain of the island, which was rocky and severe. Second, they had underestimated the strength of the Allied garrison on Crete, which numbered around 30,000 men.

The first troops landed by DFS 230 glider and were immediately destroyed. *Fallschirmjäger* followed, to receive an equally deadly reception. The fighting was fierce and all going the Allies' way, since the Luftwaffe was unable to offer support given the confused situation on the ground. But then, during the night of 21 May, Allied troops evacuated their positions on a strategically important hill. This allowed the enemy to seize the airfield at Máleme and to begin landing Ju 52/3ms there. The Junkers

Having suffered during the Battle of Britain, the Bf 110 proved well suited to operations in the desert and Mediterranean. Its long range was especially appreciated.

operated under fire, but brought in battle-winning reinforcements. The fighting continued until 25 May, when the Commonwealth forces began assembling at the port of Sfakia for evacuation.

CRETE CAPTURED

British naval units had been in operation throughout, patrolling to prevent any German naval involvement in *Merkur*. HMS *Formidable* was present with its complement of 18 Fulmars, but further air cover had to come from Egypt, which left the Hurricanes, Beaufighters, Blenheims and Marylands involved at the limits of their range and able to provide

Crete was secure, but the fighting had also cost the Germans dear. Never again did Hitler commit his *Fallschirmjäger* to combat in such an ambitious manner.

limited cover to the ships, but none to Crete. The Luftwaffe's reaction to the Royal Navy was predictable and took on a new ferocity after 22 May with the Allies in full retreat. To the Stukas were added forces of Bf 110C-4 and D-3 fighters, and Ju 88A-4, Do 17Z and He 111H-3 bombers.

The toll on shipping was heavy, with three cruisers and six destroyers

sunk. Damaged vessels included the carrier, three battleships, six cruisers and seven destroyers. Crete was secure, but the fighting had also cost the Germans dear in aircraft lost and casualties. Never again did Hitler

Below: Both the Ju 52/3m units and their *Fallschirmjäger* suffered terribly during the initial landings against Crete. Strong Allied defences and rugged terrain made for heavy losses.

Above: Float-equipped Ju 52/3m transports proved useful around the Mediterranean and Balkans. These Ju 52/3m6ge (See) aircraft were photographed over the Aegean in 1943.

commit his *Fallschirmjäger* to combat in such an ambitious manner.

In the lead-up to a new Allied offensive in the desert, Operation Crusader, Commonwealth air power concentrated on attacking Axis airfields. As the Germans came up in defence it was immediately clear that

NEW EQUIPMENT IN THE DESERT

In North Africa, after the capture of Crete and the failure of Operations Brevity and Battleaxe, it was time for the Allies to stave off any further German advances, while taking time to rearm. Among the newly arrived machines in the wake of Brevity and Battleaxe were Tomahawk Mk IIB fighters, Hurricanes, Beauforts, Beaufighters, Marylands and Boston Mk IIIs. This air power was prepared for a new offensive under Operation Crusader, beginning in November 1941. However, at the same time, new Bf 109F-2 and F-4/Trop fighters arrived with II./JG 27, while the Italians took more MC.200s and received the new MC.202 Folgore.

The DFS 230 glider, here shown during training, was towed in great numbers by Ju 52/3ms during the invasion of Crete. This example has a machine-gun above its cockpit for providing suppressive fire on landing.

the Bf 109F was in a different class to the Tomahawk and Hurricane. This discovery would have an impact on the execution of Crusader, which started well enough on the night of 18/19 November when Allied troops set out from Egypt for Tobruk. Rommel's 88mm guns and tanks engaged with ferocity, but the

Crusader forces joined with the Australian garrison, which moved out of Tobruk on 26/27 November, to lift the siege on the port on 7 December.

During the fighting Allied aircraft fared badly and were it not for the limited fuel supplies reaching the *Panzers* the aerial support provided for the offensive might not have been sufficient. As it was, Rommel's supply problems forced him to withdraw past Benghazi, taking with him elements of the Luftwaffe, some of which were forced to move to bases on Sicily. Crusader had succeeded in large part

thanks to the efficient actions of British ships and aircraft in interdicting German supplies crossing the Mediterranean. These forces were based on Malta and there would be no Axis victory in the theatre if Malta remained in Allied hands. Malta was once again to become the subject of the Luftwaffe's attention.

TARGET MALTA

With Crete, Yugoslavia and Greece all under German control, X Fliegerkorps transferred its headquarters from Sicily to Athens, moving its subordinate units variously to Germany, Greece and Crete, providing Malta with a brief respite during May 1941. Allied convoys were making it through relatively

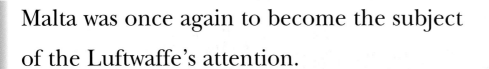

Malta was once again to become the subject of the Luftwaffe's attention.

unhindered, although the supremely skilled *Aerosiluranti*, the dedicated torpedo-bomber arm of the Regia Aeronautica, represented a constant and deadly threat, while surface craft and Italian submarines posed their own difficulties. When convoy Substance made landfall on 24 July, among its cargo were six Swordfish, which, along with a detachment of No. 272 Sqn Beaufighters, allowed Malta to begin exercising a new offensive role. By the beginning of

August Malta's air assets had multiplied considerably. During September the Halberd convoy fought its way through accurate *Aerosiluranti* attacks to deliver 50,000 tons of cargo, including fuel sufficient to last until May 1942. In the event, it was mid-August 1942 before convoys could again begin resupplying Malta.

Malta's anti-shipping work continued to have serious consequences for Axis convoys, and during September Rommel began

complaining that he was not being adequately supplied and that something must be done to protect the convoys. The reaction came late in October 1941, when Hitler ordered U-boats into the Mediterranean. He

In August 1942 the Pedestal convoy brought three merchantmen and a tanker to Malta. It included the aircraft carriers *Indomitable* (having just launched an Albacore), *Eagle* (trailing) and *Victorious* (foreground, with Sea Hurricane). *Furious* was also involved, carrying Spitfires.

No. 417 Sqn, RAF, took its Spitfires to Egypt in April 1942. These Mk VC aircraft are fitted with the clumsy Vokes tropical filter, which protected the Merlin engine from the harsh desert sand.

also insisted that Luftwaffe assets be strengthened and moved back into Sicily. During December Malta once again came under attack from Luftwaffe bombers and the U-boats began their grim work. HMS *Ark Royal* was among the vessels sunk.

In January 1942 the bombing of Malta's airfields led to the withdrawal of its Wellingtons, but the Hurricanes remained in force. Luftwaffe fighters began gathering as Bf 109F-4/Trops joined II Fliegerkorps in Sicily,

bringing its strength to around 425 aircraft. A pattern of around 65-70 bombers striking Malta each day began during the month, with the Bf 109s escorting Ju 88A-4s, as well as mounting *Jabo* attacks and flying sweeps. The Hurricane Mk II was outclassed by the Bf 109F and it came as a relief when 15 Spitfire Mk VBs were flown off HMS *Argus* and *Eagle* on 7 March. *Eagle* arrived with nine more Spitfires, Mk VCs, on 21 March.

The fighting now became even more intense when a convoy attempted to land from Alexandria on 23 March. The Spitfires and Hurricanes flew whenever possible throughout the month, with varying

degrees of success as just about every target of any significance, from shipping to runways, was hit in the near-constant bombing. *Eagle* made it through to deliver seven more Spitfire Mk VCs on 29 March, and as raids of more than 250 German aircraft each became regular occurrences, Winston Churchill gained permission to have USS *Wasp* attempt the delivery of 47 Spitfire Mk VCs.

SPITFIRE SUPREME
Only if air supremacy could be gained over Malta could the island be saved and the Spitfires seemed to be the only possibility for that to be achieved. Equipped with ferry tanks,

Air Vice Marshall Lloyd signalled London on 27 May 1942, indicating that Malta might fall if immediate reinforcement was not forthcoming.

the Spitfires were flown off *Wasp* in radio silence during the early hours of 20 April. The carrier was steaming

off Algiers and the aircraft had 1125km (700 miles) of flying ahead of them. Some 46 made it to Malta, but radio silence had been compromised and the Luftwaffe was waiting to count the Spitfires down. A pair of Bf 109s circled offshore to make the count, even as the first Ju 88s were on their way to the base at Takahli. The bombers struck not much more than an hour and a half after the last Spitfire had landed. Few of the fighters had been turned around and the raid destroyed many on the ground.

Ironically, the remaining Spitfires attracted even greater attention from the Luftwaffe and by early May 1942 only six serviceable fighters remained, their crews surviving on semi-starvation rations. Malta's air defences had been all but defeated and the island was ripe for invasion. Air Officer Commanding Malta, Air Vice Marshall Lloyd, signalled London on the 27th, indicating that Malta might

fall if immediate reinforcement was not forthcoming.

Reinforcement came, in the form of HMS *Eagle* and USS *Wasp*, which between them flew off 64 Spitfire Mk VCs. HMS *Welshman*, a fast minelayer, sailed with them, with a load of vital supplies that had to make it through. This time the Spitfires were greeted with efficiency, some being turned around in just six minutes from landing. The ferry pilots were pulled from the cockpits as the groundcrews worked, so that the fighters could be airborne with fresh pilots ready for the inevitable attacks.

The organization of 9 May was nothing short of remarkable, for when the first German bombers appeared overhead, around half of the new Spitfires were airborne and ready to fight. And fight they did, especially on 10 May, when *Welshman* made it to port and began to attract determined Ju 87 and Ju 88 raids. On 18 May, 17 more Spitfires arrived from *Eagle*. The

MESSERSCHMITT BF 109

Type: single-seat fighter

Powerplant: one 1085kW (1455hp) Daimler-Benz DB 605A-1 inverted V12 piston engine

Maximum speed: 640km/h (398mph)

Service ceiling: 12,000m (39,370ft)

Weights: maximum take-off weight 3400kg (7495lb); empty 2247kg (5893lb)

Armament: 2 x 7.92mm (0.303in) MG 17 machine-guns. 1 x 20mm (0.78in) MG 151/20 cannon

Dimensions: span   9.9m (32ft 6in)
length   8.9m (29ft 7in)
height   2.60m (8ft 2in)
wing area   16.4m² (173sq ft)

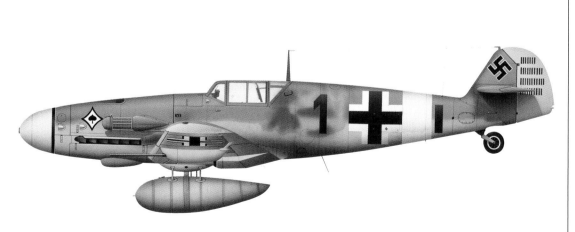

RAF began to score telling victories in the air and their effect on Luftwaffe morale revealed that the crews of II Fliegerkorps were exhausted. Operations began to suffer as Malta's defences became stronger. The invasion of Malta was shelved, but it was not until August 1942 that attacks on Allied convoys began to fall off. Nevertheless, as early as June offensive operations from Malta recommenced and its fighters were soon flying offensive sweeps over Sicily. The Luftwaffe made one more concerted effort against Malta, on 11 October 1942, for the loss of nine

A useful stopgap until better equipment became available, the Curtiss Tomahawk performed well in the desert. It was an easy match for the Italian fighters, but struggled against the Bf 109E.

> Another major German mistake was being committed and it marked the beginning of the end for the Axis in Africa.

Bf 109G-2/Trops and 35 bombers, against 30 Spitfires. These losses were too great to endure and Malta's strike assets and shipping were once again free to harry Axis convoys plying the routes to North Africa.

AT WAR IN THE DESERT

January 1942 found the Allies' Desert Air Force (DAF) squaring up to Axis forces in Libya. With attacks on Malta increasing in intensity, the entry of Japan into the war in the previous December and the reluctance of leaders at 'home' to release the latest

equipment, the DAF found itself fielding generally inferior aircraft, even though these included the latest Kittyhawk Mk I fighters. The Bf 109F still reigned supreme as it would prove in a spell of intense fighting following a new offensive launched by Rommel late in January.

Exchanges continued between the air arms at a steady pace until May 1942, then *frei Jagd* missions became more frequent and Ju 88s began bombing troop positions. A spoof manoeuvre on 26 May heralded a decisive expedition from Rommel,

Above: A large, lumbering target, the Me 323 was an essential link in the supply chain that kept German forces in North Africa. It was vulnerable to just about any aircraft with a gun!

which put the Allies on the defensive. Intensive operations cost the DAF 20 per cent of its strength between 26 and 29 May and it was forced to conserve resources. This did little to alleviate Luftwaffe attacks on Tobruk, a target with which Rommel had become obsessed. This time the port fell, its South African garrison being captured during June after a series of continuous raids on 20 June. With Tobruk gone for the loss of 32,220 men taken prisoner, it seemed that Rommel could not be stopped.

STRATEGIC ERROR

Riding on a wave of success Rommel now pushed on in his aim to reach Suez. Some within the Nazi leadership felt that already his lines of supply had been over extended and, indeed, supplies of fuel looked likely to be exhausted before June was out.

The temptation was too great, however, and the *Panzerarmee Afrika*, as Afrika Korps was now designated, thrust forward. At the same time Malta was emerging victorious from the Luftwaffe's onslaught and its air and sea units once again began attacking Axis supply convoys.

Another major German mistake was being committed and it marked the beginning of the end for the Axis in Africa. Nevertheless, for the time being Allied forces fell back towards

in the fighting prior to the 'softening-up' raids that preceded the El Alamein offensive of 19 October. The fighting proper began on 23 October. The Axis faced overwhelming Allied forces and on 24 October alone the RAF flew 1000 sorties, the USAAF adding another 147.

THE END IN AFRICA
The 8th Army broke out over the period 26 October to 4 November, with the aid of 10,405 RAF missions.

USS *Ranger* took part in Operation Torch with its F4F-4 Wildcat fighters – a VF-41 aircraft is shown here – and SBD-3 Dauntless attack aircraft.

El Alamein, while the DAF was reinforced by good-quality machines at last, including Spitfire Mk VBs diverted from Australian supplies, with the promise of US forces to come.

Although it was in retreat, the 8th Army was moving under local air superiority. During July Rommel joined battle for a month-long campaign, but Axis air power became increasingly unable to lend support thanks to a lack of fuel. A resupply effort by Ju 52/3ms could not make up for the shipping losses and through August the Axis was forced to

recoup its losses and prepare for further conflict. A renewed offensive began on 31 August as Rommel attempted to break through to the Nile around El Alamein. Every effort he made was countered by the 8th Army, now under the leadership of General Montgomery, under merciless bombardment from the air. Now Montgomery made plans to take the war back to Rommel during October 1942, but JG 27 was busy taking on new Bf 109G-2s. It would again have mastery over the best Allied fighters. The 'Gustavs' were used to good effect

Hurricane Mk IIB 'AK-W' served with No. 213 Sqn, RAF, in Egypt during 1942. Here it shares a desert landing ground with a Lockheed Hudson.

The result was rapid Axis retreat, followed, on 8 November, by large-scale Allied landings in North Africa under Operation Torch.

The Anglo-American Operation Torch put troops ashore in French Morocco and Tunisia, initially to defeat Vichy French forces and then to take on *Panzerarmee Afrika* from the rear, eventually to meet up with Montgomery's 8th Army. Some combat was fought with the French, but in other cases cooperation was received.

Operation Torch put troops ashore in French Morocco and Tunisia, initially to defeat Vichy French forces and then to take on *Panzerarmee Afrika* from the rear.

Serious opposition came first from German forces now occupying Vichy France, where reinforcements were brought in from Norway and the

Eastern Front while anti-shipping efforts were stepped up. Landings were also made in Tunisia, an army of several thousand troops being

THE AIR CAMPAIGN IN ITALY

Overwhelming air power was used against all manner of targets before the invasion of Italy, including heavy bombers from both the USAAF and RAF. Opposition to bombing raids by Bf 109Gs and MC.202s remained staunch, but the P-38, Kittyhawk, P-40 and A-36 Invader escorts were seldom bettered. A final battle between B-17s, their P-38 escorts and mortar-firing Bf 109Gs on 7 September 1943 represented the final occasion on which a massed Luftwaffe response could be put up.

assembled with the support of Bf 109G, Ju 87D and Fw 190A-4 units. These forces were to stem the Allied advance while allowing Rommel time to re-equip and regroup. They fought well and slowed the Allied advance through Tunisia to a crawl, but as Anglo-American cooperation improved and US fighter pilots gained experience, the Allies made good ground.

Late in March 1943 the newly-arrived 1st Army joined the 8th and with the Mediterranean all but closed to Axis shipping, a Luftwaffe supply effort using Ju 52/3m, Ju 90, Go 242, DFS 230, SM.81 and Me 323 transports began. This massive airlift was terribly vulnerable to Allied fighters, including the newly arrived P-38 Lightnings, and by the end of the so-called Flax operation in April 1943, around 400 transports had been lost for 35 Allied fighters. The Allies began their final offensive in Africa on

22 April. Surviving Axis troops fought hard, but the outcome was inevitable and Bf 109 and Fw 190 pilots began evacuating to Sicily with as many groundcrew as they could squeeze into their aircraft. The surrender came on 13 May and the war in Africa was over.

OPERATION HUSKY

The UK was convinced that the key to a successful invasion of northern Europe lay in attacking the Reich from the south, taking Italy out of the war in the process. Reluctantly the US agreed to this strategy and plans were drawn up for a combined airborne and amphibious assault on Sicily as a starting point. A massive warplane armada had been assembled in the Mediterranean and North African theatres, including USAAF Liberator heavy bombers, Spitfire Mk IXs and F-5 Lightning reconnaissance aircraft.

A concerted effort was made against airfields and other key military targets across Italy, Sardinia and Sicily in the build up to the assault, which was known as Operation Husky.

The invasion of Sicily was scheduled to begin at 0245 on 10 June 1943, but the operation immediately faltered. Although the Germans had guessed wrongly and decided that the forthcoming invasion was not heading for Sicily and withdrawn some forces from the island to reinforce elsewhere, the weather was against the Allies. Horsa and Waco gliders were used in the initial assault and strong winds caused 69 to come down short, in the sea. The same winds hampered paratrooping C-47s, so that their loads were strewn across a wide area. These were but setbacks, however, and with massive air support even the stiffest pockets of German resistance were eventually subdued. The fighting had been tough and protracted, but by 12 August the surviving Axis forces had evacuated.

INTO ITALY

Sicily was only a stepping stone into Italy and a three-part invasion plan was drawn up. The first part of the invasion of the mainland, Operation Baytown, landed the 8th Army at Reggio Calabria on 3 September, with

CURTISS P-40 KITTYHAWK

Type: single-seat fighter

Powerplant: one 857kW (1150hp) Packard Merlin V-1650-39 V12 piston engine

Maximum speed: 589km/h (366mph)

Service ceiling: 8839m (29,000ft)

Weights: maximum take-off weight 4173kg (9200lb); empty 2880kg (6350lb)

Armament: 6 x 12.7mm (0.5in) calibre machine-guns, external bomb load of 227kg (500lb)

Dimensions:
span 11.35m (37ft 3in)
length 9.49m (31ft 2in)
height 3.22m (10ft 7in)
wing area 21.92m² (236sq ft)

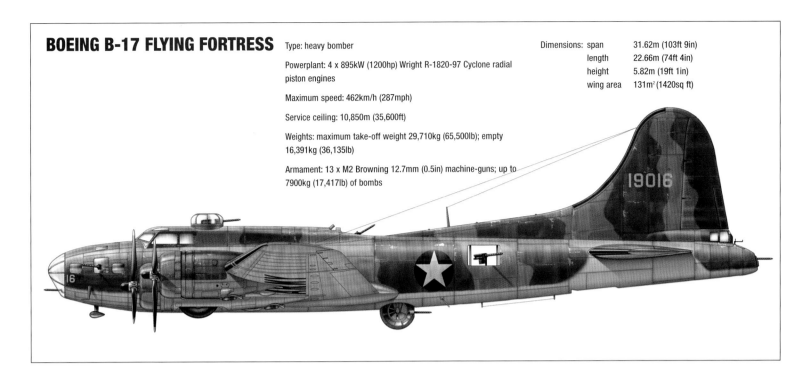

BOEING B-17 FLYING FORTRESS

Type: heavy bomber

Powerplant: 4 x 895kW (1200hp) Wright R-1820-97 Cyclone radial piston engines

Maximum speed: 462km/h (287mph)

Service ceiling: 10,850m (35,600ft)

Weights: maximum take-off weight 29,710kg (65,500lb); empty 16,391kg (36,135lb)

Armament: 13 x M2 Browning 12.7mm (0.5in) machine-guns; up to 7900kg (17,417lb) of bombs

Dimensions: span   31.62m (103ft 9in)
             length   22.66m (74ft 4in)
             height   5.82m (19ft 1in)
             wing area   131m² (1420sq ft)

Spitfire and Kittyhawk support. Operation Avalanche on 9 September put a mixed force of US and British troops down on the Italian coast in the gulf of Salerno, with massive land-based and naval fighter support. German resistance was fierce and not until 16 September did a withdrawal begin. By that time Fw 190A-5 *Jabos* and missile-armed Dorniers had hit Allied shipping hard. Finally, the relatively unopposed Operation Slapstick put troops ashore simultaneously at Taranto.

Allied advances into Italy proceeded against stiff German resistance, with Naples falling to the Americans on 1 October. Elsewhere, Italian units were beginning to defect, but Hitler determined to defend Italy to the last. The retreating Germans made clever use of Italy's terrain to establish almost impregnable defensive positions, locking the Allies into a war of attrition that could not be won with the use of air power alone. Eventual victory was inevitable, however, and the US 9th Air Force was withdrawn for operations in support of the forthcoming invasion of France. The winter of 1943 proved particularly trying, with early rains turning

airfields into quagmires and limiting the scope for operations. The advance became even more difficult, especially when it reached the German defensive system: the Gustav Line.

TAKING ROME

Fierce battles raged at Cassino through December 1943 and into 1944 as the Allies attempted to breach the Gustav Line to reach Rome. Eventually a bold landing at Anzio and Nettuno, beyond the Line, was made on 22 January, outflanking the defences and placing Allied troops just a few miles from Rome. Swift reaction from the Germans led to another stalemate, however, as US troops became surrounded at Anzio and Ju 88s were moved in from France to attack them. Equally intense fighting in the air and on the ground ensued into late February, but the

Luftwaffe could not maintain the pace of operations, especially with the need to bring units into line for the defence against Soviet forces in the east and the expected invasion of Europe from the west. The final elements of German resistance were eventually broken by heavy bomber raids, but not until early May could the Allies finally make their push on Rome. On 17 May, German forces withdrew from Cassino and US troops took Rome on 5 June.

Elsewhere, Operation Anvil dropped paratroopers into southern France on 14/15 August 1944 to begin a virtually unopposed advance up through France. Difficult fighting was still ahead in Italy, but a final offensive in April 1945 took Verona, Bologna, Ferrara and Parma. On 2 May, German forces in Italy and Austria surrendered.

The UK was convinced that the key to a successful invasion of northern Europe lay in attacking the Reich from the south, taking Italy out of the war in the process.

World War II:

The Eastern Front

1939–1945

The conflict in the east was a turning point in World War II: a clash of two totalitarian powers that would claim more lives than every other theatre of the war combined. The wider conflict began on 30 November 1939, with the outbreak of the Winter War between Finland and the USSR. Having divided Poland between them, Stalin now feared that Hitler's Germany could launch an attack on the city of Leningrad over the Gulf of Finland. To prevent this, the Soviets elected to capture Finnish territory as a buffer zone, establishing bases that could be used to repel an attack on the USSR. In 14 weeks of fighting, the Red Army struggled to overcome the well-prepared and resilient Finnish defenders on the ground, and the same pattern was reflected in the air war, although the fighting was frequently interrupted by the severe weather.

At the outset, the Finns were mainly equipped with Fokker D.XXI fighters, Blenheim Mk I bombers and Fokker C.X reconnaissance aircraft – in Finnish hands, the D.XXI in particular proved more than a match for the outdated Soviet I-15bis biplane fighter. Even Finland's single squadron of obsolete Bristol Bulldogs registered 'kills'. In the Soviets' favour were the numerical odds: almost 700 of their aircraft were deployed to face less than 150 Finnish warplanes. Eventually, the Soviets would overwhelm the Finns with sheer numbers, but not before suffering significant losses; in particular, the Soviet DB-3 (later

Spearhead of the Finnish fighter arm in the first months of the Winter War, a Fokker D.XXI is prepared for another mission. Of the Finnish air-to-air claims made against the Soviets in the Winter War, the majority were credited to pilots flying Dutch-supplied D.XXIs.

91

FOKKER C.X

Type: two-seat reconnaissance/bomber biplane

Powerplant: one 663.5kW (890hp) Tammerfors-built Bristol Pegasus XII or XXI nine-cylinder single-row radial engine

Maximum speed: 335km/h (208mph)

Service ceiling: 8100m (26,575ft)

Weights: maximum take-off 2900kg (6393lb)

Armament: two 7.62mm machine-guns: one fixed forward-firing and one trainable rearward-firing in rear cockpit; 500kg (1102lb) external bomb load

Dimensions: span   12.00m (39ft 4.5in)
length   9.2m (30ft 2.25in)
height   3.30m (10ft 10in)

designated Il-4), SB-2 and veteran TB-3 bombers suffered heavy losses during daylight raids over Finnish territory, and the Finns had 50 aerial victories by the end of the year.

On 6 January the Finns began a counterattack, the air force ranks soon bolstered by deliveries of modern Blenheim Mk IVs, plus Gauntlet and Gladiator fighters from the UK; MS.406s from France; and G.50s from Italy. On the same day, Finnish D.XXI pilot Jorma Sarvanto made history by claiming six 'kills' in a day, all DB-3s. Deliveries of new aircraft could not prevent the inevitable, however. Having boosted their numbers to 1500 aircraft, the Soviets had also introduced the I-16 monoplane fighter by January 1940 and now responded to the Finnish counter with a renewed bombing campaign, and a push towards Viipuri.

Although the outnumbered Finns held out on the ground, by March there were some 2000 aircraft facing

them. The Winter War ended with Finland signing an armistice on 13 March 1940, with much of Karelia including Viipuri now in Soviet hands.

THE BATTLE FOR GREECE

Before Hitler could begin his invasion of the USSR, the situation had to be resolved in the Balkans; the plan was to silence the Greeks and Yugoslavs, and capture the oilfields of Romania. As it was, the Balkans campaign didn't proceed as smoothly as Hitler had hoped. The efforts taken to secure Europe's southern underbelly in preparation for Operation *Barbarossa* would have a knock-on effect that arguably put the latter operation's success in jeopardy.

After having attacked Greece through Albania on 28 October 1940, Mussolini's Italian forces were struggling to subdue the Greeks, and Hitler decided to intervene. In the air, Italian MC.200s and G.50s were faced by the RAF, whose Blenheim Mk I/IVs

and Gladiator Mk Is had been deployed to bases in Greece. Although obsolescent, RAF Gladiators had claimed 30 victories against the Italians by January 1941.

On 1 March, German forces moved into Bulgaria in preparation for Operation *Marita*, the invasion of Greece. In response, additional RAF units were sent to Greece from North Africa, and these now included Hurricane Mk IA fighters. Following a military coup in Yugoslavia in March, Germany launched *Marita* on 6 April. VIII Fliegerkorps provided air support for the operation, with some 1200 aircraft including Bf 109Es and Ju 88As. At the same time, Hitler promised that Yugoslavia would be 'crushed as speedily as possible', and Do 17Zs, Ju 87Bs and Ju 88As duly hit the capital Belgrade on 6 April.

With the small Yugoslav air force – which had included both Hurricanes and Bf 109Es – effectively decimated in the first three days of operations, the remaining Greek and British aircraft in theatre were not only outnumbered, but the technological gap was also significant. The backbone of Greece's fighter force was the PZL P.24, which stood little chance against the Bf 109E. By 24/25 April, Germany had occupied Yugoslavia, devastated the port of

'PAT' PATTLE: LEADING RAF ACE

During the desperate fighting of the Greek campaign, South African-born Marmaduke Thomas St John Pattle – almost certainly the highest-scoring RAF ace of the entire war – was killed in combat with Luftwaffe Bf 110s over Athens. In a period of just nine months, Pattle had accumulated as many as 50 aerial victories, flying Gladiators and Hurricanes.

Piraeus and taken Salonika, and the RAF – which had been reduced to 28 serviceable fighters by 15 April – was forced to begin its evacuation from Greece. With the collapse of Greek and British resistance, and the fall of Athens on 27 April, the last surviving RAF assets were evacuated to Crete, together with Commonwealth soldiers. Before long, the survivors of these ragged forces would be in action again, in a vain attempt to repel Operation *Merkur* (Mercury), the German airborne invasion of Crete.

On 1 March 1940, German forces moved into Bulgaria in preparation for Operation *Marita*, the invasion of Greece.

Germany succeeded in bailing out the Italians in the Balkans, and the campaign was concluded with Greece and Yugoslavia under Axis domination. But it had taken six weeks longer than anticipated, and the result was a delay in beginning

Armed with a signature MP40 sub-machine-gun, a German NCO is photographed beside a burning farm during the early stages of Operation *Barbarossa*. Aided by near-total annihilation of the Soviet air arms in the opening phase, Germany's *Blitzkrieg* tactics saw rapid progress made.

This German aerial reconnaissance photograph reveals two bridges out of three destroyed by the Soviets on the Don. What the Soviets initially lacked in terms of efficient bombers and attack aircraft was often made up by the activities of partisans on the ground.

'We have only to kick in the door,' claimed Hitler, 'and the whole rotten structure will come crashing down.'

Hitler's main objective: the invasion of the USSR, and a subsequent showdown of Europe's two dominant 'superpowers'.

Codenamed *Barbarossa*, the Axis invasion began at dawn on 22 June 1941. 'We have only to kick in the door,' claimed Hitler, 'and the whole rotten structure will come crashing down.' The reality would be somewhat different. Despite the fact that Germany was still at war in the Balkans and Mediterranean, four

Luftflotten had been assembled across a front that stretched from the Black Sea to the Baltic, and which was covered by three army groups: North, Centre and South.

Whether Stalin was taken entirely by surprise as many historical accounts have suggested is debatable, but the fact is that the Axis invasion made rapid progress in its first weeks. It was aided by air power, and a continuation of the *Blitzkrieg* tactics that had proved so successful in Poland and in the

West. The focal point of the initial advance was Army Group Centre's front that would drive between the Baltic states and the Pripet Marshes in the direction of Moscow, covered by Luftflotte II, which would include Ju 87 Stuka dive-bombers to mop up Soviet armour.

BARBAROSSA BEGINS

Exploiting the results of earlier Luftwaffe reconnaissance flights – which had seen the use of the Ju 86P high-altitude reconnaissance aircraft – an initial, high-level force of He 111, Ju 88 and Do 17 bombers attacked 10 Soviet airfields in dawn raids. Follow-up waves of around 800 bombers and Ju 87s flying at lower level – plus fighter cover – brought further destruction to Soviet airfields, wiping out entire units on the ground: on the first day of *Barbarossa*, the Luftwaffe claimed 1800 Soviet aircraft destroyed, most on their bases.

As well as the various offensive assets thrown into the battle, the Luftwaffe and the ground forces could call upon over 1000 support aircraft detailed for a wide range of duties including reconnaissance, transport and army cooperation.

In addition to German-manned units, there were formations provided by Axis allies: a powerful Romanian air group under Luftflotte IV, tasked primarily with defending the Ploesti oilfields with He 112Bs, Hurricanes and PZL P.24s, among others; a small Slovakian contingent; and the Hungarian air force, which was based around Fiat CR.32 and CR.42 fighters and Ju 86K bombers; 'volunteer' units

A Romanian He 111 is bombed up for a mission in late 1943. Apart from Slovakia, Romania was the only Axis power involved on the Eastern Front from the outset, but Allied raids on its oilfields meant that its air force was by now on the defensive.

from Croatia, Italy and Spain would later join them.

A force of around 800 combat-ready Luftwaffe fighters – mainly Bf 109E/Fs – was available to confront those Soviet aircraft that did manage to get airborne; at this stage, the major Soviet fighter was still the I-16, a type that was hopelessly outclassed by the Bf 109s, which were frequently flown by experienced pilots.

The small number of advanced MiG-3 fighters available to the Soviets was high on the target list of the Luftwaffe. Indeed, the I-16 would remain the primary equipment of the fighter regiments until October 1942, and Luftwaffe pilots would exact a steady toll, including some extraordinary personal tallies; of the leading German aces, it is notable that most served at some point on the Eastern Front. 'Ace of aces' Erich Hartmann, for example, recorded no less than 345 of his 352 kills against Soviet opposition.

Well aware that the onset of winter could prove critical, Hitler had planned to take Moscow by Christmas, and the Luftwaffe began a bombing campaign against the capital, after air power had helped crush major Soviet pockets of resistance at Bialystok and Minsk in July, and destroy the vital rail bridge at Bobruysk. The Smolensk pocket, with around 100,000 soldiers, proved a tougher objective, despite Luftwaffe air dominance. At this stage, Luftwaffe units were jumping from one captured airfield to the next,

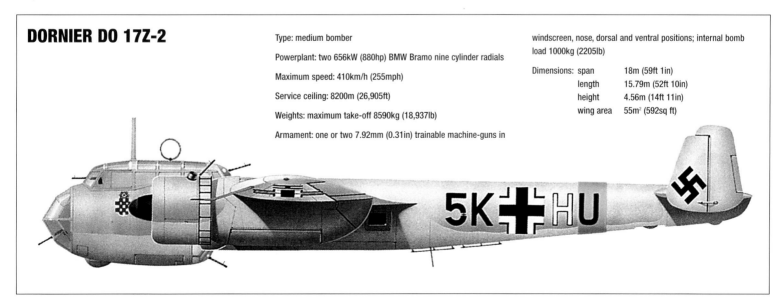

DORNIER DO 17Z-2

Type: medium bomber

Powerplant: two 656kW (880hp) BMW Bramo nine cylinder radials

Maximum speed: 410km/h (255mph)

Service ceiling: 8200m (26,905ft)

Weights: maximum take-off 8590kg (18,937lb)

Armament: one or two 7.92mm (0.31in) trainable machine-guns in windscreen, nose, dorsal and ventral positions; internal bomb load 1000kg (2205lb)

Dimensions: span 18m (59ft 1in)
length 15.79m (52ft 10in)
height 4.56m (14ft 11in)
wing area 55m² (592sq ft)

Left: Covered with camouflage netting on its unprotected airstrip, a Soviet Tupolev SB-2 bomber is prepared for a sortie. Although outclassed by the start of *Barbarossa*, Tupolev's SB-2 soldiered on in service into 1943. This example has Klimov M-103 inline engines.

Right: During the 'Great Patriotic War', Soviet air power was subordinated to the ground forces, its application dictated to a significant degree by commanders in the field, such as Zhukov, who led the Red Army to Berlin.

desperately trying to maintain cover over the flanks of the fast-moving ground forces below.

By the end of September 1941, the front stretched from Leningrad as far south as the Crimea, and by the beginning of December it had been further extended to Voronezh, Rostov and the outskirts of Moscow.

As German forces neared Leningrad, the Soviets attacked Finland on 25 June, Stalin expecting the Finns to side with the Axis forces. Again, SB-2s suffered at the lands of the Finnish air force, with 13 being claimed by G.50s on the first day of operations in what was known as the Continuation War; again, the Finns were heavily outnumbered, with around 120 aircraft available, but their US-supplied Buffalos were nonetheless more than a match for the I-16.

Leningrad, which was now within striking distance, with Bf 110s raiding airfields on the outskirts of the city in August. The Red Army held Leningrad, with the Germans switching tactics and laying siege to the city from 26 September, with air operations spearheaded by Luftflotte I. For the first time, the

SIEGE OF LENINGRAD

Despite the progress made in the north, Hitler now took the opportunity to interfere, declaring the main objective to be the Ukraine, not

Soviet air arms were able to use strength in numbers to disrupt Luftwaffe operations, and took part in a counterattack on 16 August, before

Red Army activity was suppressed with the aid of Ju 88s and Bf 110s.

As well as providing air cover for the ground forces' vast territorial gains, the early months of *Barbarossa* also saw individual highlights for the Luftwaffe. On 22 September, a raid by Ju 87s on the naval base of Kronstadt saw Hans-Ulrich Rudel sink the battleship *Murat*. Rudel would go on to become the most decorated serviceman of the war, adding the Knight's Cross with Oak Leaves, Swords and Diamonds to a tally of around 2000 ground targets destroyed, including over 500 tanks.

The raid on Kronstadt was part of a wider initiative, led by Luftflotte I and in support of Army Group North,

HITLER'S FATAL HESITANCY

As early as August 1941, Hitler's overall objective was switched from Moscow to the Crimea, the Donets industrial area, and the capture of the vital sources of oil in the Caucasus. Perhaps the fact that the army was more than half way to the Soviet capital led to over-confidence, but either way, this diversion to the south was to prove costly. Partisans, who began to launch nuisance raids on the Axis forces, sowed further confusion; autumn rains slowed the advance, and turned improvised airstrips into quagmires; and an ever-extending supply train reduced operational readiness. Hs 123 and Fi 156 aircraft were notably resilient against worsening weather conditions, but the problems of the supply train would only be exacerbated as the eastwards march towards Moscow continued.

Closer to home, and in the wake of the invasion, the Soviets undertook bombing raids against German airfields with unescorted SB-2s and DB-3s; confronted by defending Bf 109s, these outdated types suffered as they had in the Winter War.

Of more lasting value was the arrival of RAF-operated Hurricanes at Murmansk in September. These were the first foreign warplanes to fight with the Soviets, and the same aircraft were also supplied as war aid. The Lend-Lease programme, under which vast quantities of war-winning materiel – including modern aircraft – would be received by the Soviets, would follow up their initial success. In Soviet hands, certain Western types would excel in combat. Notably, the P-39 Airacobra, unloved by the USAAF, would prove a revelation when operated as a low-level fighter by the Soviets on the Eastern Front.

A TYPHOON UNLEASHED

Rapid progress in the south in September, combined with the sieges at Leningrad and Odessa, allowed Axis attention to return to the advance on Moscow, codenamed Operation *Taifun* (Typhoon).

Although successful, engagements in the Ukraine had wasted valuable time and further problems soon emerged for the aggressors: in December Luftflotte II's aircraft were reassigned to the Mediterranean. At the same time, the onset of the winter slowed down the Axis advance – *Taifun* began in early October and, although key objectives, including Orel, were captured on the way, Hitler

which targeted the Soviet Baltic Fleet and cleared a path for the advance towards Leningrad. The Soviets also launched some notable raids: although costly and ineffective, the attacks on Berlin by Il-4s, Yer-2s and four-engined Pe-8s beginning in August 1941 were a valuable

propaganda coup, launched in the wake of the first major Luftwaffe bombing raids on Moscow. These latter had taken place on 21 July, involving 200 Do 17s, He 111s and Ju 88s, but the Luftwaffe bombing campaign against Moscow was to prove little more than a token gesture.

The Soviets continued to counter, pressing the Axis forces around Leningrad and Kharkov, as well as Moscow.

failed in his aim of capturing Moscow before the weather turned for the worse; motorized formations and aircraft alike were simply bogged down by late October, and were frozen in by early December.

With the Germans faltering, Soviet commander Georgi Zhukov took the initiative, launching a major counter-offensive in the Moscow area on 5/6 December, supported by units brought in from the Far East. With the weather combining with redeployments in limiting air operations and depriving ground forces of cover, the Germans withdrew from Moscow on 8 December, and Hitler was forced to abandon his plans for the capture of the city. By now, Luftwaffe strengths had been slashed to around 1900 combat aircraft across the entire front, of which perhaps only half were operational.

The Soviets continued to counter, pressing the Axis forces around Leningrad and Kharkov, as well as Moscow. The Red Army managed to push back the Germans and achieved a major breakthrough between two German army groups – Centre and North – in February 1942. The result was the German X Corps cut off at Demyansk, south of Leningrad, with another, smaller, pocket at Kholm. It

A Soviet infantryman guards a downed Bf 109F fighter. When it first appeared during *Barbarossa*, the Messerschmitt Bf 109F variant was unmatched, but the steady development of Soviet single-seat fighters would gradually begin to turn the tables from mid-1942.

MiG-3

Type: single-seat fighter and fighter bomber

Powerplant: one 1007kW (1350hp) Mikulin AM-35A 12 cylinder Vee engine

Maximum speed: 640km/h (398mph)

Service ceiling: 12,000m (39,370ft)

Weights: empty 2595kg (5709lb); maximum take-off 3350kg (7385lb)

Armament: one 12.7mm (.50cal.) and two 7.62mm (0.30cal.) fixed forward-firing machine-guns; external rocket and bomb load 200kg (441lb)

Dimensions: span   10.20m (33ft 6in)
             length   8.25m (27ft 0.8in)
             height   2.65m (8ft 8.3in)
             wing area   17.44m² (188sq ft)

was now the turn of the Luftwaffe's transport arm to provide support, with Ju 52/3ms relieving the troops stranded in the Demyansk pocket until a land passage could be

While the Mikoyan-Gurevich MiG-3 did not meet with the same success as the succession of fighters developed by Lavochkin and Yakovlev, this sleek warplane was notably fast. However, by 1942-43 most had been demoted from the front to serve with air defence units.

established through Soviet lines in April. Meanwhile, DFS 230 and Go 242 gliders supplied troops at Kholm until this pocket was relieved in May. Demyansk was the first time that the Luftwaffe's transports would be called upon for re-supply of troops on this scale, and, although successful, it absorbed almost the entire Luftwaffe transport capacity, as well as bombers that were impressed into service in the transport role.

With the German offensive repelled at the gates of Moscow, Hitler turned his attentions south once more, and Army Group South was directed towards objectives in the Crimea and southern Ukraine. The Luftwaffe had been present on the southern flank from the outset, in the form of Luftflotte IV, supported by the Hungarian air force, covering Army Group South's front that extended from south of the Pripet Marshes to

Yak-1 pilots near the Kharkov front, with their commander, I.M. Gussarov, in the centre. Gussarov's unit claimed 15 aerial victories in the course of one week in mid-May 1942. This was the time of Marshal Timoshenko's abortive counter offensive at Kharkov.

the borders of Hungary and Slovakia.

Luftflotte IV's ultimate objective was to support the drive to the Dnieper River and Kiev, as well as suppressing air and naval activity in the Black Sea area and protecting Romanian oilfields. A separate front launched an attack towards Odessa and Moldova, supported by Romanian and Hungarian forces. The Red Army was soon on the back foot, retreating to defend Kiev from deeper positions; during its withdrawal by rail, it was harassed by He 111s and Ju 88s. When Hitler switched objectives from

Moscow to the Crimea and Caucasus, the Luftwaffe was heavily involved in pushing the Soviets back over the Dnieper from August 1941.

Bridgeheads were soon established over the Dnieper and protected by Bf 109s and Ju 87s, and Red Army positions outside Kiev were hit by the Luftwaffe in September. The battle for the city of Kiev itself ended on 26 September, with the final extinction of Soviet resistance.

GERMANY'S CASE BLUE

While the Soviets continued on the offensive in the north, a renewed German campaign in the south began in April 1942, in preparation for a

NEW EQUIPMENT IN THE EAST

In 1942, the Messerschmitt Bf 109F supplanted the Luftwaffe's Bf 109E, with the obsolescent Dornier Do 17 also having been replaced. More significant, however, was the arrival of new equipment for the Soviets in the same year. Finally, modern fighter equipment was beginning to appear in numbers, with the arrival in quantity of the monoplane LaGG-3, MiG-3 and Yak-1 fighters, as well as the Il-2 and Pe-2 ground-attack aircraft. Deliveries of these new aircraft had been limited to a certain degree as a result of the production effort being shifted to new factories in the east of the USSR, to escape the ravages of *Blitzkrieg*.

ILYUSHIN II-2

Type: two-seat close support and anti-tank plane

Powerplant: one 1238kW (1660hp) Mikulin AM-38F liquid-cooled in-line engine

Maximum speed: 404km/h (251mph)

Service ceiling: 6000m (19,685ft)

Weights: empty 4525kg (9975lb); maximum take-off 6360kg (14,021lb)

Armament: two 37mm (1.46in) fixed forward-firing cannon and two 7.62mm (0.30in) guns; one 12.7mm (0.5in) machine-gun in rear cockpit; 200 anti-tank bombs or eight rocket projectiles

Dimensions:
span   14.60m (47ft 10in)
length   11.60m (38ft)
height   3.40m (11ft 1in)

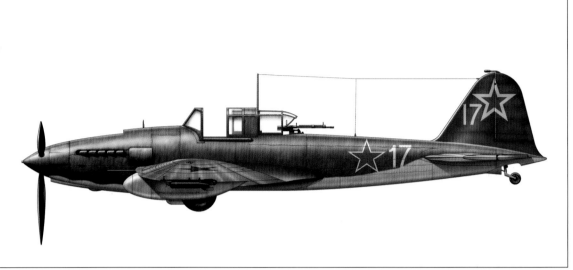

> With Stalin caught off guard by *Fall Blau*, the initial phase of the operation saw a rapid advance eastwards, with the Stukas proving especially effective.

major summer offensive codenamed *Fall Blau* (Case Blue).

This time, the Germans were seeking to gain oil for their own use as well as capturing the Crimean peninsula. Soviet losses were heavy, the Red Army failed to stop the Germans in a major counteroffensive at Kharkov in May, and the Germans again made use of widespread aerial bombing and close air support; in particular, aircraft from Fliegerkorps IV played a vital role in reversing the Soviets at Kharkov.

In a joint German-Romanian action, Operation *Trappenjagd* (Bustard Hunt) then captured the Kerch peninsula, with much use made of Luftwaffe bombers and dive-bombers. After a period of artillery bombardment and heavy raids involving as many as 600 Luftwaffe aircraft, the 'fortress city' of Sevastopol fell to the Germans on 1 July and, as they had at the opening of *Barbarossa*, the Axis forces were once again looking unstoppable.

Over Sevastopol the Axis air arms enjoyed air superiority, and the technological gains that the Soviets derived from the large-scale introduction of the LaGG-3, MiG-3 and Yak-1 would soon be completely eroded by the appearance of the Fw 190A, part of a Luftwaffe air arm that had been bolstered to a strength of around 2750 aircraft by mid-1942.

NEW FIGHTER EQUIPMENT
As well as the Fw 190, the Luftwaffe now operated the improved Ju 87D and the Hs 129 dedicated close-support aircraft. After the fall of Sevastopol, the Axis forces were ready to advance to the east, and *Fall Blau* began to push in the direction of Voronezh on 28 June; soon the Axis forces would be able to secure the vital oilfields on the shores of the Caspian. The operation involved separate German forces meeting at the Don, and encircling the Red Army; the Luftwaffe was able to

provide around 1200 combat-ready aircraft in support. With Stalin caught off guard, the initial phase of the operation saw a rapid advance eastwards, with the Stukas proving especially effective. At this point, however, Hitler made another crucial error of judgement.

With the two army groups having met at the Don on 14 July, and following the fall of Rostov on 23 July, the planned advance beyond Voronezh and to the Caucasus was effectively put on hold and attention once again turned to the capture of strategically important cities. Hitler's new objectives were Leningrad and Stalingrad: two cities that the Soviets had vowed to defend at all costs.

Meanwhile, the Axis forces had reached the first oilfields of the Crimea, but extended supply lines ensured that they would not progress much further southeast. More critically, the Luftwaffe was now so over-stretched that it could no longer ensure cover for the ground forces over the southern sectors of the front.

A pair of Polikarpov I-153 fighters on patrol over Sevastapol. These biplane fighters not surprisingly sustained heavy losses in the opening phase of *Barbarossa*, but they survived in service in lesser theatres, notably with units in Crimea and in the Far East.

Stalingrad was never going to be an easy target for Friedrich Paulus' 6th Army. The defence of the symbolic city by the Red Army was a point of prestige and the weather, as it had been at Moscow in winter 1941/42, was again in the defenders' favour.

By mid-September 1942, the Axis front extended from Leningrad and Demyansk in the north, via Voronezh in southwest Russia, to Stalingrad and beyond. The 6th Army was divided into two separate fronts in order to take the city. In the air, the Luftwaffe maintained numerical and technological superiority and unleashed a ferocious bombing campaign against the city, using

The Ju 87D-3 model was introduced in late 1942 for use in the close support role, offering improved armour protection for the engine and crew. These examples are seen in service with Schlachtgeschwader 2 'Immelmann', commanded by the legendary Hans-Ulrich Rudel.

THE QUALITATIVE BATTLE

With Luftwaffe assets stretched by mid-1942, there was no guarantee of air cover for the ground forces, and the situation for the Axis forces was worsened by the availability of a new generation of Soviet fighter aircraft: the La-5FN and Yak-9 were robust, dependable, and well-matched to Lufwaffe equipment. Locally built fighters were also supplemented by increasing numbers of Lend-Lease types, including the P-39, P-40 and Spitfire. The first of these types was to make a significant impression in Soviet hands, although the propaganda machine tended to downplay the achievements of Western equipment. In opposition, the Luftwaffe could put up a total of just over 1000 combat types at Kursk – amounting to almost their entire inventory on the Eastern Front. A technological advantage was provided by the arrival of the latest Bf 109G variant, but the more important events would unfold on the ground, where the German commanders now had powerful Tiger I and Panther tanks.

He 111s and Ju 88s, although the arrival in significant numbers of the capable La-5 and Pe-2 on the Soviet side represented a significant advance, and was a sign of things to come. One of the Soviet heroes of the battle was Lydia Litvyak, the top-scoring female fighter ace of all time. Litvyak claimed her first kill – a Ju 88 – over Stalingrad on 13 September.

The following month, a reconfigured Red Army formation launched Operation Uranus, which closed around Stalingrad in a pincer

Covered with branches serving as field camouflage, an La-5FN is refuelled by groundcrew. A match for most German fighters, the Lavochkin La-5FN offered a fuel-injected ASh-82FN engine, top speed of 620km/h (385mph) and excellent manoeuvrability.

movement, encircling the Axis forces: around 300,000 soldiers. With the Axis troops trapped, it was left to the Luftwaffe's transport fleet to maintain a lifeline for the 6th Army. By now, winter had arrived, and the Soviets put their artillery to good use, bombarding the airfields used by the German transport aircraft: mainly Ju 52/3m and other transports, but also including He 111 and He 177 bombers. By mid-January 1943, the Luftwaffe was down to just two remaining airfields and was forced to drop supplies by parachute. By February the 6th Army had ceased to exist, and Hitler's eastward advance was stopped in its tracks.

THE KURSK CAULDRON

The Soviets having successfully blunted the Axis eastwards advance at Stalingrad, Hitler ordered a new offensive to take place on the central sector of the front, to begin in June 1943. Both Red Army and Axis forces were standing at loggerheads in the area south of Moscow. The target of the new campaign was the major concentration of Soviet forces in the Kursk salient, to the west of Voronezh.

At the beginning of *Barbarossa*, events in the Mediterranean had intervened to cause a critical delay in starting the offensive, and the same happened at Kursk. With Hitler expecting an Allied offensive in the Mediterranean, the Kursk offensive –

One of the Soviet heroes of the Battle of Stalingrad was Lydia Litvyak, the top-scoring female fighter ace of all time, who claimed her first kill on 13 September 1942.

codenamed Operation *Zitadelle* (Citadel) – was put on hold. In the event, *Zitadelle* began on 5 July 1943, by which time the Soviets had assembled three air armies of almost 2500 operational aircraft for the offensive – plus significant reserves.

SOVIETS ON THE OFFENSIVE

Among the aircraft on strength were large numbers of Il-2 and Il-2M3 ground-attack aircraft, which would prove devastating against armour and troops on the ground; the Soviet war plan was a model combined-arms offensive – similar 'Soviet *Blitzkrieg*' tactics would now be the norm, and from now on the Luftwaffe was on the defensive. As well as being outnumbered, the Luftwaffe was suffering from the combined effects of raids by partisans and a lack of fuel.

The showdown at Kursk would be primarily land based, as the Germans geared up for an armoured assault against the Red Army. The result was the biggest tank battle of all time. Around 3000 tanks clashed, while above them specialist anti-tank aircraft were able to make an impact; chief among these were the Hs 129 and Ju 87D adapted for anti-armour operations, and the Il-2. The *Stuka* was also up-gunned to produce the Ju 87G, armed with a pair of 37mm cannons, while the Ju 88 received a 75mm gun to produce the Ju 88P; both types were deployed in time for Kursk. After a week of fighting, the Germans appeared to hold the advantage, but in response, Marshal Georgi Zhukov deployed an entire new tank army, plus additional Il-2s.

Around 3000 tanks clashed; above them specialist anti-tank aircraft made an impact.

Generalfeldmarschall Erich von Manstein realized that the Axis position was now precarious, and favoured a withdrawal. Hitler stepped in, ordering the offensive to continue. The front was being widened by the Soviets, however, and the Soviet air forces were increasingly gaining the upper hand. While the Red Army pressed towards Orel in the north, Luftwaffe losses mounted. By the end of the battle, the Axis forces had lost around 900 aircraft, compared to 600 for the Soviets.

Following the decisive defeat of the Axis forces at Kursk and the loss of Luftwaffe air superiority, Hitler's Eastern Front campaign increasingly appeared to be a lost cause. Meanwhile, the situation on the home front was becoming increasingly concerning, such

LUFTWAFFE NIGHT RAIDERS

In order to reduce losses, the Luftwaffe also began to turn increasingly to night sorties, resulting in the creation of dedicated *Nachtschlachtgruppen* (Night-Attack Groups). This tactic reflected Soviet air force success in the night-harassment role and, while the Soviets employed the venerable Polikarpov U-2 (later designated Po-2) in the role, the Germans impressed Gotha Go 145 and Arado Ar 66 biplane trainers, among others.

that large numbers of aircraft – notably Bf 110s – were being withdrawn from the Eastern Front for the defence of the Reich. There were some positives for the Luftwaffe in the east, however, such as the continued replacement of the increasingly vulnerable Ju 87D with Fw 190F ground-attack variants, the latter type first being introduced in early 1943. By the winter of 1943/44, the Soviet air arms greatly

outnumbered the Luftwaffe, and the previous qualitative advantage enjoyed by the Germans had generally been eroded. The Soviets took advantage of the Axis weaknesses to launch a major offensive in the Kiev area,

Bell's mid-engined fighters, both the Airacobra and Kingcobra, were highly prized by the Soviets for their low-altitude performance. Seen here with his P-39 Airacobra is Fedor Shikunov, who scored 25 victories in just 52 combats before falling to flak in March 1945.

RETURN TO FINLAND

While the Red Army continued to flush the Axis forces out of the Ukraine, in the north, the offensive was taken into Finland, which was invaded through Karelia on 10 June 1944. In the same month, the USAAF's 8th and 15th Air Forces began their shuttle bombing raids from Soviet territory. The Luftwaffe responded with a series of bomber raids on the Allied bombers' bases, but these did little to effect their fighting capacity. The Luftwaffe could still call upon some 2000 aircraft by mid-1944, but against this total, the Soviets could raise around 13,000 aircraft, and industry was producing new equipment at an astonishing rate to make good losses incurred.

Air power played a major role on both sides during the battle for Finland, but the numerical superiority of the USSR (which threw some 750 aircraft into the fight) eventually overcame the combined Finnish and German defences. Nevertheless, the Finns succeeded in taking a heavy toll on the Soviets, as they had in the Winter War. This time they had the benefit of more modern fighter equipment, most notably in the form of the Bf 109G-6. After Viborg fell into Soviet hands, the Finns agreed to a ceasefire on 4 September 1944.

January 1944 the Red Army made a major advance to the west, pushing through towards Zhitomir.

As they had been previously at Demyansk and Stalingrad, the Axis ground forces (elements of Army Group South) found themselves cut off once again, this time in the Korsun-Cherkassy pocket. Again, their only reliable means of supply was by airdrops, but it was another lost cause, and the pocket was liquidated in mid-February. Meanwhile, in the north, the Germans suffered final defeat on the Leningrad front. Although the Luftwaffe succeeded in boosting its aircraft numbers from 240 to 400, the Soviets held the city, aided by partisans who were supplied by airdrops, and by U-2 biplanes active in the nocturnal harassment role.

German troops examine a Po-2 forced down in Latvia in 1944. Of decidedly antiquated appearance, the Po-2 – known to the Germans as the 'sewing machine' – gave good service in general reconnaissance, casualty evacuation, liaison and night harassment duties.

beginning in late 1943. The Germans were hit hard through their third winter on the Eastern Front, and in

This Bf 109G-6 was flown by Eino Luukkanen, Finland's third-ranking ace (behind Ilmari Juutilainen and Hans Wind) in 1944. Luukkanen achieved 56 victories on the D.XXI, Buffalo and the Bf 109 and was involved in the intense aerial fighting over Karelia in June 1944.

> By December 1944, the front had shifted to a line that ran between the Niemen River, to the east of Warsaw, and south to Budapest.

The siege of Leningrad was finally lifted on 27 January, after 880 days, with the final German resistance breaking down to the south of the city.

The Red Army's successful winter offensive of 1943 was given renewed impetus in spring 1944, with the aim of driving the Germans out of the Ukraine. By May 1944, the last Luftwaffe aircraft had evacuated the Crimea, which had previously survived as a pocket of Axis resistance. With air superiority ensured, the Soviet air arms stepped up attacks on retreating Axis forces. While the Soviets had some 3000 aircraft available, the Luftwaffe was struggling to make 300 fighters operational each day across the entire front.

During July 1944, the Red Army was at times advancing west at a rate of some 40km (25 miles) per day. By the time the Soviets entered Wilno (now Vilnius) on 9 July 1944, Belarus was effectively safe in Red Army hands and the stage was set for a concerted westwards push, in which the increasingly beleaguered German forces would be harried all the way back to their own borders, with air power playing a major role.

RACING WESTWARDS

The Soviet advance to the west drove through two corridors: the first advanced into northeast Poland, while the second moved south, from where Marshal Ivan Konev's forces would push towards the Vistula. Initial Red Army progress was fast, and they were soon at the limits of their supply train. By the end of the month Brest-Litovsk was in Soviet hands, and the Vistula had been crossed.

The Soviet generals now shifted their attentions to the south, and in particular the Balkans. A renewed offensive began on the Odessa front on 20 August, aimed at Romania, and supported by around 1700 aircraft. The Romanians and their German allies were soon overwhelmed and the Romanian government was brought to its knees after just three days. The result was the vital oilfields of Ploesti secure in Allied hands. On 8 September Bulgaria fell to the Soviets, but the Luftwaffe continued the struggle in the Balkans, waging war on the Soviets, and still assisted by their Hungarian allies.

By December 1944, the front had shifted to a line that ran between the

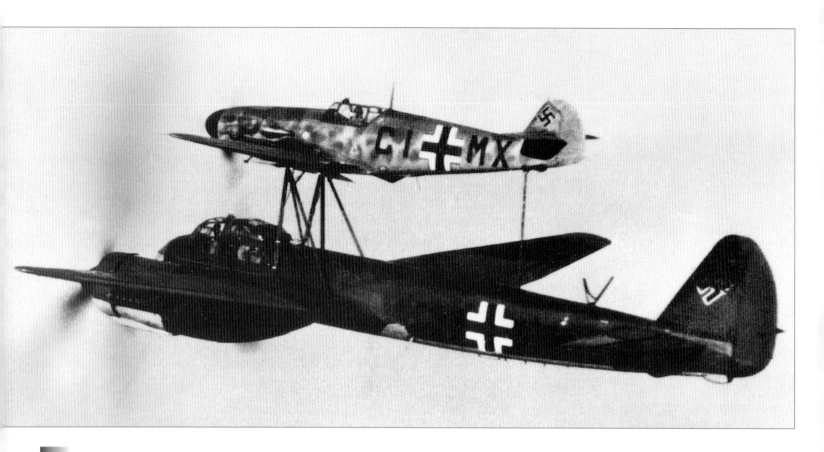

The Luftwaffe attempted to bolster its fighter arm in an attempt to wrest air superiority from the Soviets, redeploying aircraft to defend the German capital.

Above: Typical of the increasingly desperate measures taken by the German military, the Mistel (Mistletoe) combinations allied a redundant bomber airframe, packed with explosives, to a fighter that would guide it to the target. The Ju 88A and Bf 109F seen here were combined to form the Mistel 1, used operationally against bridges over the Oder.

Niemen River, to the east of Warsaw, and south to Budapest. The Soviets could call upon around 15,500 combat aircraft, and their effective use had reduced Luftwaffe totals across the front to just 2000 aircraft. Stalin's forces were also making swifter progress than the Western Allies struggling through the Ardennes, and the Red Army had reached East Prussia by 13 January 1945.

FINALE IN THE EAST

East Prussia would be the scene of bitter fighting on the ground and in the air, and stiff German resistance combined with dismal weather to hold up the Red Army at Königsberg.

However, a significant objective fell to the Soviets on 17 January, with the capture of Warsaw. In the course of February, the Soviets crossed the River Oder, and found themselves within 80km (50 miles) of Berlin. By now, the defenders were resorting to ever more desperate measures, and it was against this backdrop that the Luftwaffe's Mistel composite aircraft were thrown.

At the same time, the Luftwaffe attempted to bolster its fighter arm in an effort to wrest air superiority from the Soviets, redeploying aircraft to defend the capital. However, not only were the Luftwaffe's dwindling resources – both materiel and personnel – stretched over two fronts, but the Soviets had by now introduced the La-7 and Yak-3, superior in most respects to the bulk of the Germans' fighter equipment.

An exception to the trend was the handful of Me 262 jet fighters that the Luftwaffe had managed to put into service. Even these were not invulnerable, however, and leading Soviet ace Ivan Kozhedub claimed one of the swept-wing fighters in combat over Frankfurt-Oder on 19 February; his eventual tally amounted to 62 'kills'. The odds were stacked in the Red Army's favour, and Berlin was duly overrun by the Soviets in May.

In an image that sums up the level of superiority enjoyed by the Soviets by 1945, an La-7 (nearest camera) heads an impressive line-up of Yak-3s. The La-7 could outclimb and outmanoeuvre an Fw 190, while the Yak-3 was arguably the most agile fighter of the war.

World War II:
The Pacific
1941–1945

The timing for the numerous Japanese operations against Oahu in the Hawaiian Islands, the Philippine Islands, Hong Kong and Malaya on 7/8 December 1941 was dictated to a large extent by the fact that the US Pacific Fleet was generally at anchor in Pearl Harbor on a Sunday morning. The Japanese gambled all on a series of operations designed to neutralize US and British naval and air power in the Far East and Pacific theatres as a preliminary to the creation of the 'Greater East Asia Co-Prosperity Sphere'. Having established this and created a ring of defensive positions around its perimeter, the Japanese hoped to be in a position to gain a peace on the basis of the status quo. Located on bases in the south of Indochina, the 3rd Hikoshudan (air corps) of the Imperial Japanese Army Air Force (JAAF) and the 22nd Air Flotilla of the Imperial Japanese Navy Air Force (JNAF) were to provide support. The Formosa-based 5th Hikoshudan and the 21st and 23rd Air Flotillas were to strike at the US Far East Air Force in Luzon.

The vessels of Vice Admiral Chuichi Nagumo's 1st Koku-Kantai departed Japan on 26 November 1941, and were based on the sister carriers *Kaga* and *Akagi*, *Hiryu* and *Soryu*, and *Zuikaku* and *Shokaku*, with 135 A6M2 fighters, 135 D3A1 dive-bombers and 144 B5N2 torpedo-bombers.

Japan precipitated her own and the US entry to World War II with the devastating attack on Pearl Harbor in the Hawaiian Islands. The Japanese concentrated their air attacks on the warships in Pearl Harbor and also on the US air installations on Oahu Island.

AICHI D5A2

Type: two-seat carrier-based dive-bomber

Powerplant: one 969kW (1300hp) Mitsubishi
Kinsei 54 14-cylinder, air-cooled radial engine

Maximum speed: 430km/h (267mph)

Service ceiling: 10,500m (34,500ft)

Weights: empty 2570kg (5654lb); maximum
take-off 3800kg (8360lb)

Armament: three 7.7mm (.303cal.) MGs: two
fixed forward-firing, one flexibly mounted in
rear cockpit; 370kg (814lb) bomb load

Dimensions: span   14.37m (47ft 2in)
          length   10.20m (33ft 6in)
          height   3.85m (12ft 8in)
          wing area 34.90m² (373sq ft)

By 0300 on 7 December the 1st Koku-Kantai had reached the fly-off position 320km (200 miles) north of Oahu. The initial attack wave of 189 aircraft left from 0600, while the second wave of 170 aircraft lifted off their carriers at 0715.

The most important targets were the ships anchored or moored in Pearl Harbor, while the A6M2 and D3A1 aircraft provided cover and attacked the airfields at Wheeler, Hickam, Ewa, Kaneohe and Ford Island. By 0750 the attack had begun, and was wholly devastating. Torpedoes struck the battleships USS *West Virginia*, *Arizona*, *Oklahoma*, *Nevada* and *Utah*, and the cruisers *Helena* and *Raleigh*. These and the battleships USS *California*, *Maryland* and *Tennessee*, and the repair ship USS *Vestal*, were also hit by D3A1 and B5N bombers. Less damaging blows were inflicted on the battleship USS *Pennsylvania*, the cruiser USS *Honolulu* and the destroyers USS *Cassin*, *Downes* and

Shaw. By 0830 the Japanese had completed their mission. Out of 353 aircraft, losses amounted to just nine A6M2, 15 D3A1 and five B5N2 machines. In the air and on the ground the US Army Air Force losses were 71 aircraft, those of the US Marine Corps 30 aircraft and those of the US Navy 66 aircraft. Some 2403 personnel were killed and 1176 wounded.

LIMITED RESISTANCE
The 4th Koku-Kantai, centred at Truk in the Caroline Islands, was responsible for covering the occupations of Wake, Guam and the Gilbert Islands. Only at Wake was there determined resistance. Even so, as early as 8 December, 36 G3M2 bombers of the Chitose Kokutai, flying from the 24th Air Flotilla's base at Roi-Namur in the Marshall Islands some 1160km (720 miles) away, bombed the aircraft dispersal area on Wake, destroying seven of 12 F4F-3

Wildcat fighters. On the following day the G3M bombers returned for an attack with fragmentation bombs, but lost two of their number. The first

WHERE ARE THE CARRIERS?

The one failing in the Japanese attack plan, created by Admiral Isoroku Yamamoto, was that the Pacific Fleet's aircraft carriers were absent from Pearl Harbor and therefore could not be attacked: the USS *Enterprise* was ferrying from Wake Island, the USS *Saratoga* was being refitted at San Diego, and the USS *Lexington* was ferrying to Midway Island.

Japanese landing attempt, on 10 December, was beaten back with support from the three surviving F4Fs, so the Japanese diverted the *Hiryu* and *Soryu* from their return to Japan, and heavy attacks by D3As and B5Ns covered the final invasion, leading to the garrison's surrender on 23 December.

In Malaya, Air Chief Marshal Sir Robert Brooke-Popham, the British commander-in-chief in the Far East, commanded elements of the Royal Air Force and Royal Australian Air Force, most of them flying obsolescent aircraft. The Japanese invasion forces were initially spotted by a Hudson of the RAAF on 6 December while 133km (82 miles) east-southeast of the southern tip of Indochina. The Allied forces were put on alert, and the plan to occupy Singora in southern Thailand was readied, but already the Ki-21 and Ki-48 bombers of the 3rd

Hikoshudan were active, bombing many targets. By the evening of the 6th the Japanese had landed at Singora and Patani. On 8 December Force 'Z' (the battleship HMS *Prince of Wales*, battlecruiser HMS *Repulse* and four destroyers) departed Singapore to search out and destroy the Japanese invasion fleets, but lacked any air cover. About 128km (80 miles) due east of Kuantan, on 10 December, Force 'Z' was attacked by the 22nd Air

The initial attack wave of 189 Japanese aircraft left from 0600, while the second wave of 170 aircraft lifted off at 0715.

Battleships of the US Navy under attack in Pearl Harbor's 'Battleship Row' during the Japanese attack of 7 December 1941. The Japanese failed to destroy the all-important tank farms and repair facilities, and the US Navy was fortunate that its carriers were all absent from the base.

Both the *Prince of Wales* and *Repulse* were sunk for the loss of only four aircraft.

Flotilla from Saigon. In a carefully orchestrated attack, the G3M2s bombed from medium altitude as the G4M1s undertook low-altitude torpedo runs, and both the *Prince of Wales* and *Repulse* were sunk for the loss of only four aircraft.

By the end of December the British situation in Malaya was strained beyond limits as the Japanese advanced south under cover of the Ki-43 and Ki-27b fighters of the 3rd Hikoshudan. The losses of the RAF and RAAF were heavy, and by the end of January the British were bottled up on Singapore Island, where they surrendered on 15 February 1942. The campaign had cost the Japanese 92 aircraft, while the British and Australians lost 390.

On 10 January 1942 the ABDA (American, British, Dutch, Australian) command was created to coordinate the Allied defence of the theatre, and could call on only some 310 obsolescent aircraft, 160 of them Dutch, for the defence of the Dutch East Indies. Supplemented by the JNAF's 21st and 23rd Air Flotillas, transferred from Formosa to Davao in the Philippines early in January, the Japanese campaign in the Dutch East Indies started on 11 January with the aid of the 22nd Flotilla and the JAAF's 3rd Hikoshudan. The 21st Air Flotilla supported the central drive from

Throughout the first six months of the war the Japanese struck at many points in East and South-East Asia, always with great vigour and under cover of decisive air power which often caught the Allied aircraft on the ground. Here Japanese troops examine wrecked British aircraft.

NAKAJIMA KI-43 HAYABUSA 'OSCAR'

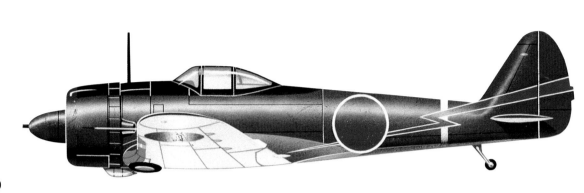

Type: single-seat land-based interceptor

Powerplant: one 858kW (1150hp) Nakajima
HA-115 radial piston engine

Maximum speed: 530km/h (329mph)

Service ceiling: 11,200m (36,750ft)

Weights: empty 1910kg (4202lb); maximum
take-off 2925kg (6435lb)

Armament: two 12.7mm (0.50cal.) machine-
guns and up to two 250kg (550lb) bombs

Dimensions: span 10.84m (35ft 6in)
     length 8.92m (29ft 3in)
     height 3.27m (10ft 9in)
     wing area 21.40m² (230sq ft)

Davao to Bali via Jolo Island, Tarakan, Balikpapan and Bandjermasin, which was also aided by the aircraft of the light carrier *Ryujo*. The eastern drive to take Sulawesi, and then to move south against Manado, Kendari, Ambon, Makassar and Timor, was supported by the aircraft of the seaplane tender *Chitose* and the light carrier *Zuiho*, supplemented by the 23rd Air Flotilla. The carriers *Kaga*, *Akagi*, *Hiryu* and *Soryu* also played major roles. Japan swept to victory in the Dutch East Indies by 8 March.

THE FALL OF RABAUL

Even as the campaigns in Malaya, Burma, the Philippines and Dutch East Indies were being fought, the Japanese moved southeast to secure the Bismarck Islands and capture positions on New Guinea, and thus be in the position to attack the sea and air routes linking Australasia and the US. After a number of preliminary air attacks, on 20 January Rabaul on New Britain was attacked by 120 A6M2, D3A1 and B5N2 aircraft of the *Zuikaku*, *Shokaku*, *Kaga* and *Akagi*.

On 23 January a Japanese task force landed on New Britain, and took Rabaul by midday. The important port and airfield at Kavieng, in New Ireland, were also occupied by the same task force.

Rabaul was a key component in the plan for an extension of Japanese power towards Australia via New Guinea, and into the New Hebrides, the Fijian and the Samoan Island groups. From Rabaul the G3M2, later joined by the G4M1, was within range of the Allies' Port Moresby base on the southern coast of Papua, and the first attack on Port Moresby occurred during 3 February. On the night of 7/8 March, Japanese forces landed at Lae and Salamaua on the north coast of New Guinea to march over the Owen Stanley mountains to strike at Port Moresby. In the meantime Lae

WAR IN THE PHILIPPINES

In the Philippines, General Douglas MacArthur's US Forces Far East (USFFE) was supported by Major General Lewis H. Brereton's US Far East Air Force (FEAF), which included the B-17D bombers of the 19th Bombardment Group and the P-40B fighters of the 24th Pursuit Group; there were also limited numbers of naval aircraft. About 160 US and 29 Philippine aircraft were available on the morning of 8 December 1941, when the initial Japanese air attacks were delivered. The first occurred at Davao, where the carrier *Ryujo*'s 13 B5N2 bombers and nine A5M4 fighters achieved total surprise. Other raids followed against Baguio and Tuguegaro in northern Luzon, by Ki-49 bombers of the 8th Sentai and Ki-21 bombers of 14th Sentai, both of the 5th Hikoshudan. The main attack by the JNAF's 21st and 23rd Air Flotillas, also based on Formosa, was delayed by fog over their airfields, but reached their targets at 1245 to devastate the complex of airfields round Manila using 108 G3M2 and G4M1 bombers escorted by 87 A6M2 fighters of the 1st, 3rd, Takao and Tainan Kokutais. The Japanese attacks on 8 December destroyed 108 aircraft, leaving only 17 B-17s and fewer than 40 P-40 machines. This dwindling force fought at odds during the following weeks as the Japanese landed and moved against the USFFE. By 25 December the remnants of the FEAF had been pulled back to Australia, and the US ground forces surrendered on 6 May 1942. After the fall of Manila on 2 January 1942, the 5th Hikoshudan was moved west to take part in the Burma campaign.

MITSUBISHI A6M2

Type: single-seat carrierborne and land-based fighter and fighter-bomber

Powerplant: one 708kW (950hp) Nakajima 14 cylinder two-row radial engine

Maximum speed: 534km/h (332mph)

Service ceiling: 10,000m (32,810ft)

Weights: empty 1680kg (3704lb); maximum take-off 2796kg (6164lb)

Armament: two 20mm (0.79in) wing cannon; two 7.7mm (0.303in) MG in forward fuselage; 120kg (265lb) external bomb load

Dimensions:	span	12.00m (39ft 4.5in)
	length	9.06m (29ft 8.75in)
	height	3.05m (10ft)
	wing area	20.00m² (199sq ft)

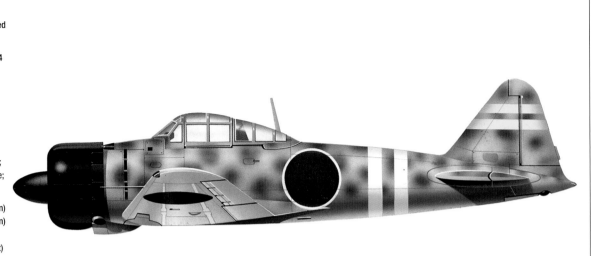

would form an advanced fighter base for Rabaul's air elements, which by a time early in April comprised the new 25th Air Flotilla.

CARRIER STRENGTHS

By January 1942 the commissioning of the *Shoho* gave the Japanese navy a strength of six fleet and three light carriers, whereas Admiral Chester W. Nimitz's US Pacific Fleet had only four carriers in the form of the large USS *Lexington* and *Saratoga,* and the medium-size USS *Yorktown* and *Enterprise.* The USS *Hornet* was currently on a shake-down cruise, and was destined for San Diego to partake in training with the USAAF for a raid on Tokyo. The force was cut to three on 11 January when the *Saratoga* was damaged by a torpedo.

After their efforts at Pearl Harbor and Wake, the *Kaga, Akagi, Zuikaku* and *Shokaku* returned to Kyushu to refit, but the *Hiryu* and *Soryu* steamed to Truk, where they were joined by the other four carriers on 14 January, and were then used in support of the conquest of the Dutch East Indies. In preparation for the invasion of Timor the *Kaga, Akagi, Hiryu* and *Soryu* joined forces off Peleliu in the Palau Islands: the carriers reached a position 320km (200 miles) northeast of Darwin on the morning of

19 February for an attack coinciding with that of the G3M2 and G4M1 land-based bombers of the Kendari-based 1st Air Attack Force. Some 81 B5N2, D3A1 and A6M2 aircraft reached Darwin at 0950: the B5N2s bombed from medium altitude, the D3A1s dive-bombed the harbour and airfields, and the A6M2s strafed shipping and aircraft on the ground, and at the same time saw off an interception attempt by the USAAF's 33rd Pursuit Squadron, which lost none out of 10 P-40E fighters. At 1145 some 53 twin-engined bombers of the 1st Air Attack Force bombed the town and harbour. Some 15 USAAF and RAAF aircraft had been destroyed, and five merchantmen, one Australian destroyer and two other craft sunk. Darwin was then frequently attacked by the 23rd Air Flotilla from its bases at Kendari and Timor-Penfui.

The 1st Air Fleet next steamed into the Indian Ocean and Bay of Bengal. The *Akagi, Soryu, Hiryu, Zuikaku* and *Shokaku* were tasked with raids on Ceylon in an effort to draw

out the Royal Navy's Eastern Fleet for a decisive battle, while the *Ryujo* undertook an anti-ship raid into the Bay of Bengal. The carriers had 377

Land-based bombers such as the Mitsubishi Ki-21 were classified by the Japanese as heavy bombers, but were at best medium bombers. These warplanes had good range, but lacked essential features such as defensive armour and self-sealing fuel tanks for most of the war.

aircraft, and for support the 22nd Air Flotilla had transferred its G3M2 and G4M1 bombers from Gloembang to Sabang in northern Sumatra. Warned by patrol flying-boats, the British knew what to expect, and on 5 April, 127 Japanese warplanes arrived over Colombo harbour, where the defence was largely unprepared. Some 26 Hurricane Mk IIAs and six Fulmar Mk IIs were scrambled, but these were no match for the A6M2 fighters, which destroyed two Catalinas, 10 Hurricanes (another five being damaged), and six naval aircraft for the loss of seven of their own number. In the harbour a merchant vessel and a destroyer were sunk. To the south, 53 B5N2 and D3A1

On 5 April 1942, 127 Japanese warplanes arrived over Colombo harbour, where the defence was largely unprepared.

warplanes spotted a British cruiser force, and the dive-bombers sank HMS *Dorsetshire* and *Cornwall*. The *Ryujo*'s aircraft struck the ports of Vizegapatam and Coconada on 6 April, but achieved little success. The Japanese carriers returned on 9 April to attack Trincomalee and China Bay, sink the carrier HMS *Hermes*, and shoot down eight British fighters and five Blenheim Mk IV light bombers.

After the occupation of Thailand on 8/10 December 1941, the JAAF's 10th Hikodan (air brigade) of the 5th Hikoshudan moved to airfields in that country. Then the 7th Hikodan of the 3rd Hikoshudan was sent from Malaya, where there was no real air opposition, to boost the Japanese air strength in Thailand. On 23 December 1941, in preparation for the invasion of Burma, the 7th and 10th Hikodans flew their first raid on

Rangoon, whose defence was entrusted to the RAF's No. 221 Group, comprising Nos 60 and 67 Squadrons with the inadequate Buffalo fighter. Formed at Toungoo early in 1941, three squadrons of the American Volunteer Group (AVG), equipped with Hawk 81A fighters, had been defending the Burma Road providing the only land link with China, and its 3rd Squadron was currently based at

By May 1942 the Japanese imperial headquarters had extended its ambitions.

Mingaladon outside Rangoon: Allied fighter strength was some 37 aircraft.

The first Japanese raid on Rangoon by 60 Ki-21s and escorting fighters was tackled by the two British and one US squadrons, whose pilots claimed nine

bombers and one Ki-27b fighter in exchange for two Hawk 81A fighters. Eight RAF and AVG fighters were lost in the course of a second raid by 200 or more aircraft on 25 January, but as a result of their losses the Japanese switched to night raids from 4 to 23 January. By the latter date, marking a return to day attacks in an intense campaign up to 29 January, the whole of the 5th Hikoshudan had reached Thailand from the Philippines. Even so, the Japanese lost more than 50 aircraft in the period 23/29 January. Though strengthened by Hurricane Mk IIB fighters, No. 221 Group was barely able to maintain a defence, but then the defence of Burma crumbled.

BATTLE FOR BURMA

By the middle of March 1942 the 5th Hikoshidan (flight division, a command replacing the Hikoshudan throughout the JAAF during this period) moved to Rangoon to control all JAAF units in the Burma theatre, and soon overwhelmed the surviving British air strength. The Japanese pressed their advance to the north, and by 29 April the Japanese had severed the Burma Road at Lashio. Mandalay fell in May 1942 and, just over one week later, the Japanese advance guard had reached the Chindwin river before monsoon rains ended the advance.

By May 1942 the Japanese imperial headquarters had extended its

Japanese troops prepare to land at an Allied port already devastated by the attentions of the Japanese air forces. In the fast-moving campaigns of the Pacific War's first six months, the Japanese swept all before them with such tactics.

In April 1942 the US achieved a psychological success when North American B-25 Mitchell twin-engined bombers of the USAAF took off from the US Navy's carrier USS *Hornet* to attack Tokyo and start to bring home to the Japanese the real implications of their assault on the US.

ambitions beyond those envisaged in December 1941 to include Midway Island in the east, the Aleutian Islands in the north, and Australia in the south via the stepping stone of Port Moresby in Papua, shielded from the east by the occupation of Tulagi in the Solomon Islands. The seizure of these objectives was allocated to the 4th Fleet, based at Rabaul and coordinating the required transport groups, the Mobile Force (5th Carrier Division with the *Zuikaku* and *Shokaku*), the Support Group (centred

THE 'DOOLITTLE RAIDERS'

On 18 April 1942 a daring and ingenious raid was made on Tokyo, Kobe, Yokohama and Nagoya on Honshu Island by 16 adapted North American B-25B Mitchell twin-engined bombers, embarked on the *Hornet* on 1 April. The carrier sailed from the US on the following day and joined the *Enterprise*, the two then heading for the selected launch point some 725km (450 miles) east of Tokyo. At 0738 on 18 April a Japanese picket vessel was sighted and, fearing that his security had been compromised, Vice Admiral William F. Halsey ordered the fly-off at 0800 when the *Hornet* was still some 1290km (800 miles) from Japan. All the B-25s managed to take off, and bad weather aided the raid in securing total surprise as the aircraft attacked. Most crews bailed out safely over China, two aircraft force-landed in Chekiang, one landed at Vladivostok in Soviet Siberia, and two landed in Japanese territory, their crews being beheaded. The damage caused by the bombers was minimal, but the raid had enormous consequences in raising US morale and persuading the Japanese to commit an immediate offensive on Chekiang, which they believed to be the starting point of the attack, and to establish two JAAF fighter Hikodans (air brigades) for home defence.

THE BATTLE OF CORAL SEA

At 1200 on 7 May 1942 an air attack by the aircraft of the *Zuikaku* and *Shokaku* hit only the tanker *Neosho* and the destroyer USS *Sims*. Then, tailed by B-17E bombers and with her covering fighters occupied, the *Shoho* was attacked by the *Yorktown*'s aircraft and soon sank. On 8 May the aircraft of the *Yorktown* and *Lexington* hit the *Shokaku*, which had to be sent back to Truk. Meanwhile B5N2 and D3A1 warplanes from the Japanese carriers attacked TF-17. The *Lexington* was hit by a torpedo, but still managed to recover her aircraft, but then fumes spread and at 1247 she was ripped by a huge explosion. During the evening the crew abandoned the ship, which was then sunk by US destroyers. Some 80 Japanese and 66 US aircraft had been lost in the first major carrier battle in the Pacific theatre, and the world's first naval battle in which the combatants' vessels did not come within sight of each other.

Nimitz prepared a counter-move which led to the Battle of the Coral Sea. At Noumea on 1 May Rear Admiral Frank J. Fletcher took command of the new Task Force 17 (TF-17) including the *Yorktown* and *Lexington* with 143 F4F-3, TBD-1 Devastator and SBD-3 Dauntless warplanes. The Japanese operation began on 3 May with the unopposed landing at Tulagi, and late in the morning the *Shoho* was therefore detached to the Port Moresby invasion groups. During the following morning the *Yorktown*'s aircraft attacked Tulagi, after which the two US carriers joined

on the seaplane tender *Kamikawa Maru*), and the Covering Group with the light carrier *Shoho* (12 A6M2 and nine B5N2 aircraft) and four heavy cruisers. Most of these elements where to sweep through the Solomons to approach Port Moresby from the southeast, while the *Zuikaku* and

Shokaku (with 125 aircraft) were to counter any US moves. Land-based air support was to be furnished by the 25th Air Flotilla at Rabaul. The 45 fighters and 45 bombers of the Tainan and Genzan Kokutais were due to reach Rabaul on 4 May. US intelligence warned of the plan, and

Below: US naval aviators at first lacked the experience and skills of their opponents, who continued to sink US warships, but soon built up their capabilities and, aided by more modern aircraft, turned the tables from mid-1942.

Right: In the first stages of the Pacific campaign the US Navy was phasing out older aircraft such as the TBD Devastator torpedo-bomber and placing more reliance on more modern types such as these SBD Dauntless dive-bombers.

in the morning of 5 May. The Battle of the Coral Sea began two days later.

BUILD-UP TO MIDWAY

From May 1942 the Japanese naval operations in the Pacific were designed to extend Japanese influence to the east along three routes to the western Aleutians, Midway Island not far to the northwest of Hawaii, and Port Moresby as a stepping stone towards the southeast and New Caledonia, Samoa and Fiji. Admiral Yamamoto's Midway operation was the most important Japanese undertaking of the summer, and was conceived as a means to take Midway and also to draw the US Pacific Fleet into the desired 'decisive battle'.

The occupation of Midway was to be preceded by a diversionary attack on US bases in the Aleutians: on 5 June 1942 Japanese troops were to be landed at Kiska and Attu in the Aleutian chain and to establish defensive bases, while the Midway invasion also took place following a period of intensive aerial bombardment by aircraft of the light carrier *Ryujo* and new fleet carrier *Junyo*, with the light carrier *Zuiho* offering support.

The Japanese strike and transport forces which set off towards Midway in the period 25-28 May were huge and complex in their organization, and included Nagumo's 1st Koku-Kantai comprising the *Kaga*, *Akagi*, *Hiryu* and *Soryu* with 72 A6M2, 72 D3A1, 81 B5N2 and two D4Y1-C Suisei dive-bomber aircraft; the elderly light carrier *Hosho* with eight B5N2s; and the seaplane tenders *Nisshin* and *Chiyoda*. But having broken the Japanese naval code, the US Navy knew what the Japanese planned and prepared to ambush Yamamoto's fleet.

USS *LEXINGTON*

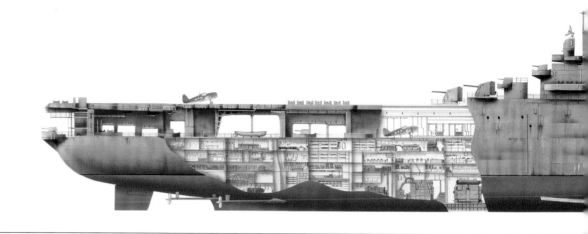

Type: aircraft carrier

Powerplant: Quadruple screw turbo electric drive

Maximum speed: 33.2 knots

Range: 18,900km (10,500nm) at 10 knots

Displacement: 48,463 tonnes (47,700 tons)

Crew: 2327

Armament: eight 203mm (8in), 12 127mm (5in) guns, 80 aircraft

Dimensions: length 270.6m (888ft)
width 32.2m (105ft 8in)
height 9.9m (32ft 6in)

Core of Fletcher's TF-17, the *Yorktown* was repaired and readied for sea in an extraordinarily short time. The *Enterprise* and *Hornet* were the heart of Rear Admiral Raymond A. Spruance's TF-16. Some 232 aircraft were carried by the US ships, and 119 more naval and Marine Corps aircraft operated from shore bases. Based also at Midway, the US 7th Army Air Force contributed 19 B-17E Flying Fortresses and four B-26A Marauders.

The Japanese task forces bound for Midway were first located by PBY-5 flying-boats on 3 June about 1125km (700 miles) west of Midway.

INVADERS UNCOVERED

In the morning of 4 June the Japanese launched their first wave of 108 aircraft, but these were spotted by a PBY-5, while another such machine located the Japanese carrier force 257km (160 miles) northwest of Midway. As the Japanese aircraft

neared the island, all of the land-based aircraft were launched, but suffered heavy losses without gaining any real success. As the aircraft of the first Japanese attack returned, they were refuelled and rearmed for a second attack. At this point Nagumo was informed that there were US carriers in the area, and decided to

The crews of torpedo squadron VT-6 board their Douglas TBD-1 Devastator aircraft on board USS *Enterprise* prior to the Battle of Midway.

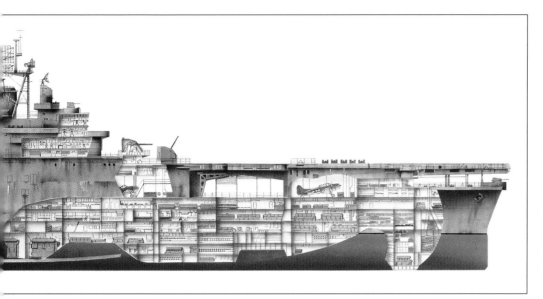

But the *Hiryu* was undamaged and retaliated, her aircraft hitting the *Yorktown*, which was abandoned and later scuttled. Finally, the *Hiryu* was found and sunk by SBD-3s of the *Hornet* and the *Enterprise* at 1705. This effectively ended the battle as a huge US strategic victory. As well as the four carriers, the Japanese lost one heavy cruiser, 332 aircraft, and 216 highly experienced and irreplaceable pilots. The US losses were one carrier, one destroyer, and 150 aircraft.

have the aircraft rearmed for the anti-ship task. During this period of delay, an attack by obsolete TBD-1 torpedo-bombers was effectively slaughtered, losing 35 of the 41 aircraft as well as three escorting F4F-4 fighters.

The dive-bombers of the *Yorktown* and *Enterprise* now located the Japanese carriers as they recovered their fighters, and in a sustained attack the SBD-3s hit the *Akagi*, *Kaga* and *Soryu*, all of which caught fire.

Island bases to the west of the Hawaiian Islands were key air outposts for the US forces, and a magnet for Japanese attack. The Japanese assault on Midway triggered the decisive Battle of Midway, in which the Japanese lost four aircraft carriers and the strategic initiative in the Pacific.

Japanese troops were landed on Guadalcanal by destroyers, cruisers and transports and engaged the 1st Marine Division in some of the bitterest fighting of the war.

Though small and carrying only a modest bomb load, the Douglas SBD Dauntless was a vital asset for the US Navy in 1942 and 1943. Flown by steadily more skilled crews, the Dauntless was able to plant its bombs with devastating accuracy.

The focus now moved southwest to the Solomon Islands region. Savage fighting continued along the 'Kokoda Trail' across the Owen Stanley mountains as the Japanese pushed their overland, but doomed drive on Port Moresby from the north coast.

The whole situation in the theatre was then changed by the landing of the US 1st Marine Division on Tulagi and Guadalcanal on 7 August.

The US forces quickly overran the small Japanese garrisons and set about completing the airstrip, which the Japanese had started to build on Guadalcanal, at Henderson Field.

ASSAULT ON GUADALCANAL

The Japanese decided that the US lodgement at Lunga Point on Guadalcanal must be retaken, for US aircraft from Henderson Field could attack the Japanese forces right

It was not all one-way traffic in the Pacific, and the listing deck of the USS *Yorktown* during the battle of Midway attests to the fact that the Japanese were able to strike back with bomb or torpedo.

along the Solomons and in New Guinea, and attack bases as far distant as Rabaul and Kavieng. Japanese air attacks started almost immediately, and air reinforcements were hastened to the bases in the Bismarck Islands.

Over the following five months the Japanese navy made a great effort to dislodge the US forces from Guadalcanal, transferring to Rabaul and Kavieng an ever larger number of units drawn from the 21st, 22nd, 23rd

and 24th Air Flotillas, and as early as September transferring the headquarters of the 11th Koku-Kantai from Tinian to Rabaul to oversee the naval air operations. Japanese troops were landed on Guadalcanal by destroyers, cruisers and transports and

engaged the 1st Marine Division in some of the bitterest fighting of the war. As US air power on Guadalcanal became stronger, with aircraft of the US Navy and US Marine Corps supplemented by the P-38F, P-39D and P-40 fighters of the USAAF, the losses

SOLOMONS NAVAL BATTLES

The air defence of the US position on Guadalcanal rested initially on the F4F-4s of one Marine squadron on Henderson Field, and there also took place a series of naval battles near Guadalcanal. In the Battle of the Eastern Solomons on 23 August the Japanese lost the *Ryujo*, and in the Battle of Santa Cruz on 26 October the US lost the *Hornet* sunk, while the Japanese lost 102 aircraft and suffered damage to the *Zuiho* and *Shokaku*. In October the land fighting continued as the Japanese land forces were enlarged by seaborne reinforcements.

A decisive factor in the Pacific War was the ability of the US to turn out considerably larger numbers of warships than the Japanese could achieve, and these ships were also qualitatively superior to the vessels which the Japanese could get into service.

of the 25th and 26th Air Flotillas escalated enormously.

The *Enterprise* returned, and reached the scene during November, and on 12 November her aircraft sank the battleships *Hiei* and *Kirishima* in the Battle of Savo Island.

MOUNTING LOSSES

On 4 January 1943 the Japanese decided to yield Guadalcanal, and the remnants of their 17th Army were withdrawn by 9 February. At the same time the Japanese had been driven from Buna in Papua and pulled back to Lae and Salamaua, ending the threat to Port Moresby. In the battles of Guadalcanal the Japanese navy had lost one carrier, two battleships, four cruisers, 11 destroyers, six submarines, and about 350 aircraft that carried the cream of its pilots and crews.

On 9 November 1942 the first-line strength of the JNAF was 1721 aircraft, 465 of them carrierborne, while the first-line strength of the JAAF, which was now organized as air armies (Kokugun) in Japan, China, Manchuria, Burma, Sumatra and Malaya, amounted to 1642 aircraft.

The year 1943 saw the real development of the US challenge to the Japanese in the Pacific Area and the Southwest Pacific Area (SWPA) theatres. Japan had by now lost the war, although she refused even to consider the reality of the situation. US aircrews were now better trained, and had formidable new carrierborne aircraft including the F4U-1 Corsair and F6F-3 Hellcat fighters, and the SB2C Helldiver bomber. Moreover, US shipyards were beginning to complete

Japan had by now lost the war, although she refused even to consider the reality of the situation.

the first of the powerful 'Essex'-class fleet carriers, each carrying up to 110 aircraft, for service from June 1943.

The increasing capability of Allied air supremacy was revealed on 3 March, when aircraft of Major General George C. Kenney's US 5th Army Air Force (AAF) intercepted a convoy carrying most of the Japanese 51st Division from Rabaul to Lae: in the Battle of the Bismarck Sea, RAAF Beaufighter Mk VIC attack fighters, B-17s of the 43rd Bombardment Group (BG), B-25s of the 3rd BG and A-20s of the 38th BG sank all but four destroyers out of the convoy of 16 ships. This ended Japanese attempts to reinforce their strength on New Guinea by sea.

Yamamoto flew to Rabaul on 3 April 1943 to supervise a maximum-effort campaign to eliminate Allied air

RUSSELL ISLANDS AND NEW GEORGIA

The ever-increasing number of US air elements serving in Guadalcanal came under the Air Solomons Command, which was supplemented over New Guinea by the US 5th Army Air Force (AAF) and from December 1942, the new 13th AAF. As a prelude to their advance up the chain of the Solomon Islands, US forces landed on the Russell Islands on 21 February; from here the Japanese airfield on New Georgia lay within easy range, and conditions on New Georgia soon became untenable for the JNAF.

power in the Solomons, but wrongly believing that they had sunk one cruiser, two destroyers and 25 transports sunk, and destroyed 134 Allied aircraft (losses were only three ships and fewer than 20

aircraft), the Japanese ended their campaign prematurely on 12 April.

The Japanese war effort was then seriously affected by the death of Yamamoto, whose aircraft was

Conceived as a carrierborne bomber, the Avenger was also an effective attack aircraft in the island campaigns that typified the Southern and Central Pacific elements of the war.

129

In the battles of the Solomons and Rabaul from 7 August 1942 to 20 February 1944, Japanese naval air power was defeated with the loss of 2935 navy aircraft.

intercepted and shot down on 18 April by P-38 fighters of the USAAF after US intelligence had worked out the admiral's itinerary.

After the capture of Buna in January 1943 MacArthur pushed his SWPA forces west along the north coast of New Guinea in a series of air-supported amphibious landings ending at Sansapor on the western tip on 30 July 1944. Pacific Area forces had also reached the northwestern tip of the Solomon Islands chain on 3 February 1944 with the landing of New Zealand forces on Green Island.

In both campaigns Allied air power was wholly dominant, and an ever-courageous Japanese air defence was crippled by lack of modern aircraft, shortages of vital equipment, spares and fuel, and the increasingly poor standard of the pilots and aircrews delivered by Japan's overburdened and under-equipped training programme. In the battles of the

A ceiling of shells bursting above a US aircraft carrier during the Battle of Santa Cruz demonstrates the ever-increasing strength of the anti-aircraft batteries carried by the US Navy's ships to beat off Japanese air attacks, which were always delivered with great determination.

Solomons and Rabaul from 7 August 1942 to 20 February 1944, Japanese naval air power was defeated with the loss of 2935 navy aircraft. By this time it had been decided not to assault New Britain and New Ireland, now deemed irrelevant, but to leave their impotent Japanese garrisons isolated and thus to 'wither on the vine' for the rest of the war.

ISLAND-HOPPING CAMPAIGN
After the forces of the South Pacific Area had advanced through the Solomons, and as MacArthur's SWPA forces were moving along the north coast of New Guinea, the elements of Nimitz's Central Pacific Area were driving west through the Gilbert Islands (20-23 November 1943) and Marshall Islands (1-23 February 1944) for naval and air bases that would allow attacks farther to the west, against Japanese bases such as Truk.

After the attack on Truk and the landings in the Marshall Islands, three fleet and three light carriers of TF-58 (otherwise the Fast Carrier Task

These USAAF Republic P-47 Thunderbolts are seen leaving on a routine patrol shortly after the capture of an island in the Marianas chain.

Force) moved to attack Japanese strength in the Marianas Islands. At Tinian and Saipan were the remnants of the 22nd and 26th Air Flotillas, recuperating after the recent spate of massive losses. On 21 February 1944, the day before the US strike, the recently formed 1st Koku-Kantai despatched from Kanoya in Japan to Guam, Tinian and Saipan 120 aircraft,

F6F-5 HELLCAT

Type: single-seat carrier-based fighter

Powerplant: one 1492kW (2000hp) Pratt &
Whitney Double Wasp 18-cylinder radial piston

Maximum speed: 620km/h (380mph)

Service ceiling: 11,500m (37,500ft)

Weights: empty 4191kg (9200lb); maximum
take-off weight 6991kg (15,400lb)

Armament: six 12.7mm (.50cal.) Browning M2
machine-guns; up to 907kg (2000lb) bomb load;
six 127mm (5in) rockets

Dimensions: span   13.08m (42ft 10in)
length   10.23m (33ft 7in)
height   3.99m (13ft 1in)
wing area 31.03m² (334sq ft)

but at dawn on the following day a US carrierborne fighter sweep destroyed all of them. TF-58's aircraft then attacked the 26th Air Flotilla's remnants on the Palau Islands, claiming more than 100 more of its aircraft on 30/31 March, provided air support for the SWPA's landings at Aitape and Hollandia between 21-24 April, and struck the re-equipped 22nd Air Flotilla as it passed Truk on 29/30 April.

The US assault on the Marianas Islands comprised the hard-fought conquests of Saipan, Tinian and Guam between 15 June and 10 August. The Japanese launched a maximum-effort operation to destroy the US Navy's forces off the islands.

This effort would lead to the Battle of the Philippine Sea.

DECISION IN THE PHILIPPINES

The Japanese operation was based on a re-formed carrier force backed by land-based air power. The 1st Mobile Fleet had been created on 1 March 1944 with nine carriers, carrying 452 aircraft, in three carrier divisions each with its own air group. Centred upon the new fleet carrier *Taiho* with the veteran *Zuikaku* and *Shokaku* was the 1st Kokusentai. Its 601st Kokutai had 71 A6M5s, 10 A6M2 fighter-bombers, 81 D4Y2s, nine D4Y1-C reconnaissance aircraft and 56 B6N2s. The *Hiyo, Junyo* and *Ryuho* formed the 2nd Kokusentai with the 652nd Kokutai of 108 aircraft

OPERATION HAILSTONE: ATTACK ON TRUK

On 17 February 1944 the remnants of the 24th and 26th Air Flotillas on airfields in the Truk atoll complex totalled about 155 serviceable aircraft as well as floatplanes and transports, and 180 aircraft under repair. From a point some 145km (90 miles) northeast of Truk, 72 F6F-3s were launched from the carriers *Enterprise, Yorktown, Belleau Wood, Essex, Intrepid, Cabot, Bunker Hill, Monterey* and *Cowpens* under the command of Admiral Marc A. Mitscher. The Japanese responded with 45 A6M5s of the 204th Kokutai and 18 A6M2-Ns of the 902nd Kokutai, and in the fight which followed the Japanese lost about 30 fighters and the US just four. There followed a series of devastating attacks on surface targets, and by the fall of night on the following day the Japanese had lost more than 200,000 tons of shipping and 252 aircraft.

plus 27 D3A2 dive-bombers. The smaller carriers of the 3rd Kokusentai were the *Zuiho, Chitose* and *Chiyoda* carrying 90 aircraft.

By June 1944 JNAF land-based air power in the Pacific totalled 484 aircraft directly under the 1st Koku-

The US-led campaign to advance west along the north coast of New Guinea saw the use of airborne landings to secure key areas, such as airfields, behind the Japanese lines, as amphibious forces landed from the sea at a nearby location.

The Japanese launched a maximum-effort operation to destroy the US Navy's forces off the Marianas Islands.

Kantai in the Marianas, 114 of the 61st Air Flotilla on Yap Island and in the Palaus, plus the 22nd Air Flotilla at Truk, the 23rd Air Flotilla at Sorong in western New Guinea, and the 26th Air Flotilla at Davao in Mindanao.

From 12 June TF-58's fighters flew sweeps over 1st Koku-Kantai airfields on Guam, Saipan and Tinian, shooting down 81 aircraft and destroying another 29 on the ground on the first morning. Turning north, TF-58 then attacked airfields on

Chichi Jima and Iwo Jima. The 1st Mobile Fleet sailed from Tawi Tawi on 13 June to approach the Philippine Sea, and on 19 June the first wave of Japanese aircraft lifted off in the form of 43 A6M2s each with one 250kg (551lb) semi-armour-piercing bomb, seven B6N2s and 14 A6M5 escort fighters of the 1st Special Attack Unit.

'TURKEY SHOOT'

The force was intercepted by 197 F6F-3 fighters: the Japanese scored only one hit on a battleship, but the fighters and ships' 40mm AA guns destroyed 42 of the Japanese aircraft. US submarines now torpedoed and sank the *Taiho* and *Shokaku*.

Admiral Jisaburo Ozawa launched four attacks on 19 June totalling 373 sorties, but lost 243 aircraft with another 33 severely damaged in what was the greatest air battle of the Pacific War. Retiring to the west, the 1st Mobile Fleet was tackled by TF-58's attack aircraft (77 dive-bombers, most of them SB2C-1s, and 54 TBF/TBM-1 torpedo-bombers) escorted by 85 F6F-3s, and lost the *Hiyo* while also taking heavy damage to the *Ryuho* and *Chiyoda*.

Returning after dark and short of fuel, 80 US aircraft ditched or were lost in crashes, most of their crews being saved. The 1st Mobile Fleet's air strength had been destroyed, and so too had been the land-based elements of the 1st Koku-Kantai, which was to

The Japanese were reliant on shipping for the support of their bastions in South-East Asia and the Pacific, so Japanese transport vessels and the ports they frequented were devastated by US air attacks, often delivered deep into Japanese-held areas by carrierborne aircraft.

have provided the carrierborne aircraft with support.

The 1st Koku-Kantai was now transferred to Manila in the Philippines to join the 26th Air Flotilla at Davao, and by a time early in September the JNAF strength in the Philippines had risen to some 500 aircraft. However, in the course of pre-invasion air attacks by TF-38 in the period 9-14 September, the JNAF strength was crushed, and by

30 September, the 5th Base Air Force (otherwise the 1st Koku-Kantai) had been reduced to fewer than 100 serviceable aircraft.

With the US landing on Leyte Island in the Philippines scheduled for 20 October 1944, TF-38 struck at the Japanese bases in the Ryukyu Islands, including Okinawa, with 1392 sorties on 10 October. On 12 October TF-58 attacked air bases on Formosa,

US Navy pilots in celebratory mood in front of a Grumman F6F Hellcat's tailplane. From 1943 US warplanes were decidedly better than the obsolescent types still operated by the Japanese, were available in larger numbers, and were flown by more experienced pilots.

The attacks continued on Formosa and Luzon Island, and in one week of air fighting the JNAF lost 492 aircraft and the JAAF 150.

where there were some 630 aircraft of the 6th Base Air Force (2nd Koku-Kantai) and the JAAF's 8th Hikoshidan, the F6F-3s shooting down more than 100 of a 200-strong Japanese force for the loss of 30 of their own. The attacks continued on Formosa and Luzon Island, and in one week of air fighting the JNAF lost

492 aircraft and the JAAF 150.

The US invasion of Leyte was supported by some 500 aircraft of TF-77.4's 17 escort carriers. More distant cover was provided by TF-38 (Fast Carrier Task Force) with 1074 aircraft on nine fleet and eight light carriers. Allied land-based air power later came into play after airfields on

Leyte were captured or built, and was at this time widely deployed. It comprised Kenney's Far East Air Force, created in July 1944 with the 2500 aircraft of the US 5th and 13th AAFs, and another 420 of the RAAF.

EPIC CONFRONTATION

The Japanese navy tried to destroy the initial landings in the four-part Battle of Leyte Gulf, which was fought between 23-26 October and remains the world's largest-ever sea battle. The four Japanese forces involved were

The Japanese navy tried to destroy the initial landings in the four-part Battle of Leyte Gulf, which was fought between 23-26 October and remains the world's largest-ever sea battle.

three attack groups and one decoy group, the last based on the surviving carriers with only 116 aircraft, and the components were the Battles of the Sibuyan Sea, Surigao Strait, Samar and Cape Engano.

Included in the Japanese losses were four carriers and 500 aircraft, while the US losses included one light carrier, two escort carriers (including the USS *St Lo* to the *kamikaze* air attacks now adopted by the

Japanese pilots), and more than 200 aircraft.

In the Battle of the Sibuyan Sea, US submarines located the Japanese Force 'A' as it entered the Palawan Passage from the South China Sea, informed Halsey and then sank two heavy cruisers and damaged another. The Japanese steamed on, but were then assailed by

A member of the deck crew scrambles to free a pilot possibly trapped in the cockpit of his Grumman F6F Hellcat fighter-bomber, which has come to grief on landing on board USS *Enterprise* and caught fire.

A scene typical of the later stages of World War II in the Pacific: photographed from the deck of USS *Coral Sea* during operations off Saipan in the Marianas in 1944, a Japanese warplane plunges in flames, its pilot possibly trying to strike the US aircraft carrier below it in a *kamikaze* attack.

CHINA, MANCHURIA AND BURMA

While naval battles raged in the Philippines, the Japanese army was concerned with China, Manchuria and Burma. By June 1942 some 1560 of the JAAF's front-line aircraft were in this area in three air armies (Kokuguns). The 1st Kokugun was based in Japan with only modest numbers of fighters. Fearing war with the USSR despite a non-aggression treaty, the JAAF had its 2nd Kokugun with 550 aircraft in Manchuria. The 3rd Kokugun was responsible for the Southern Area (Thailand, Burma, Malaya, Sumatra, and the East Indies) and China. The subordinated 5th Hikoshidan supervised four Hikodans (the 4th, 7th, 3rd and 12th in Burma, Malaya and Thailand, Java and Sumatra respectively), as well as the 21st Dokuritsu Hikotai in Indochina. In August 1942 the 3rd Kokugan's 3rd Hikoshidan returned to China and, established at Nanking, became the nucleus of the new 5th Kokugun from March 1943.

carrierborne aircraft which, over two days, sank the super-battleship *Musashi* and damaged several other ships before the Japanese apparently turned back.

Japanese land-based aircraft meanwhile harassed a division of TF-38, most of the aircraft being shot down, but the light carrier USS *Princeton* was sunk and a cruiser severely damaged. After dark, the Japanese reversed course once again and made for the San Bernardino Strait. In the Battle of Surigao Strait only ships were involved at first, but aircraft became involved in the later stages of the rout.

Force 'A' had meanwhile passed through the San Bernardino Strait as it tried to link, north of Samar, with

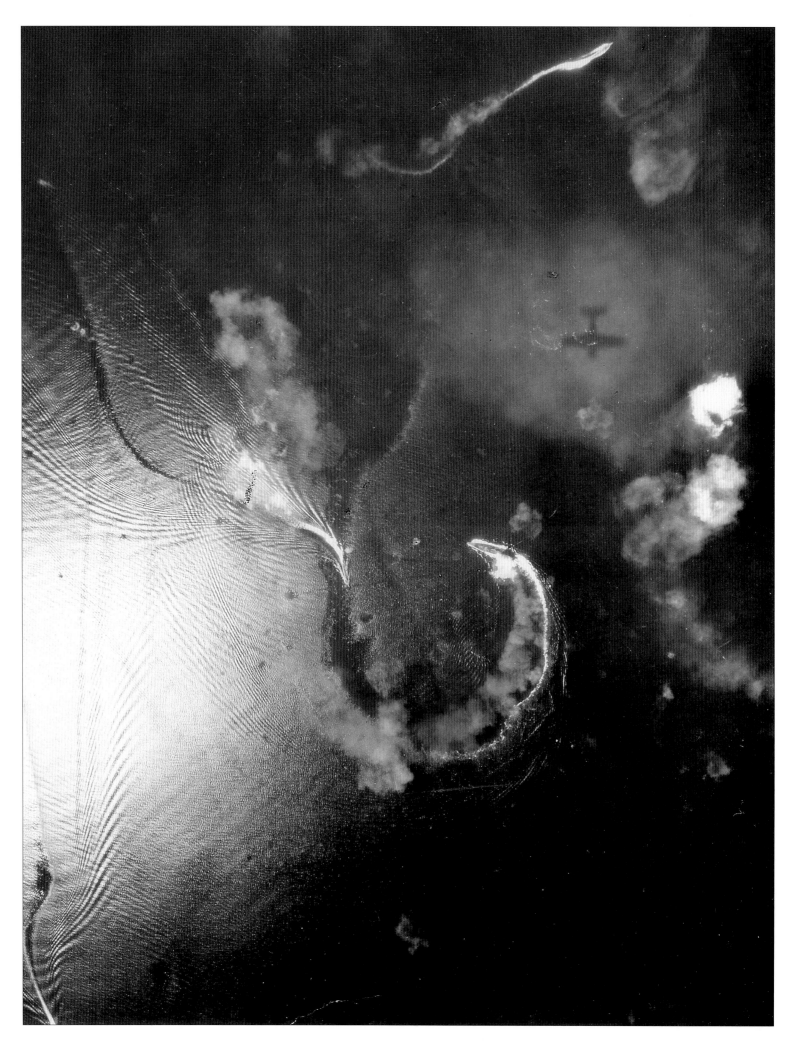

In an image thoroughly redolent of the Pacific War of World War II, bombs explode in the water and warships manoeuvre at speed in an effort to evade the attentions, or at least the aim, of attacking aircraft.

Force 'C' trying to reach this area via the Surigao Strait. Force 'A' turned

south as Halsey's 3rd Fleet steamed north in pursuit of the carriers of the Japanese Decoy Force.

In the Battle of Samar, Force 'A' fell on the six escort carriers and seven escorts of Task Group 77.4.3 with four battleships, six heavy cruisers, two light cruisers and 11

destroyers. The US aircraft, armed only with fragmentation bombs for support of the ground operations, harassed the Japanese ships, while the destroyers made torpedo attacks.

MIRACULOUS ESCAPE

The US Navy fought off disaster in the Battle of Samar, losing only one escort carrier and three escorts. But aircraft from other escort carrier groups now attacked and Kurita fell back under severe US air attacks.

> In the Battle of Samar, US aircraft, armed only with fragmentation bombs for support of the ground operations, harassed the Japanese ships, while the destroyers made torpedo attacks.

Some British aircraft, such as these Supermarine Spitfire fighters, saw service in the South-East Asia part of the Pacific War, largely in the hands of Australian and New Zealand pilots.

In the Battle off Cape Engano, Halsey closed the gap between his 3rd Fleet and the retiring and essentially harmless Decoy Force, and in three waves of air attacks sank four Japanese carriers and another five ships.

The Allied air elements in South-East Asia grew steadily in strength and capability between mid-1942 and the end of 1943 with the arrival of

The greatest threat faced by US Navy aircraft carriers late in World War II was a direct hit by a *kamikaze* aircraft, such as this attack on the USS *Bunker Hill*. US carriers had no armoured flight deck, unlike their UK counterparts.

more units and better aircraft. A US presence in India arrived with the formation of the US 10th Air Force in March 1942, which included six squadrons of the 7th Bombardment Group and the 23rd and 51st Fighter Group (FGs), and before August 1942 the 23rd FG, the 16th Fighter Squadron (FS) of the 51st FG and the 11th Bombardment Squadron (BS) of the 7th BG had been reallocated to Brigadier General Claire L. Chennault's China Air Task Force (CATF).

With the Japanese severance of the Burma Road in April 1942, China was

reduced to a state of siege, with heavy reliance placed on the supply of materiel by C-47s and LB-30s flying the hazardous route over the 'Hump' to Kunming. By the end of 1942 the 10th AAF had 259 aircraft, and the intensity of air operations over China increased steadily during 1942 and 1943, and the CATF also contributed to the air war over South-East Asia.

AIR FORCE REORGANIZATION
In March 1943 the CATF became the new US 14th Air Force, and this was soon in action and being reinforced. In January 1944 the 14th AAF had 194

fighters, 38 medium bombers and 50 heavy bombers on strength.

To a lesser extent the same type of situation prevailed over Burma, where Allied air units, predominantly British, gradually gained a clear ascendancy over the JAAF, which was increasingly beset by the obsolescence of its aircraft in the face of Allied receipt of more advanced warplanes, shortages of fuel and other essentials, and the steady decline of the quality of its aircrews as experienced, skilled men were killed and replaced by men of far lower capability. Thus the Allies gained a clear air superiority over Burma. Here the British 14th Army finally gained victory in the Battles of Imphal and Kohima between March and June 1944. By this time the Allies had total air superiority over the remnants of the 3rd Kokugun, whose strength had fallen by November 1944 to just 159 aircraft scattered

through Burma, Thailand, Sumatra and Java. The Battle of Mandalay in April 1945 opened the way for the advance to Rangoon, which fell on 3 May 1945, effectively ending the war in Burma.

Meanwhile, over the Philippines the JAAF was performing better than had been expected. The strength of the 4th Kokugun was increased to about 400 aircraft on bases in Luzon, Bacolod and Negros Islands. The JAAF made a major effort during and after the landings on Leyte, but on 27 October the US Army completed repairs to the Tacloban fighter strip, allowing land-based aircraft to operate from within the lodgement area. Even so, the air combat of October and November 1944 was intense.

FOOTHOLD IN THE PHILIPPINES
On 9 January 1945 the US 6th Army landed on Luzon Island with the

The most capable fighter-bomber used by the US Navy and US Marine Corps in the later part of World War II was the Vought F4U Corsair. A capable air-combat fighter, the Corsair could also carry bombs, napalm and rockets (seen here) for use in the ground-attack role.

support of the US 3rd and 7th Fleets, but by this time the total Japanese air strength in the Philippines was only some 150 aircraft, many of them expended in *kamikaze* attacks. US air power was also evident in the other island operations of the Philippine campaign.

The object of taking Iwo Jima – in an invasion which started on 19 February and ended on 26 March after very hard fighting – was to establish advanced bases for the 20th AAF operating against Japan from the Marianas. Softening operations against Iwo Jima started as early as August 1944, B-24J bombers of the 7th AAF based in Saipan flying regular attacks. During the battle for Iwo Jima the 3rd Koku-Kantai on Honshu sent many of its 400 aircraft on conventional and *kamikaze* attacks on the US 5th Fleet, sinking the escort carrier USS *Bismarck Sea* and damaging the *Saratoga*. Before the

F6-5 and F4U-1s fought about 100 Japanese fighters and shot down some 40 of them in the first of these attacks, while other US aircraft attacked targets of opportunity.

Above: The way the war was won: apart from the numbers, skill and fighting determination of their fighting men, the US forces depended for victory on the US Navy's ships, especially its carriers and submarines, and the warplanes of the US Navy, US Marine Corps and USAAF.

invasion, on 16/17 February 1945 TF-58 undertook the first major carrierborne air attacks on Japan. F6F-5s and F4U-1s fought about 100 Japanese fighters and shot down some 40 of them in the first of these attacks, while other US aircraft attacked targets of opportunity. TF-58 flew 2761

Left: *Enola Gay*, flown by Colonel Paul Tibbets, was the Boeing B-29 Superfortress four-engined bomber of the US Army Air Force which lifted off from the Marianas Islands to drop the world's first atomic bomb on the Japanese city of Hiroshima on 6 August 1945.

sorties and claimed 341 aircraft shot down and another 190 destroyed on the ground, for the loss of 60 US aircraft shot down and 28 in accidents.

Allied aircraft continued to roam over Japan until 15 August when, after the atomic bombings of Hiroshima and Nagasaki by USAAF B-29s on 6 and 9 August, Emperor Hirohito agreed Japan's surrender.

ASSAULT ON OKINAWA

The scale of the *kamikaze* attacks suffered by the US forces over the Philippines and Iwo Jima was small compared with that over Okinawa, whose invasion started on 1 April after the island's defences had been softened up by the air attacks of the US TF-58 and the British TF-57. The fighting lasted to 22 June, and throughout this period Allied ships came under sustained *kamikaze* attack by units based on Formosa and Kyushu. Out of 36 ships sunk and 368 damaged to varying degrees, *kamikaze* attacks were responsible for 26 and 164 respectively. The battle for Okinawa was very hard fought, with major losses on each side, those of the Allies including 763 aircraft as 458 falling in combat and 305 succumbing to operational causes. The Japanese navy fought its last battle when the super-battleship *Yamato*, sent to Okinawa on a one-way mission, was caught at sea on 7 April and destroyed by TF-58's aircraft.

World War II: Strategic Bombing 1939–1945

Interwar Royal Air Force (RAF) planners had become convinced that in future conflicts the bomber would be a war-winning weapon. Much had therefore been invested in establishing a force of almost 500 bomber aircraft, under Bomber Command. These aircraft were poor by comparison with those of the Luftwaffe and in some cases obsolete even before war broke out in September 1939.

Of them, the Wellington medium bomber was perhaps the most capable, while the Whitley heavy bomber barely had the performance for operations in anything less than ideal conditions. The Hampden was too lightly armed to survive, while the Battle light bomber was a travesty of an aircraft in which to send young men to war. Finally, the Blenheim, cornerstone of the fleet, was a light bomber that had steadily put on weight as it evolved for military operations, to the point where its performance had become marginal. None of Bomber Command's fleet had self-sealing fuel tanks, leaving them horribly vulnerable to enemy fire, and all relied on primitive bombsights for daylight operations only. All navigation was by dead reckoning – using map, stopwatch and compass.

In doctrine Bomber Command was radically different to the Luftwaffe's bombing force, which had developed its bombers for short- to medium-range use in support of an advancing army. Communications, fuel and ammunition dumps behind the front line were its key targets, while Bomber Command primarily trained to attack strategic targets deep inside enemy territory. That it was woefully equipped to do so, soon became clear.

The city of Sheffield suffered sporadically under German bombing from August 1940 until July 1942. The heaviest attacks were delivered on the nights of 12 and 15 December 1940.

14 December 1939 caused the RAF to switch its bombing operations from daylight to night-time attacks. That these aircraft were lost to a poor-quality force of Bf 109E and Bf 110 fighters was almost as big a blow as the fact that Bomber Command was now fighting in darkness, unable to bomb targets with accuracy, always assuming that its poorly equipped navigators could find them in the first place.

REPRISAL ATTACKS

Bomber Command had thus far been denied any real opportunity to engage strategic targets, but this changed on 15/16 May 1940. The Luftwaffe's devastating raid on Rotterdam on 14 May won reprisal in the form of a 99-aircraft attack against oil and steel facilities in the Ruhr. The Hampdens, Wellingtons and Whitleys primarily attacked targets around Duisburg, setting the pattern for a series of raids against similar targets, plus communications and aircraft factories that was to follow. The operation also marked the beginning of a massive strategic campaign that continued with little let-up until VE-Day, as well as demonstrating just how difficult it was going to be to get bombs on Ruhr targets with any telling effect.

Initially Bomber Command was limited to shipping targets. Wellingtons and Blenheims flew its first raids on 4 September 1939. Of the 14 Wellingtons sent against Brunsbüttel, two were lost, while the Blenheims had more luck at Schillig Roads, with the first Bomber Command attack against the enemy being pressed home. Anti-shipping operations continued into 1940 when operations in support of British forces in Norway, the Low Countries and France began. These proved disappointing, while the destruction of 10 Wellingtons out of a force of 24 tasked against Schillig Roads on

The destruction of 10 Wellingtons out of a force of 24 tasked against Schillig Roads on 14 December 1939 caused the RAF to switch its bombing operations from daylight to night-time attacks.

Bomber Command played an important role in the Battle of Britain. Continued attacks on oil and aircraft production targets were important, but it was the Command's strikes against the enemy invasion fleet assembling at ports in France and Belgium that contributed mightily to Hitler's decision to delay his invasion of Britain. Most importantly, by luck rather than design, the first attack against Berlin, on the night of 25/26 August 1940, so incensed Hitler that he ordered his bombers against London. With Fighter Command almost broken, this relieved the pressure on its bases sufficiently for it to turn the tide of the Battle, and the opportunity for invasion was lost.

Given the current state of bombing technology – the RAF had not invested in the radio direction finding aids that the Luftwaffe enjoyed – it was simply impossible to put enough bombs onto a single target, such as a factory, to knock it out. A heavy raid on Berlin on 23/24 September 1940 achieved very little and to the frustration of Bomber Command's leaders was added the fury of the UK

FIRST OF THE 'HEAVIES'

The RAF desperately needed new aircraft and August 1940 saw the first of its true heavy bombers, the Stirling, accepted into service. This giant of an aircraft, powered by four Bristol Hercules engines, was joined by the four-engined Halifax later in the year, while the Manchester twin began military testing in December. All three types began operations in 1941, proving more capable on the long raids into Germany, but still their bombing was inaccurate.

government following the devastating Luftwaffe attack on Coventry. It was clear that attacks on area targets containing installations of military or strategic importance was the way forward, regardless of civilian casualties. This tactic was made more palatable to the politicians after the Coventry attack, and the order to 'Coventrate' German cities was given.

The first Bomber Command area attack was flown against Mannheim on 16/17 December 1940, but it was poorly executed and the only real damage inflicted was to housing.

The intention of Bomber Command's leader, Air Marshall Sir Richard Peirse, was that resources be aimed against the Reich. The UK's

position into 1941 precluded such ambitions, as the Admiralty called for sustained attacks against shipping and U-boat pens in an effort to relieve the bitter war in the Atlantic, and Fighter Command needed bombers to act as the bait in its set-piece offensive operations over occupied France.

The Stirling (10/11 February), Manchester (24/25 February) and Halifax (10/11 March) all flew their first operations against naval targets, while the only type really taking the

Later in its career a twin-fin arrangement was adopted for the Avro Manchester. An otherwise useful heavy bomber, the Manchester was hamstrung by the poor reliability of its Vulture engines.

THE LUFTWAFFE'S NIGHT-FIGHTER ARM

The strategic campaign was executed by night from autumn 1941. To the RAF's chagrin the Luftwaffe had recognized the night-time threat posed by Bomber Command early on. From relying simply on flak and searchlights to provide defence against night bombers, it had instigated a force of Bf 109D night-fighters late in 1939. Experimental night-fighting began with Bf 110C-1 aircraft over Denmark in the spring of 1940 and with attacks against the Ruhr increasing, a formal night-fighting force was formed in June. German airborne radar was primitive, but the *Nachtjagdgeschwadern* could rely on an excellent system of early warning radars and highly developed tactics. Soon the Bf 110, Ju 88C-2 and Do 17Z-10 night-fighters were beginning to make nocturnal operations difficult. Indeed, not only were the depredations of the night-fighters added to the dangers of the flak, but also from September weary bomber crews could expect to find long-range Ju 88C-2 and Do 17Z-10 intruders operating over their bases to strike them on their return. Fortunately for the RAF, the value of these operations was not clear to everyone within the Luftwaffe's high command and opposition to them arose. They were eventually stopped on 10 October 1941 by order of Hitler. Bomber Command was also suffering politically. Even given its new aircraft, the accuracy of its operations remained poor and little was being achieved for great expense in resources, effort and lives. Between July and December 1941 the Command recorded that 605 aircraft failed to return, while a further 222 were destroyed on operations. Such losses could not be sustained and calls for the dissolution of Bomber Command were made.

war to the Germans was the Blenheim, during coordinated Circus raids.

On 27 April Bomber Command again began to engage German targets in daylight, Stirlings attacking Emden in bad weather. The new Fortress, whose performance and advanced bombsight should have made it a weapon of significance, also flew such raids at very high altitude. The type was used badly by the RAF,

Left: Although it introduced the RAF to reliable heavy bomber operations, the Stirling was hampered by its inadequate ceiling. Its stalky main undercarriage was also prone to collapse.

Right: This Lancaster was dropping bundles of 'Window' during a raid on Duisburg on 14 October 1944. It was also equipped with ABC – note the fuselage aerials – for jamming enemy radio signals.

however, and little was achieved by it as a bomber in British hands.

Daylight operations continued into August 1941, with major attacks against *Scharnhorst, Gneisenau* and *Prinz Eugen* at Brest on 24 July, and

Cologne on 12 August. With the Luftwaffe heavily engaged on the Eastern Front it was reasonable to expect light fighter opposition to these raids, but losses to fighters and flak remained heavy, even given the escorting Spitfire Mk IIs on the Brest attack. Worryingly, the Halifaxes involved seemed no less vulnerable than the Wellington and the RAF was once again convinced of the need to concentrate on nocturnal operations.

BOMBER COMMAND RESURGENT

The year 1942 brought with it developments of critical importance to Bomber Command and, ultimately, for the Allied war effort. Crucially, the issue of accuracy had to be addressed. A radio direction finding aid had been developed under the designation Gee Mk I. This promised a navigation accuracy of around 3.2km (2 miles) over a range of 563km (350 miles) and although it was likely to be detected and jammed by the Germans relatively quickly, it would present the RAF with a window of opportunity.

On 12 February *Scharnhorst, Gneisenau* and *Prinz Eugen* evaded all attempts to stop them as they transited the English Channel from Brest, but at least they were no longer

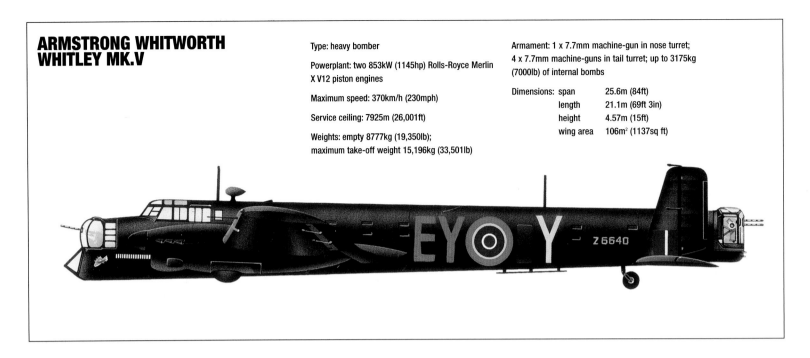

ARMSTRONG WHITWORTH WHITLEY MK.V

Type: heavy bomber

Powerplant: two 853kW (1145hp) Rolls-Royce Merlin X V12 piston engines

Maximum speed: 370km/h (230mph)

Service ceiling: 7925m (26,001ft)

Weights: empty 8777kg (19,350lb); maximum take-off weight 15,196kg (33,501lb)

Armament: 1 x 7.7mm machine-gun in nose turret; 4 x 7.7mm machine-guns in tail turret; up to 3175kg (7000lb) of internal bombs

Dimensions: span 25.6m (84ft)
length 21.1m (69ft 3in)
height 4.57m (15ft)
wing area 106m² (1137sq ft)

on Bomber Command's list of regular targets. Their escape coincided with a change of command, Air Marshall Arthur Harris becoming Air Officer Commanding-in-Chief Bomber Command later in February. Harris was a tactician of some skill and a leader ruthless in his aims. He was

tasked against the same strategic targets as his predecessor, with the same area bombing policy in force, but Harris determined that in order to ensure success against strategic targets he would destroy the Reich house by house if necessary. His was the leadership that would make

Bomber Command a truly effective fighting force.

NEW BOMBERS ARRIVE

Finally, Bomber Command at last received the equipment that it so desperately needed. The Wellington was still in first-line service, while the Stirling was proving deficient in altitude performance, the Halifax Mk I and Mk IA could offer only marginal performance and the Manchester was proving a disaster, largely thanks to its complex and unreliable Rolls-Royce Vulture engines.

From the Manchester, however, was to emerge one of the greatest bomber aircraft of all time. Stretching the aircraft's wingspan in order to allow it to mount four Rolls-Royce Merlin engines – as already proved in the Hurricane and Spitfire – revolutionized the Manchester, turning it from a heavy bomber of potential into a heavy bomber of devastating effect. Early in 1942 the first of these new Avro Lancasters were undergoing trials for service entry in the spring.

Left: Chief of Bomber Command Arthur 'Bomber' Harris, shown here at centre studying maps and reconnaissance photographs, masterminded the RAF's strategic bombing campaign.

The night-fighters had begun to wreak a telling toll over Germany, but using Gee Bomber Command could send its bombers out in concentrated streams, saturating the defences and placing them over the target for as short a time as possible. The first such attack took place on 3/4 March 1942, against the Renault plant at Paris-Billancourt, and although the raid was far better executed than had previously been the case, the factory was soon back in business.

A similar raid against Essen used flares and incendiaries dropped by Gee-equipped aircraft as target markers – copying a tactic used by the Luftwaffe over the UK – but proved that Gee was not providing quite the accuracy expected of it. It remained a system of importance, however, but was best used against coastal targets. Thus the port of Kiel was hit with some effect on 12/13 March.

EASY TARGET

The city of Lübeck lay beyond the range of Gee, but was nevertheless selected by Harris as the ideal target to demonstrate the new found power and will of Bomber Command. Lübeck's port status justified it as a target, while its light defences and largely wooden housing made it a relatively easy one. Some 191 bombers, dropping a high percentage of incendiaries, caused massive damage over 121 hectares (300 acres) of the city and demonstrated to the German leaders and populace alike that Bomber Command was adopting a new and savage policy.

Similar raids against other cities followed, leading Hitler to order

The RAF came to regularly use weapons of much higher weight than those used by US and German bombers. The 1,814kg (4000lb) Cookie was a typical RAF bomb, here with a Wellington.

THE AUGSBURG RAID

One of the earliest Lancaster raids has remained as one of the type's most noteworthy. Squadron Leader Nettleton led Nos 44 and 97 Sqns against the MAN diesel engine works at Augsburg in a daring low-level, daylight raid on 17 April 1942. Diversionary raids went awry and losses were heavy for minimal results, but the raid demonstrated the qualities of the Lancaster, the capability of Bomber Command to hit a precision target and earned Nettleton a Victoria Cross. In the grand scheme of the bombing war Augsburg was little more than a distraction, since Harris was already looking towards an even greater military and propaganda coup. He wanted to put 1000 bombers over a single target.

retaliatory raids against British cities of historic importance. Named after the Baedeker travel guides, the so-called Baedeker Blitz hit several

Setting out at twilight for a raid against the UK, these Do 17Zs were typical of the type that formed an important part of the Luftwaffe's bomber force. The Dorniers were heavily engaged in attacks on the UK.

historic cities, including Exeter, Bath, Norwich and Canterbury, causing widespread damage.

On 30/31 May 708 Hampdens, Wellingtons and Whitleys joined 388 Halifaxes, Lancasters, Manchesters and Stirlings for a raid on Cologne. Instructors and trainee crews flew many of the aircraft, but good use was made of Gee to achieve accurate

and concentrated bombing. Significantly, four of the superlative new Mosquito B.Mk IV light bombers were over the city early the next morning, to confirm massive fires and huge devastation. In fact, 243 hectares (600 acres) of the city had been destroyed, with 250 factories badly hit, 486 people killed and 59,100 left without homes. Losses to Bomber Command had been sustainable, and similar raids were flown against Essen on 1/2 June when the Krupps works escaped damage, and Bremen on 25/26 June, when night-fighters scored notable success. No further 1000-bomber raids followed, but again the capabilities of Bomber Command had been demonstrated with great effect.

Less ambitious, but nevertheless damaging raids continued, but with the Germans now jamming Gee, more

Above: The Focke-Wulf Fw 190A demonstrated instant superiority over anything the RAF had to offer. A-1 machines began facing the Allies in 1941 and soon A-4s were engaging the heavy bomber fleets.

emphasis was placed on accurate dead-reckoning navigation on moonlit nights. Losses to night-fighters thus began to increase, while accuracy still needed to be improved. A Pathfinder Force (PFF) was therefore created. Under the leadership of Group Captain Don Bennett, the PFF consisted of experienced Stirling and Lancaster crews whose task it was to locate and mark targets for the following Main Force of bombers. Initially relying on Gee Mk I, the benefits of the PFF were minimal, but soon new technologies, added to the brilliance of its crews, would begin to prove its worth.

Elsewhere, German resources were increasingly being consumed by the bitter struggle in North Africa and around Stalingrad, and the US was entering the war in Europe. The seeds that would grow into the combined bombing offensive with the mighty 8th Air Force (AF) were being sown.

During January 1943 Allied leaders, political and military, met at Casablanca for a conference to map out the conduct of the remainder of the war. Among its many ramifications was the Casablanca Directive, issued on 21 January to both Bomber Command and VIII Bomber Command stating that: 'Your primary objective will be the progressive dislocation of the German military, industrial and economic system, and the undermining of the morale of the German people to a point where their capacity for armed resistance is fatally weakened'. A list of target sets was also issued, in order of priority: U-boat yards, aircraft factories, transportation, oil installations and 'other targets in enemy war industry'. To Arthur Harris the directive came as a licence to continue the campaign he had already started. To VIII Bomber Command, whose 8th AF had been engaged in Europe since August 1942, it represented a new era.

USAAF RAIDS BEGIN

Bombers of the United States Army Air Force (USAAF) had first arrived in the UK during February 1942, but not until 17 August had their first raid been flown, to Roen-Sotteville. The USAAF's B-17s and B-24s had been tasked against targets in northern France, operated in Circus missions and attacked U-boat bases. The US tactic was to attack in daylight, using

> German resources were increasingly being consumed by the bitter struggle in North Africa and around Stalingrad, and the US was entering the war in Europe.

THE 'DAMBUSTERS' RAID

While Main Force attacks remained its priority, Bomber Command also fielded a number of one-off, precision strikes against key targets. One such was Operation Chastise, a daring plan to breach the Eder, Sorpe and Möhne dams, which generated hydroelectricity for Ruhr industry. It was thought that the loss of this power would severely affect the Ruhr's production capability and great ingenuity was displayed in the development of a 'bouncing bomb', known as Upkeep, for the attacks. No. 617 Sqn was formed for Chastise and its 19 Lancasters set out on the night of 16/17 May 1943. Even given the precise operational parameters of Upkeep, the unit managed to breach both the Möhne and Eder dams, for the loss of eight Lancasters and the award of the Victoria Cross to Wing Commander Guy Gibson who led the mission. Flooding was widespread, but the effect on hydroelectricity output minimal and damage was soon repaired. In strategic terms Chastise achieved very little, but in propaganda it was worth a great deal – it seemed to the British people that Bomber Command could strike anywhere it pleased, against the most difficult targets.

Upkeep was the codename for the 'bouncing bomb' used on the dams raid by No. 617 Sqn's Lancasters. It required the bombers' weapons bays to be specially modified, as seen here.

tight formations where the bombers offered mutual support in their massed firepower. To a degree the tactic worked, until III./JG 2 began head-on attacks late in 1942.

Now the bombers' vulnerability had been exposed and when raids into Germany began, the bomber crews would suffer terribly. Nevertheless, the first mission to Germany, on 27 January 1943, was relatively successful, despite lacking fighter escort. The Luftwaffe's Fw 190A-4s and Bf 109G-1s fought hard, but losses were light and several

Right: Gibson was just 25 years old when he led Operation Chastise. Here he poses after the raid, with an aerial photograph of the Möhne dam.

fighters fell. The bombing did not go entirely as planned, but the flak offered little trouble and the future seemed bright.

Daylight missions continued, with losses mounting slowly as the Luftwaffe's fighter opposition strengthened. Germany's fighters were defending the Reich by day and night when, in February 1943, Bomber Command reached a new level of capability, some 35 of its 50 squadrons being equipped with the latest Lancaster B.Mk I, Halifax B.Mk II or Stirling B.Mk III 'heavies'.

TECHNICAL DEVELOPMENTS

More capable weapons, a developed system of target marking and a Mk II version of Gee that was less vulnerable to jamming, were also introduced. Crucially, two new pieces of equipment were provided to the PFF. Oboe became operational on the Mosquito from December 1942 as a radio location system, while H2S was a radar that provided an image of the ground to aid in navigation and target finding. Neither of these systems was perfect, with Oboe only just having sufficient range for targets in the Ruhr and H2S providing a confusing 'picture' that made it most useful against coastal targets, but both represented a leap forward in targeting capability.

So armed, Harris instigated a new series of attacks against Ruhr industry, in what would become known as the Battle of the Ruhr. The first raid was

HANDLEY PAGE HALIFAX

Type: heavy bomber

Powerplant: four 1205kW (1615hp) Bristol Hercules XVI piston engines

Maximum speed: 454km/h (282mph)

Service ceiling: 7315m (24,000ft)

Weights: maximum take-off weight 24,675kg (54,400lb)

Armament. 4 x 7.7mm (.303in) Browning machine guns in dorsal turret, 4 x 7.7mm (.303in) Browning machine guns in tail turret), 1 x 7.7mm (.303in) Vickers K machine gun in nose; 5897kg (13,000lb) of bombs

Dimensions: span 31.75m (104ft 2in)
length 21.82m (71ft 7in)
height 6.32m (20ft 9in)
wing area 110.6m² (1190sq ft)

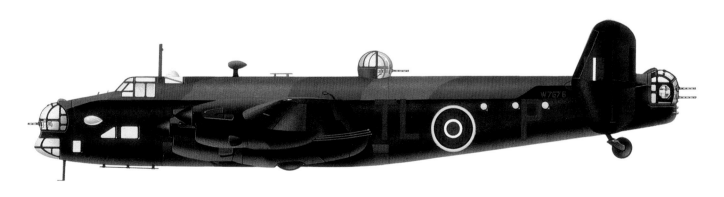

Boeing's B-17 Flying Fortress could carry only a relatively light bombload without sacrificing range. This B-17G demonstrates the variant's undernose turret, added to counter the Luftwaffe's head-on attacks.

flown against the Krupps works at Essen by 442 aircraft and employed target marking from PFF bombers. Losses to night-fighters and flak amounted to 14, but the bombing was more effective than had ever before been the case against this difficult target. The Battle consisted of 26 large raids and continued into June. It cost Bomber Command 628 bombers, and while bombing accuracy was improving drastically, something clearly had to be done to counter the

The Battle of the Ruhr cost Bomber Command 628 bombers. Bombing accuracy was improving drastically, but something clearly had to be done to counter the menace of the night-fighters.

menace of the night-fighters and their radar guidance systems.

A militarily more significant raid was flown on 28/29 June, when Oboe-equipped Mosquitos used parachute flares above the cloud base to mark Cologne. A Main Force of 540 bombers, all equipped with Gee Mk II,

bombed on these markers in the first demonstration of mass blind bombing. The results were devastating. Still the losses to fighters were appalling, however, and while the RAF sought to combat night-fighters, the USAAF strove to protect its bombers by day. UK-based Spitfires

could only provide escort on the bombers' outbound legs or on their return, while even P-47s equipped with the new drop tanks had insufficient range to fly with the bombers to their targets and back. Meanwhile, the Luftwaffe began pulling quantities of fighters back from the Eastern Front to bolster the defence of the Reich.

BLITZ WEEK AND GOMORRAH

The USAAF was struggling to maintain its precision bombing campaign in the face of fierce enemy defences and the European weather. Its B-17s and B-24s were equipped with Norden bombsights, which were considered to provide great accuracy. Bombing through a typical European overcast, however, bombardiers were struggling to achieve results even close to those that were possible in the clear skies of their US training grounds.

The depredations of the Luftwaffe's fighters were of even greater concern and Major General Ira Eaker saw bombing attacks on aviation factories as the only means of defeating the enemy air threat. Thus a concentrated

effort, known as Blitz Week, began on 24 July. As well as bombing fighter production, its intensity would also draw fighters into combat more readily, depleting crews and aircraft. In fact, the result was heavy losses for both sides, at a rate that the 8th Air Force could not sustain, especially with units being posted to the Mediterranean for missions in support of the forthcoming invasion of Sicily and campaign against Italy. Blitz Week was not a success.

The RAF had more luck with its scheme to neutralize the night-fighter threat. The success of the fighters lay in the tight control they received from their ground controllers. This relied on three radars for each fighter under control. One unit constantly scanned for targets, a second locked onto and tracked an individual bomber, while a third tracked the night-fighter and allowed the controllers to guide it onto the bomber. At this point the fighter's onboard radar took over to complete the intercept.

British scientists realized that metallic strips, cut to a precise length and dropped in massive bundles,

---

REPUBLIC P-47C THUNDERBOLT

Type: fighter-bomber

Powerplant: One 1715kW (2300hp) Pratt & Whitney R-2800-59 supercharged piston engine

Maximum speed: 696km/h (433mph)

Service ceiling: 12,800m (42,000ft)

Weights: maximum take-off weight 6769kg (14,925lb); empty 4490kg (9900lb)

Armament: 8 x 12.7mm (0.5in) Browning M2 machine guns; 907kg (2000lb) of bombs; 10 x 127mm (5in) rockets

Dimensions: span 12.43m (40ft 9in)
length 11.03m (36ft 2in)
height 4.44m (14ft 6in)
wing area 27.87m² (300sq ft)

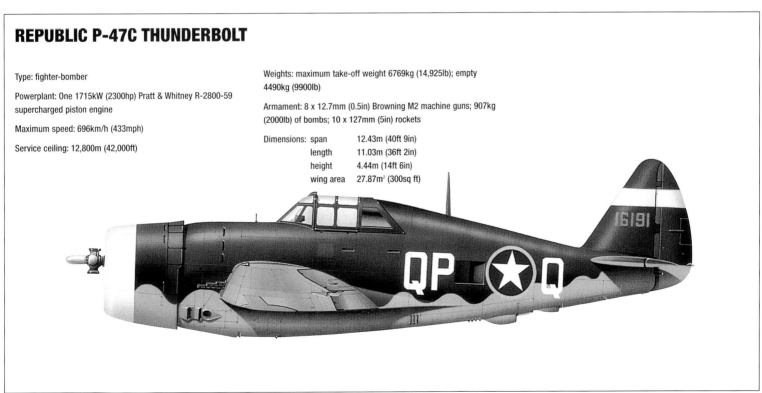

Above: German fire crews work on burning debris after a raid on Cologne. As well as dedicated fire and air-raid personnel, 'criminal assistants' were also employed, their sentences being to work with unexploded ordnance.

would reflect energy directly back to the ground radars, saturating them with returns and hiding bomber formations. Operation Gomorrah was the first to use this so-called 'Window' and it took the form of a series of raids against Hamburg. The first, on 24/25 July 1943, was terribly effective.

Not only were the night-fighters blinded, but the radar-directed searchlights and flak batteries were also robbed of direction.

The bombers returned on 27/28 July, visiting more destruction on a city that was still burning. The result was a new phenomenon, the firestorm, which created superheated tornados and temperatures exceeding 1000°C (1832°F). Still there was no let up, the bombers returning to Hamburg on 30/31 July and again on 2/3 August. At least 41,800 people were killed and German propaganda minister Dr Josef Goebbels described the destruction of Hamburg as 'a catastrophe, the extent of which simply staggers the imagination'.

In response, the Reich's defences were further strengthened and

OPERATION JUGGLER

Juggler was planned as a coordinated 8th Air Force effort against the Messerschmitt plant at Regensburg and the ball bearing factory at Schweinfurt on 14 October 1943. Bomber forces heading for both targets were to swamp the fighter defences, but poor weather over England caused the vital timings for the raid to be missed. In the event, the Regensburg aircraft served to ensure that a huge Luftwaffe strength was airborne to meet the Schweinfurt raiders. Losses amounted to 24 Regensburg B-17s and 36 of the Schweinfurt aircraft. These losses were great, but a follow-up raid on Schweinfurt was deemed necessary and on 21 October a further 60 B-17s were lost. Subsequent strikes against Germany also suffered terribly. Unescorted daylight raids could no longer be considered.

Right: Some 316 Lancasters and four Mosquitos hit Berlin on the night of 3/4 September 1943. Twenty-two Lancasters were lost, while 422 people in the city were killed, with 170 missing.

Of little military significance, the V-1 flying-bomb was terribly effective against civilians, thanks to its noise, explosive power and indiscriminate, unpredictable targeting.

counters to 'Window' were soon developed. In the meantime, unguided night-fighting tactics were refined, but elsewhere the war was going badly, with the invasion of Sicily and further losses in the USSR.

Early in November 1943 Arthur Harris announced to Winston Churchill the certainty of Hitler's defeat in the face of a concentrated bombing campaign, incorporating US aircraft, with Berlin as its lead target.

The first raid of what was to become the Battle of Berlin went in on the night of 18/19 November. It was followed by a series of Main Force attacks throughout the winter, with the last on 24/25 March 1944. Harassing missions by Bomber Command's Mosquitos added to the horror of these attacks. The result was 492 aircraft lost and a war that still raged. Berlin had not been broken, Bomber Command was suffering equally severe losses on other raids, and the thrust of the assault was already moving towards transport and other targets in preparation for the invasion of France.

ATTACK FROM THE SOUTH

Even as the 8th AF was licking the wounds it had sustained during October, the 15th Air Force, based in southern Italy, was preparing to start attacks against targets in Austria and the southern parts of France and Germany, in addition to its duties in support of Allied forces advancing through Italy. It began these operations on 2 November 1943 with a raid on Wiener-Neustadt, but its missions were unescorted and losses accordingly high.

Perhaps the most important result of these raids from the south was that

NORTH AMERICAN P-51B MUSTANG

Type: single-seat fighter

Powerplant: one 1029kW (1380hp) Packard V-1650-3 (Rolls-Royce Merlin 68) piston engine

Maximum speed: 692km/h (430mph)

Service ceiling: 12,649m (41,500ft)

Weights: maximum take-off weight 5080kg (11,200lb); empty 3102kg (6840lb)

Armament: 4 x 12.7mm (0.5in) machine guns; 907kg (2000lb) of bombs

Dimensions:
span	11.3m	(37ft 1in)
length	9.82m	(32ft 3in)
height	4.16m	(13ft 8in)
wing area	21.64m²	(233sq ft)

Few aircraft have revolutionized a campaign in the way that the P-51 changed the Allied strategic bombing campaign against Germany. This machine is a P-51B, with the early style cockpit glazing.

Luftwaffe resources had to be further stretched to counter them.

MUSTANG ARRIVAL

On 5 December 1943, P-51B Mustangs flew a Rodeo mission. The Merlin-powered Mustang had finally arrived and its long range and superb fighting abilities were to revolutionize the US bombing campaign, although not before Eaker himself had stepped in to prevent these precious fighters being sent to overseas and reconnaissance units!

The 8th AF began penetrating deeply to German targets again on 11 January 1944, with P-47 and P-38 support, but the turning point came

THE BATTLE FOR OIL

The US first struck at Axis oil production with a largely ineffective raid by B-24 Liberators flying out of North Africa in June 1943. Their target was the huge oil refinery complex at Ploesti in Romania, and this same target received more attention from B-24s on 1 August 1943. This time units of the 15th and 8th AFs were involved, all flying from Libya at low level. The results were again disappointing. Major attacks on industrial and military targets continued throughout early 1944, while the first of the new round of anti-oil attacks came on 5 April. Ploesti was again the target, the 15th AF delivering the blow. A massive effort now concentrated on oil production in Germany itself, with the result that the 195,000-ton output achieved in May had fallen to just 7000 tons by September. Now the Luftwaffe really began to suffer, with flying limited only to the most crucial units – those in France and those defending the Reich – and even these curtailed operations. To add to their woes, some of the fiercest fighting of the bombing campaign thus far had erased the majority of the fighter arm's most experienced pilots. The RAF was now able to return to daylight raids over France, while the campaign against German targets continued unabated. The Luftwaffe still rose against the bombers, albeit in limited numbers, but the lack of skilled pilots resulted in increased loss rates. Allied air superiority had been secured and the bombers could now attack almost at will.

This USAAF B-24D Liberator was being bombed up at Hardwick, Norfolk. The aircraft, named *Shoot Luke*, was being prepared for its 28th mission, during April 1943.

on 25 February, when the Mustang escorted a raid for the first time. Bomber losses continued, but now the escorts could combat the defenders all the way to the target and back.

'BIG WEEK'

The first Mustang operation coincided with 'Big Week', a concerted effort by the 8th and 15th Air Forces, and Bomber Command, against German aircraft industry and V-1 launch sites in France. Massive missions were staged between the first on 19/20 February and the last on the 25th. Bomber losses were heavy, but

bearable, while the toll on Luftwaffe fighters was more telling. It was noted that the new escort fighters would have to be countered, while for the first time concerns arose that fighter production might be badly affected. With raids continuing through to April and the US fighter pilots becoming ever more aggressive, losses

in experienced German pilots also began to be felt.

The RAF suffered its worst losses yet against Nuremburg on 30/31 March, but generally the campaign was going the Allies' way. Orders to begin 'softening up' Europe for invasion diverted some of the bomber strength away from the Reich,

> Bomber losses continued, but now the escorts could combat the defenders all the way to the target and back.

With the B-29 the USAAF was able to take the war directly to Japan's home islands. The aircraft wrought terrible damage, especially with incendiaries.

but a new target was soon to draw Allied attention: oil production.

PACIFIC BOMBING

The air war in the Pacific was generally one of tactical and naval operations, but towards its conclusion the strategic bomber arrived to help bring Japan to its knees.

As soon as suitable airfields in the Marianas could be constructed, the USAAF began moving in B-29 Superfortress bombers. The B-29 was a new type of warplane. It carried a huge bombload, offered pressurized accommodation to its crew for high-altitude operations, and attacked over long ranges at high speeds. The Japanese developed desperate measures to defend against the B-29, but ultimately the sustained raids, typically containing more than 300 aircraft each, were just too powerful for the defenders.

The first B-29 attack, on 24 November 1944, was unsuccessful, but soon the USAAF was turning in devastating raids, using a large proportion of incendiaries and creating firestorms in Japanese cities whose housing was largely of wood.

Tokyo, Nagoya, Osaka and Kobe were all terribly hit, but with the Japanese will to wage war unbroken, the Allies decided to use the ultimate weapon. Faced with the prospect of firebombing Japanese cities into non-existence and a 1946 invasion of

Japan that was estimated to cost at least one million Allied lives, the Allied leaders sanctioned the use of atomic weapons against Hiroshima and Nagasaki.

Little Boy, dropped by *Enola Gay* on 6 August 1945, destroyed 12.7km² (4.7 sq miles) of Hiroshima and killed in excess of 70,000 people. A second B-29, *Bock's Car*, dropped the Fat Man weapon on Nagasaki three days later. Japan surrendered on 15 August.

Strategic bombing had ended the war in the Pacific theatre and contributed immeasurably to the end of the war in Europe.

A mushroom cloud rises over Nagasaki on 9 August 1945. The Japanese could fight on no longer, but the use of atomic weapons drew the world into a new era of Cold War.

Air Wars in the Insurgency Era

1948–1988

While the Western Allies that had contributed to the defeat of Nazi Germany concentrated on the situation in the now divided Berlin – a political tinderbox epitomized by the Berlin Airlift that ran from 1948-49 – and the deteriorating relationship experienced with the USSR both in the former German capital and elsewhere in Europe, the Cold War suddenly became 'hotter' on the other side of the world. On 25 June 1950, North Korea invaded US ally South Korea with seven infantry and one armoured divisions, with the aim of reunifying the two countries under the communist flag. The North Korean advance was covered by Soviet-supplied La-9 and Yak-7 piston-engined fighters, and Il-10 ground-attack aircraft (the latter a development of the wartime Il-2), which were mainly used to strafe South Korean airfields during the initial invasion.

The tense standoff between the US and the USSR that formed the backdrop of world political and military affairs in the latter half of the 20th century saw a range of different responses to global crises and flashpoints, depending on the exact nature of superpower relations at that time and the particular strategic value assigned to any given theatre of war. In

Republic of Korea Air Force F-51 Mustangs prepare to take off for a mission in May 1951. A single RoKAF squadron (later wing) operated US-supplied Mustangs on fighter-bomber duties from Kangnung air base for the duration of the war in Korea.

Left: Prior to the surprise outbreak of war in Korea, attentions of the Western powers were firmly focused on another early Cold War flashpoint: the blockade of Berlin and its subsequent supply by airlift. These C-47s are at Berlin's Tempelhof Airport in 1948.

with 27 June seeing the first B-29 bombing raids launched from Okinawa against railway lines and bridges. The following day B-26 Invader bombers went into action, once again flying from bases in Japan to attack objectives near Seoul. In the first weeks of action, the USAF B-26 and B-29 units were mainly used for attacking troop concentrations and armour.

COMMUNIST OFFENSIVE

By 29 June, Seoul was in communist hands, and US ground forces were fighting on the ground by the beginning of July; initial air support for the troops was provided by F-80 fighter-bombers of the USAF, as well as US Marine Corps F7F Tigercat night-fighters. The F-80s were initially flown from their bases in Japan, and were equipped with long-range fuel tanks, while F-51s were based in South Korea, as close to the front as possible. The first of the F-51s to be forward deployed arrived in South Korea in mid-July, and the type excelled in the close air support (CAS) role, at least while unopposed,

the case of the Korean War, the response was engineered by the United Nations (UN) and was led on the military level by the US. With North Korea armed and trained by the USSR and backed by China (communist since 1949), the situation risked escalation into a new global conflict, but it remained a 'limited war' and one in which air power played a major role.

The first step in the UN strategy on Korea was to assist South Korea, and among the military materiel supplied were F-51 (previously P-51) Mustang fighters. US Air Force F-82 Twin Mustang night-fighters then covered a civilian evacuation in the wake of the invasion, before the deployment of armed forces from 17 nations, together with associated naval and air power.

The initial aim was to push the communist forces out of South Korea, and back beyond the dividing 38th

Parallel. Among the first of the UN aircraft into the fray were USAF F-80 Shooting Stars from bases in Japan, while an F-82 crewed by William G. Hudson and Carl Fraser duly claimed the first air-to-air victory of the war, a North Korean Yak-9, on 27 June.

As North Korean forces pressed towards the South Korean capital, Seoul, US air power went into action,

NAVAL AIR POWER OVER KOREA

Almost from the outset, there was significant involvement in the Korean air war by carriers of the US and Royal Navies. Aircraft from Task Force 77 (TF-77, initially comprised of USS *Valley Forge* and HMS *Theseus*) would remain on station for CAS, air defence work and reconnaissance until the end of the war, although the composition and number of carriers would regularly change. When naval aircraft attacked North Korean targets on 3 July 1950, it marked the first use of naval jets in warfare – in this case, the jets were F9F Panthers. In mid-July 1950, an attempt was made by the UN to break out of the Pusan pocket, and an amphibious landing was made to this end at Pohang, supported by carrier aircraft.

The first Marine jet squadron in theatre, VMF-311 flew its F9F Panther jets on ground-attack missions from Korean land bases. Note the underwing rockets on these aircraft, and the pierced steel planking (PSP) that provides a basic runway.

making an impression on North Korean troops and armour and interdicting supplies.

The focus on CAS operations throughout the war demanded close cooperation with ground forces, and to this end saw widespread use of airborne forward air controllers (FACs). These were provided under separate USAF, US Navy, US Marine Corps, British Army and Republic of Korea Air Force (RoKAF) initiatives, but all had in common the use of slow-flying 'spotters' in the class of the T-6 Texan and L-19 Bird Dog. As well as the USAF-operated F-51s that operated in the CAS role, the Royal Australian Air Force (RAAF) and South African Air Force (SAAF) also sent their Mustangs to the war zone.

From August onwards, the USAF bombers switched their focus from the battlefields to strategic industrial targets in the north, where they wrought destruction in multi-aircraft raids. While the B-29s relentlessly hit industry and infrastructure, the B-26s were used primarily for night interdiction work, attacking military supply lines and railways. August 1950

also saw the aircraft of the US Marine Corps in action for the first time over Korea. Initially flying F4U Corsairs and F7Fs from land bases, among the first tasks of the USMC aircraft included support of UN troops in the Pusan area. The USMC also pioneered the art of helicopter combat rescue during the war, and a Marine HO3S Dragonfly was

From August onwards, the USAF bombers switched their focus from the battlefields to strategic industrial targets in the north, where they wrought destruction in multi-aircraft raids.

THE BATTLE FOR 'MIG ALLEY'

November 1950 saw the communist MiG-15 jet fighters enter the fray for the first time to challenge the previous air dominance of the UN forces. Although an example of the new fighter was claimed by an F-80 flown by Russell Brown on 8 November in what was recorded as the first jet-versus-jet 'kill' in history, the MiG-15 would prove a menace to the UN forces for the remainder of the conflict. (According to Soviet accounts the first 'true' jet-versus-jet 'kill' occurred a week before Brown's claim, an F-80 falling to the guns of a Soviet MiG-15.) Flown by Chinese, North Korean and Soviet pilots, the swept-wing Soviet fighter was initially a generation ahead of the UN jet equipment in theatre: the F-80 and F-84 Thunderjet of the USAF, and the RAAF Meteor. The latter proved so vulnerable to the MiG that it was soon relegated to ground-attack duties. The USAF's RB-45 Tornado photo-reconnaissance jets also encountered the MiGs, during their missions to check the strength of communist forces across the border in China. Following the naval blockade of the Yalu, the next objective for the carrier aircraft was the destruction of bridges over the river in November, and these raids saw the first clashes between US Navy F9F and communist MiG-15 fighters. The USAF's bombers – which were by now using primitive guided bombs to destroy high-value 'hard' targets – were equally at risk from MiG attacks during daylight raids. Prior to the MiG's arrival, UN air assets could go about their interdiction and CAS duties relatively unmolested, enjoying air superiority, but from now on they would be under continued threat when operating over the Yalu – soon dubbed 'MiG Alley'. The solution to the MiG problem was the F-86 Sabre, an aircraft at least as equally advanced and which would eventually turn the tables of the air war in its favour, generating an enviable kill ratio against the MiG-15, against which it was otherwise well matched – superior USAF training provided a major advantage. The first F-86s were rushed to the theatre on 11 November, and a first Sabre 'kill' followed on 17 December, when Bruce H. Hinton downed a Soviet-flown MiG-15.

21 September and a renewed breakout from the Pusan pocket was launched.

MARINE SUPPORT

The USMC played a key role in the air campaign over Inchon and Seoul, notably in the pre-invasion 'softening up' of ground targets, with their aircraft now operating from USN carrier decks, and they also covered the first Marines entering the South Korean capital. Also covering the landings and subsequent advance from the carriers were aircraft of Task Force 77 (TF-77), which provided support for the troops on the ground as well as directing naval artillery fire.

By early October the US generals changed their aim to reunification of

Right: Seen in June 1951, these F-86A Sabres are from the 4th Fighter Interceptor Group, the first USAF Sabre wing to deploy to Korea. The 336th Fighter Interceptor Squadron flew the type's first Korean missions from K14 air base in mid-December 1950.

Below: Commander of UN forces in Korea for the early part of the war, General Douglas MacArthur observes Operation Chromite, the amphibious landings at Inchon in September 1950. These received air support from US Navy and Royal Navy carriers.

responsible for the first such aircrew rescue on 10 August.

With UN forces pinned back by the North Korean formations to an area around Pusan by August, General Douglas MacArthur planned an ambitious amphibious landing behind North Korean lines at Inchon, within 32km of Seoul, which would sever communist supply lines. Supported by carrier aircraft and the widespread use of air-dropped napalm and rockets, as well as by bombers reassigned to the tactical support role, the Inchon landings of 15 September were a great success. The UN had reached Seoul by

The devastating effects of B-26 Invader bombing in 1951. USAF B-26s were involved in the conflict from the outset. Initially flying from Japan, two wings were moved to Pusan and Kunsan in summer 1951 to undertake interdiction missions, mainly by night.

Chinese had been pushing the UN forces further back down the peninsula, and by 5 December, Pyongyang was taken back by the communists, and the UN troops would soon be below the 38th Parallel again, the communists having broken a renewed UN offensive that had begun under MacArthur's instigation in November.

Communist gains in territory meant losses in terms of airfields for the UN, and F-86s had to be briefly withdrawn to Japan, leaving the F-84 to go on the offensive. The F-84 fighter-bomber had been introduced to the war in December, and could carry a more useful warload than the F-80, which had not been designed for offensive duties; piston-engined attack aircraft, meanwhile, had effectively been rendered too vulnerable by the arrival of the MiG-15, at least when flying in daylight hours.

In response, continued use of bombing on behalf of the UN meant that the communists were deprived of airfields in North Korea, and the MiGs had to be kept at bases north of the Yalu for their own safety. The appearance in the skies of the improved MiG-15bis variant prompted the USAF to send the latest F-86E model to the theatre, and it soon found success. The RF-86A, meanwhile, was the result of a crash programme to give a reconnaissance capability to the Sabre, and these aircraft proved much more survivable than the RF-51s, RF-80s and RB-26s previously used in the role.

Another new entrant to the war, on the naval side, was the F2H Banshee jet fighter, which had

the two Koreas – under their terms. This was the signal for China to enter the war, as it had promised to retaliate if US troops crossed the 38th Parallel. Therefore, by the time US and Republic of Korea (RoK) forces were fighting for Pyongyang, the North Korean capital, Chinese troops had crossed the border in the north, despite the attentions of B-29s tasked with the destruction of bridges over the Yalu River. UN carriers attempted a naval blockade of the entrance to the Yalu, and this also involved

attacks on North Korean airfields in the area; the Royal Navy's Sea Fury units were particularly active in this period.

After Pyongyang had fallen to the UN on 19 October, UN and Chinese forces clashed at the Yalu River, on the China/North Korea border, later that month. Meanwhile, another landing had taken place, this time at Wonsan, with the bulk of air support put up by units of the USMC, and latterly in the face of fierce Chinese 'human wave' counterattacks. However, by now the

Despite mounting 'kills' on the UN side, the communist MiG-15s still held a trump card of a kind – their Chinese airfields were off limits for the UN air forces.

arrived to complement the F9F from autumn 1950. From December 1950, the USMC was also flying jets in the combat zone, in the form of the F9F.

At the end of December, the Chinese crossed the 38th Parallel and were in a position to begin a new offensive in January 1951, employing sheer weight of numbers to their advantage. In the course of the operation the communists recaptured Seoul on 4 January, before facing off the UN forces along a line between Suwon and Wonju. Communist gains were short-lived, however, and in March the UN retook Seoul and crossed the 38th Parallel once more before the end of the month.

In April, MacArthur gave way to General Matthew Ridgway, amid frustration back in the US at the slow rate of progress being made in the conflict by the UN side.

OPERATION STRANGLE

A communist spring offensive turned the tide again, and UN troops were pinned back to positions to the north of Seoul. At much the same time, the UN began Operation Strangle, a concerted effort by USAF, USMC and USN air assets to disrupt communist supply lines running from China. On the USN side, F9Fs and AD Skyraiders were especially active in the interdiction role; the latter type made a notable raid on the dam at Hwachon on 1 May.

More successful than the efforts of Operation Strangle was the career of F-86 pilot James J. Jabara. On 21 May 1951 he shot down a pair of MiG-15s – his fourth and fifth, to make him the world's first jet ace. Despite mounting 'kill' tallies on the UN side, the communist MiG-15s still held a trump card of a kind – their Chinese airfields were off limits for the UN air forces, and they could exploit this fact to mount 'hit and run' attacks across the border, and would tend to remain at height, with the aim of using their

Douglas Skyraiders from the US Navy's VA-55 unleash air-to-ground rockets at a North Korean target in October 1950. Flying the AD-2 model of the venerable 'Able Dog', the prototype of which first flew in March 1945, VA-55 was one of the first US Navy squadrons in Korea, aboard the USS Valley Forge.

1951: FROM NEGOTATION TO STALEMATE

As early as summer 1950 the UN had begun to look for a political resolution to the conflict in Korea, but it would take another two years before an armistice could be brokered. In the meantime, air power was used to force the communists – namely the truculent Chinese – to the negotiating table. UN forces took Pyongyang again in June 1951, allowing ceasefire talks to commence in July. The UN ground-attack aircraft continued their assault on Chinese supply routes, and made concerted efforts to take out rail networks in the second half of 1951, but without making a significant impact on the course of the war, and they were increasingly harassed by MiGs when operating around the Yalu. Nevertheless, the UN kept up its aerial interdiction effort into the following year, and from August 1951, B-26s were stationed in South Korea rather than in Japan and continued their anti-convoy work by night. In September 1951, the arrival of the HRS-1 allowed the USMC to begin the first sustained troop transport effort using helicopters. 23 October saw a huge air battle fought over North Korean airfields, when a force of B-29s and escorts met large numbers of MiGs. Losses were such that future B-29 raids would only be conducted by night. Another prominent operation of this month involved the first large-scale air assault of the war, conducted north of Pyongyang on 20 October. On this occasion, paratroopers were dropped by C-47 Skytrains and C-119 Flying Boxcars, and the city was successfully cut off from communist supply lines.

speed in a dive when launching an attack on an F-86.

Another communist initiative was the 'Bedcheck Charlie' nocturnal nuisance raid; launched by Po-2 biplanes and Yak-18 trainers to harass UN airfields. One counter to the 'Bedcheck Charlies' was the F-94 jet night-fighter, although the Marines' piston-engined and radar-equipped F4U-5N Corsair proved a more suitable solution, flying from land bases. Indeed, a USN pilot flying the F4U-5N in this role became that service's only ace of the conflict.

On the political side, talks had broken down by January 1952, and the tempo of B-29 raids against bridges picked up the following month as a

Below: Korea was the first war to see the widespread use of helicopters for troop transport. Most capable of available rotorcraft were the HRS-1s flown by the USMC, a type that arrived in the war zone in September 1951.

reaction to this. UN naval assets, under Operation Moonlight Sonata, briefly pursued night attacks in early 1952, with limited success.

STRATEGIC RAIDS

In June a major air campaign took aim at North Korean airfields and the hydroelectric system before large-scale bombing of Pyongyang in July and August. The raids on the power system were successful, closing down industrial production, and taking out

most of the North Korean national grid. The carefully planned attacks were mainly prosecuted by F-80s and F-84s, with F-86s flying top cover to ward off attention by MiGs; USN aircraft were also heavily involved, with AD Skyraiders bearing the brunt of carrier-based offensive duties. Other ground targets were 'mopped up' by USMC F4Us, diverse USN fighters and USAF F-51s. USMC assets were also heavily involved in both the dams raids and the Pyongyang attacks.

Paratroopers disembark from C-119 transports over Korea. The first airborne operation of the war was undertaken in October 1950, when the elite US 187th Regimental Combat Team was successfully deployed north of Pyongyang.

By July, the definitive F-86F version of the Sabre was deployed to the war zone, this aircraft offering increased power, and eventually a redesigned wing tailored for high-altitude manoeuvrability, and both the communists and UN air forces were

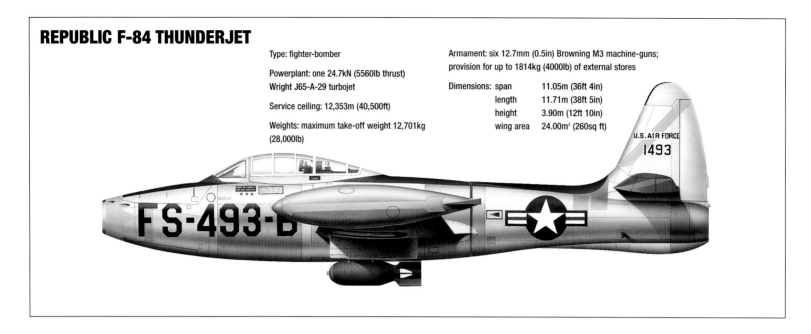

REPUBLIC F-84 THUNDERJET

Type: fighter-bomber

Powerplant: one 24.7kN (5560lb thrust) Wright J65-A-29 turbojet

Service ceiling: 12,353m (40,500ft)

Weights: maximum take-off weight 12,701kg (28,000lb)

Armament: six 12.7mm (0.5in) Browning M3 machine-guns; provision for up to 1814kg (4000lb) of external stores

Dimensions:
span 11.05m (36ft 4in)
length 11.71m (38ft 5in)
height 3.90m (12ft 10in)
wing area 24.00m² (260sq ft)

U.S. AIR FORCE
1493

FS-493-B

using ground control intercept radar in the air battles from spring 1952.

Among the most successful means used by the UN of making a mark on the MiG-15 numbers was a bombing campaign of targets around the Yalu. This had the effect of bringing the MiGs into low-level combat, where large numbers fell to F-86s.

Modernization of UN air arms in the region continued apace, however, and the USAF's last F-51s were finally withdrawn in January 1953, and the following March the final F-80s in theatre were replaced by F-86s. As far as negotiations were concerned, a hard line was maintained as regards China, with air power used as a brokering tool in the months that followed; in May, a campaign was begun against North Korean irrigation facilities, with mixed results, although the raids were credited with speeding the conclusion of peace talks; B-29 attacks on airfields, meanwhile, had

been almost constant since the latter half of 1952, and were increased for the duration of the talks. However, the threat of attack against China was not enough to prevent the People's Republic from launching one last offensive on the ground in June 1953.

On 27 July a ceasefire was signed, although North and South Korea effectively remain on a war footing, with periodic clashes of opposing aircraft over their borders and coastlines in the years that followed.

COLONIAL CONFLICTS

The years following the end of World War II saw the UK involved in a number of 'emergencies' in its former colonies. These were sometimes the result of the power vacuum left in the wake of the previous war creating conditions in which pro-communist movements could flourish. In other instances, the UK confronted nationalistic independence

movements or other anti-colonialist initiatives that had gained various degrees of popular support, leading to potential flashpoints. Where insurgents were involved, the UK more often than not called upon some degree of air power to resolve the situation, and in so doing established much of the groundwork for the use of air power in a counter-insurgency (COIN) capacity.

In the Far East, Malaya remained under UK control at the end of World War II, but by 1948 it was not nationalistic anti-colonialism, but the local communist party that was causing concern, having gained a large body of support, especially among the large Chinese population. Meanwhile its military wing, which had been armed and supplied by the British during World War II, was preparing for guerrilla war.

The situation became critical in 1948, and the UK launched Operation Firedog in response to the rebellion. While the guerrillas took their war to the civilian population, the RAF – ultimately supported by both the RAAF and Royal New Zealand Air Force (RNZAF) – struck against communist jungle positions, initially using Spitfires and Beaufighters. Improved intelligence allowed the UK

US NAVY FIGHTERS IN ACTION

In October 1952, the UN risked a major diplomatic crisis when US Navy F9F Panthers engaged Soviet air force MiG-15s in the Vladivostok area, and claimed at least one Soviet fighter destroyed. The following month witnessed the arrival in the combat zone of the USMC's F3D Skyknight jet night-fighter, which saw some success against the MiGs.

Navy F4Us returning from a mission over Korea wait to land back on the USS *Boxer*. The carrier is in the process of launching F9F Panthers, overseen by an HO3S plane-guard helicopter, the latter seen just above the carrier's island.

to make more significant inroads from 1949, with Spitfires and Beaufighters again being used for strikes, together with the occasional deployment in the offensive role of Sunderland flying-boats, which were otherwise tasked with maritime patrol. In the same year, further support was provided by Tempests, and by carrier-based Seafires and Fireflies from HMS *Triumph*, before the arrival of the Brigand ground-attack fighter and in 1951 the Vampire – the latter the first jet in theatre. At the same time, the

Tempest was replaced by the twin-engined Hornet, which continued ground-attack missions, before being superseded by the Venom jet fighter-bomber in the mid-1950s.

In addition to attacks on particular guerrilla camps, the RAF undertook the bombing of large areas of jungle in an effort to flush out the communists and extinguish their resolve. This 'carpet bombing' effort was first spearheaded by the Lancaster, followed by the Lincoln from 1950, and finally the jet-powered Canberra

from 1955. For photo-reconnaissance work, the RAF called upon the Spitfire and Mosquito, and later the Canberra, and it was in this role that a Spitfire made the type's last operational sortie with the RAF, in 1954.

As well as aerial bombing and ground-attack – often using Auster

FACs in support – aircraft were used to support the 'search and destroy' raids in the jungle, in which communists were hunted down by small bands of troops led by Dyak trackers, natives of Borneo. Dakotas and later Valettas were therefore used to drop supplies to the raiding parties, and on occasions also dropped special forces paratroopers. Later transport assets deployed included the Hastings and Beverley, from the late 1950s.

Two years after the end of the Malayan Emergency, the focus of UK attention turned to Borneo, which was the centre of the Indonesia-Malaysia confrontation, in which these two nations claimed the island. While the UK wished to unite the northern provinces of Borneo within a wider

Malaysian Federation, Indonesia opposed the move, and sought to bring the island into its 'empire', arguing that the formation of a Malaysian Federation was an extension of UK colonialism in the region. Indonesia itself had been granted independence by the Dutch in 1950, with support from both the UN and US.

UNREST IN INDONESIA
The Indonesian Confrontation that took place between 1962-66 would be characterized on the Indonesian side by a campaign of sabotage and small-scale raids by infiltrators, focused upon the border between Indonesian-controlled Kalimantan and the northern provinces of Borneo:

Above: The UK's contribution in Korea included Seafires from No. 800 Squadron, seen here in the Mediterranean prior to the conflict. This unit, together with the Fairey Fireflies of No. 827 Squadron, were on the first RN carrier to deploy to the war zone, HMS *Triumph*.

independent Brunei, and the UK colonies of Sarawak and British North Borneo. Guerrillas from the Indonesian province of Kalimantan first launched an attack into Brunei in 1962, prompting the UK to send Gurkhas from Singapore to restore order, and these troops were initially flown in by Beverley and Britannia transports. Closer to the front, troops were moved by Twin Pioneer STOL transports and Belvedere helicopters, while Hunters and Canberras were available for ground-attack and CAS work. Further British and Commonwealth troops were brought in by RAF, RAAF and RNZAF transports, as well as by Whirlwind and Wessex helicopters from the carrier HMS *Albion*.

The initial Indonesian-instigated rebellion that targeted Brunei was put down successfully, but trouble flared again in 1963, in conjunction with the official establishment of the Federation of Malaysia in the same year. This new wave of violence initially took the form of an Indonesian-inspired attack against positions on the Indonesian border with Sarawak, and this precipitated a sustained campaign of cross-border raids. Once again, troops were required, and they were brought into action by Whirlwind, Sycamore and Belvedere helicopters, as well as by

'HEARTS AND MINDS' IN MALAYA

As part of the 'hearts and minds' campaign that aimed to extinguish support for the communists among the local Malayan population, aircraft including the Auster and Dakota were used extensively to drop propaganda leaflets and broadcast messages. For medical evacuation (medevac), the helicopter soon became available, first in the form of the Dragonfly in 1950, and later both the Sycamore and Whirlwind. The larger Whirlwind also permitted use in the heliborne assault role, but the smaller rotorcraft were also used to transport troops, and to deliver defoliant, together with Austers. Playing a similar trooplift role to the helicopters, the Pioneer STOL (short take-off and landing) transport also proved capable of operating from jungle airstrips. The Malayan Emergency was effectively concluded by 1954, with independence subsequently granted in 1957, but the conflict only officially ended in 1960. By then, Valiants and Vulcans had also been deployed to the theatre in shows of force, together with RAAF Sabres, the most advanced fighters to see action in the conflict.

Hastings and Argosy transports.

As small-scale Indonesian attacks continued, the RAF sent Javelin all-weather fighters and Hunter ground-attack aircraft to the island to dissuade any incursions by Indonesian B-25s and P-51s. After an assault on Kalabakan in North Borneo in 1964, the UK sent further reinforcements to the area, aided by Malayan transport assets. Meanwhile, Indonesia re-equipped with Soviet-supplied Il-28 and Tu-16 bombers and MiG-17 and MiG-19

fighters, leading to further RAF Javelin fighters being deployed as a defensive measure.

Another negative development was the appearance of Indonesian regular soldiers, part of an escalation of attacks in the course of 1964 that included the use of paratroopers dropped by C-130. The Indonesians

Deployed to the theatre from early 1953, the RAF's short take-off and landing (STOL) Pioneers proved valuable in Malaya for the re-supply of isolated jungle garrisons, and they proved more reliable than the helicopters used in this role.

also launched a number of amphibious raiding parties against West Malaysia, but these were similarly put down with British and Commonwealth assistance.

Another response by the UK was to launch ground-attack sorties by RAF Hunters targeting Indonesian forces. In order to bolster the air defences of northern Borneo against further Indonesian incursion, Royal Navy Gannet AEW aircraft were tasked with monitoring airspace, further Javelins were sent, RAF Meteors put on alert in Singapore and RAAF Sabres alerted in Malaysia, while additional Canberras were deployed as a

dissuasive measure. Hunters and Canberras were soon in action, mopping up Indonesian infiltrators, but the air defences nevertheless proved incapable of preventing small-scale raids by Indonesia's World War II-era B-25 and B-26 bombers.

CROSS-BORDER RAIDS

As in Malaya, the RAF also turned to psychological warfare to try and turn the tide of the Indonesian incursions, using Argosy and Hastings transports, and from 1965 the UK began to mount its own cross-border raids into Indonesian territory. The result of the latter was a decrease in activity by the insurgents, who were now forced to

abandon much of their efforts in attacking UK and Malaysian bases along the border, and were instead put on the defensive. The beginning of the end of the Indonesian Confrontation came with a coup attempt in Indonesia in 1965, and incursions soon began to decrease. In 1966 the conflict in Malaya came to an official end with the signing of a peace treaty between Indonesia and Malaysia.

Below: An RAF Transport Command Belvedere of No. 66 Squadron takes off from a jungle clearing in Borneo during operations against the guerrillas. In the background is a Royal Navy Wessex HU.Mk 5 commando helicopter, detached from HMS *Albion*.

In 1960 Cyprus gained independence, with violence between Greek and Turkish factions being the predictable result. Once again Austers and Whirlwinds proved useful for peacekeeping duties.

Equipped with underwing rocket projectiles, a Hunter FGA.Mk 9 ground-attack aircraft of No. 20 Squadron, assigned to the RAF's Far East Air Force, patrols the Malayan coastline. The type was used to attack Indonesian troops on the island.

In the colony of Cyprus, the UK faced a situation in which a majority Greek-Cypriot population was pushing for amalgamation with Greece, beginning an armed campaign to further their cause in 1955. The response was a state of emergency and British troops were sent in, together with Sycamore helicopters and Auster 'spotters', and later Pioneer STOL transport aircraft, for army cooperation. From 1956 Whirlwind helicopters were used to move troops trying to round up the combatants, and Royal Navy Sea Venoms carried out limited ground-attack sorties in 1958. A year later, the emergency ended, but the helicopter had again shown its value in missions directed against the terrorists.

In 1960 Cyprus gained independence, with violence between Greek and Turkish factions being the predictable result. In this instance, forces from the UK were active under a UN mandate to restore peace, and once again Austers and Whirlwinds proved useful for peacekeeping duties. In 1964, the Turkish air force entered the conflict, with F-84 Thunderjet and F-100 Super Sabre

fighter-bombers attacking targets around Nicosia.

SUEZ CRISIS

The Suez Crisis of 1956 represented a disastrous intervention by the UK and France in global affairs; it was a conflict in which air power played a significant role from start to finish. The starting point was an Arab

blockade against Israel and closure of the Suez Canal to Israeli shipping. Amid hostile Western reactions, Egypt's leader, Colonel Nasser, announced in July that the Canal would be nationalized. With their commercial interests at stake, the UK and France prepared a military response, launched in conjunction with Israel. The centrepiece was a

Above: Armée de l'Air Noratlas drop 500 men of the 2nd Régiment de Parachutistes Coloniaux (RPC) on Fuad during the Suez operation on 5 November 1956. A second force of 450 men from the RPC followed this initial wave.

combined naval and airborne assault on Port Said, however, Israeli forces were to enter the Sinai in advance, and were to reach the Canal Zone first, thereby precipitating and justifying an Anglo-French move.

From 31 October, the RAF began a bombing campaign against Egyptian airfields, as Canberras and Valiants attempted to knock out the Egyptian air force on the ground on the first night. Follow-up reconnaissance missions flown by French RF-84F and RAF Canberra aircraft revealed only

> The Suez Crisis of 1956 represented a disastrous intervention by the UK and France in global affairs; it was a conflict in which air power played a significant role from start to finish.

limited success, and French F-84Fs were called in to knock out surviving Il-28s on the ground. RAF Hunters and further F-84Fs then made follow-up raids on 1 November.

The arrival on station of Royal Navy carriers allowed Sea Hawks and Sea Venoms to continue anti-airfield strikes, before the focus turned to Egyptian ground forces, hit by RAF Venoms and RN Wyvern strike aircraft on 2 November; on the same day, French carriers entered combat, with F4Us bearing the brunt of Aéronavale

Below: Seen armed with underwing machine-gun pods, the T-28 Fennec was a French development of the North American T-28 Trojan and was tailored for the demands of the counter-insurgency campaign fought over the deserts of Algeria in the late 1950s.

TURKISH INVASION OF CYPRUS

A decade after the Greek-Turkish fighting during the Cypriot Civil War, a Cypriot coup precipitated a return to warfare on the island, and Turkish forces invaded in July 1974. A combined-arms operation saw Turkish paratroopers dropped by C-47 and Transall transports, and AB 204 helicopters inserted ground troops. While an amphibious force was landed, Turkish air force F-100 Super Sabre and F-104 Starfighter fighter-bombers struck military targets, as well as sinking a Turkish destroyer in a 'friendly fire' incident. After concentrating on the Cypriot capital, Nicosia, Turkish forces' attentions turned to Famagusta, which was raided by F-100s, before a ceasefire came into action in August, with Cyprus divided into Greek and Turkish zones.

ground-attack operations. The next phase from 3 November saw air attacks on targets closer to the Canal Zone itself, and final preparations for the assault were made on 4 November, with carrier-based RN aircraft seeing much action.

On 5 November, Hastings and Valettas dropped UK paratroopers over the Canal Zone, before capturing Gamil airfield under air cover, with RN warplanes using 'cab rank' tactics to keep aircraft on station. French paratroopers were dropped at the

HAWKER SEAHAWK

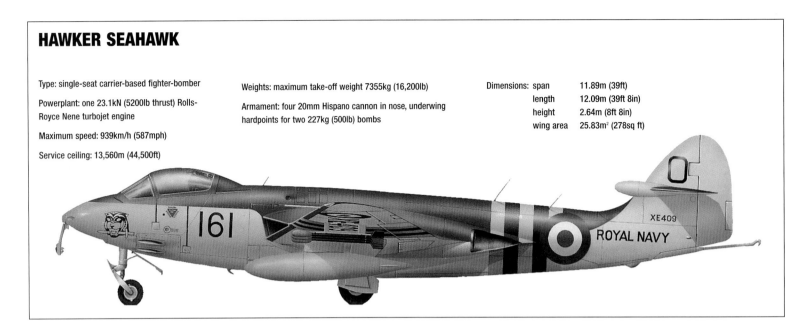

Type: single-seat carrier-based fighter-bomber

Powerplant: one 23.1kN (5200lb thrust) Rolls-Royce Nene turbojet engine

Maximum speed: 939km/h (587mph)

Service ceiling: 13,560m (44,500ft)

Weights: maximum take-off weight 7355kg (16,200lb)

Armament: four 20mm Hispano cannon in nose, underwing hardpoints for two 227kg (500lb) bombs

Dimensions: span 11.89m (39ft)
length 12.09m (39ft 8in)
height 2.64m (8ft 8in)
wing area 25.83m² (278sq ft)

same time, by C-47 and Noratlas, and also captured their objectives, including vital bridges, before subsequent packets of French paratroopers took Port Fuad, supported by F4Us.

On 6 November 1956 the naval assault on Suez began, with UK troops landing at Port Said and French troops reaching Port Fuad, both to be met by further 'cab rank' air support. Further troops then arrived via a heliborne assault, with Whirlwind and Sycamore helicopters flying off HMS *Ocean* – the action was a success, and marked the first occasion in which rotorcraft had been used in this manner on such a large scale. Despite military success, UK and French troops surrounding Port Said, and the possibility of capturing the entire Suez Canal, the intervention drew criticism from the US and USSR and soon led to an embarrassing climb-down. A ceasefire therefore came into being on 7 November. The UN moved into the Canal Zone, and UK and French

prestige in the Middle East was seriously damaged.

Armed groups within the French colony of Algeria began seeking independence from the early 1950s,

with the armed wing of the Front de Libération Nationale (FLN) being established in 1954. The French were intent on suppressing anti-colonialist rebellion in North Africa, but initially

An Aéronavale F4U-7 Corsair from 14 Flotille on the deck of a French navy carrier, two of which (*Arromanches* and *La Fayette*) were deployed to Suez in 1956. Corsairs provided close support to the troops taking key Egyptian objectives on the ground.

had limited air power available in the country: primarily Mistral jet fighters, French navy F4U Corsairs and assorted transport and support machines, none of which was suited to the COIN operations demanded. The French response was to hurriedly develop COIN adaptations of existing light aircraft and trainers, and they were among the first to press the T-6 Texan/Harvard into this role.

INFLUENTIAL DOCTRINE
Following France's lead, aircraft like the T-6 and T-28 would go on to see widespread use in putting down insurgencies in Africa and elsewhere; the French use of communications and close cooperation between land and air forces would also prove influential. However, in Algeria, it was the lesser-

known Morane-Saulnier MS.500 (a development of Germany's wartime Fieseler Fi 156) and MS.733 that were the first aircraft to be used by dedicated anti-guerrilla units in 1955, followed in 1956 by the T-6, and subsequently by the Sipa S.111/S.12 (which originated in the Arado Ar 396 design). Early successes had seen most of the rebels

pushed into mountainous areas and into the cities and thereafter much of the air activity focused on urban areas.

When General Maurice Challe was appointed commander of the French war effort in Algeria in 1959, he ensured that the ageing T-6 was replaced by the T-28, known as the Fennec in French service. Challe

One of the more potent warplanes deployed by the French to Algeria was the Armée de l'Air's supersonic F-100 Super Sabre strike fighter. From 1959 these aircraft were used to attack targets direct from their base at Rheims in France, with a stopover at Istres.

presided over a shift in tactics, as France moved onto the offensive with larger scale operations that would aim to annihilate the rebels. The air operations now involved bomber units equipped with B-26 Invaders, and Skyraider ground-attack aircraft, and also saw cooperation between fixed-wing aircraft and heliborne troops.

Algeria was one of the first conflicts that saw the widespread use of helicopters in the troop transport and assault roles, the first equipment comprising Bell 47Gs and H-19s deployed in 1955. Far more capable in the assault role was the S-55 and the twin-rotor H-21, which arrived in

1957, and the former was also adapted for use as a gunship.

Although Challe's campaign was an apparent success, France could no longer sustain its efforts in Algeria, and despite the introduction of

Right: Portuguese paratroopers disembark from Alouette IIIs during operations in a hamlet in Mozambique. With a major base at Nacala, the helicopters were often used to deliver troops to stamp out guerrilla activity in trouble spots.

AERITALIA G.91

Type: single-seat fighter-bomber

Crew: 1

Powerplant: one 22.2kN (500lbf) Bristol-Siddeley Orpheus 803 turbojet

Maximum speed: 1075km/h (668mph)

Service ceiling: 13,100m (43,000ft)

Weight: maximum take-off weight 5500kg (12,100lb)

Armament: four 12.7mm (0.50in) M2 Browning machine guns; 500kg (1100lb) of bombs

Dimensions: span 8.56m (28ft 1in)
length 10.3m (33ft 9in)
height 4.0m (13ft 1in)
wing area 16.4m2 (177sq ft)

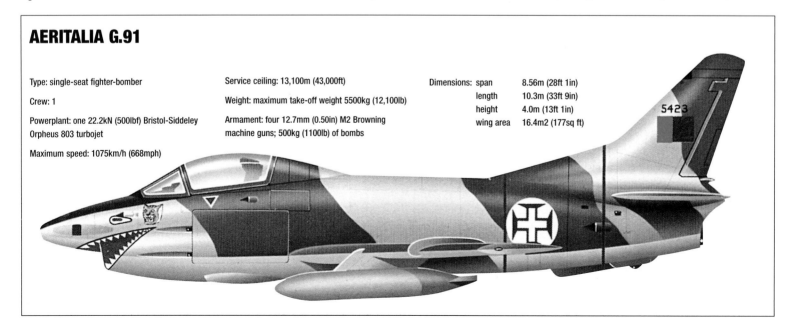

AIR WAR IN ANGOLA

In Angola, Portugal was confronted by the Marxist Movimento Popular de Libertação de Angola (MPLA) and other anti-colonialist agencies, and in 1959 called upon C-47s and PV-2 Harpoons to support the army in putting down the rebellion. Such was the lack of equipment that Portugal employed civilian Beech 18s and DC-3s as makeshift bombers, while Piper Cubs and other light aircraft were outfitted as basic ground-attack aircraft. In 1961 Portugal introduced the F-84G to the conflict, and together with the PV-2 these were widely used to attack rebel troops. In the same year, paratroopers were dropped by C-47 transports, but US sanctions limited Portugal's options in terms of offensive air assets. Despite these restrictions, Portugal managed to attain a handful of B-26s in 1965 to make up for F-84G attrition, while Alouette IIs, DC-6s, Do 27s and Noratlas arrived to bolster the transport arm. The Noratlas was soon involved in dropping paratroopers, as Portuguese ground forces attempted to round up the rebels, while B-26s, T-6s and Do 27s attacked ground targets. Despite a combined defoliation and re-settling effort, the MPLA was making gains by 1972 and the Portuguese maintained their tempo of air attacks. In 1972, G.91Rs arrived from Mozambique, and at the same time increasing use began to be made of heliborne troops to reach outlying combat zones, deployed by the larger Alouette IIIs, and finally Pumas.

Above: A tank commander looks on as an Alouette III supports an offensive in Angola. More often than not, the Alouette family of helicopters found itself the workhorse of various counter-insurgency campaigns waged in Africa.

supersonic jet equipment to the war – namely the F-100, used from 1959 on raids from bases in France – Charles de Gaulle eventually accepted terms for Algerian independence in 1962.

OTHER FRENCH ACTIONS
The conclusion of the Algerian war did not spell the end of French military activity in Africa, and in subsequent years French air power has been regularly called to intervene in the civil war and subsequent strife in Chad from 1968, in support of Morocco against the Polisario Front from 1977, and in Zaire to protect French interests in 1978.

Portuguese air force losses to Guinean ground fire were increasing – including to surface-to-air missiles (SAMs) – and the enemy also had access to Nigerian MiG-17s for reconnaissance and limited ground-attack duties.

By 1967, Portugal was responding to the increasingly precarious situation in Guinea by forward-deploying G.91R battlefield support aircraft, additional T-6s and Do 27 liaison aircraft, with Alouette III helicopters arriving in 1969. The aim of the air campaign was to wipe out guerrilla supply lines and to provide fire support for Portuguese troops on the ground, and the air campaign escalated from the early 1970s. At the same time, Portuguese air force losses to Guinean ground fire were increasing – including to surface-to-air missiles (SAMs) – and the enemy also had access to Nigerian MiG-17s for reconnaissance and limited ground-attack duties. By 1973 the situation on the ground was that of stalemate, and the former Portuguese Guinea was ready to declare its independence.

CRISIS IN MOZAMBIQUE

Mozambique saw the emergence of the Frente de Libertação de Moçambique (FRELIMO) independence movement in 1962, and an outbreak of serious violence in

Angolan troops examine the remains of a napalm bomb dropped by the Portuguese air force (FAP) in 1961. FAP activity in the early years of the campaign included the large-scale use of napalm and fragmentation bombs against positions in the Dembos Mountains.

1964. Available Portuguese C-47s and T-6s were pressed into use in a COIN role from 1962, and were soon supplemented by further ground troops plus PV-2s, Do 27s and Alouette IIIs, as well as C-47 and Noratlas transports. Eventually, Portugal had more forces in the country than in either Guinea or Angola, and aircraft were making routine use of forward strips, with Do 27s undertaking spotting duties, and T-6s responding with ground-attack and CAS sorties. Meanwhile, Alouettes inserted small packets of troops, and larger drops of paratroopers were made by Noratlas.

A concerted Portuguese air campaign began in 1968, and before long G.91Rs were also taking the fight to the FRELIMO rebels. A major Portuguese campaign of 1970 saw large-scale use of Alouette IIIs for trooplift, while fixed-wing aircraft subsequently contributed through CAS, defoliation and psychological warfare missions.

By 1973, FRELIMO's network was expanding, and the guerrillas had access to SAMs. Despite combined operations with Rhodesia, the Portuguese military failed to make a decisive breakthrough by 1974.

SOUTH AFRICA IN ANGOLA
Following Portugal's experiences, South Africa made early advances in

South Africa made early advances in Angola, but the arrival in numbers of Cuban forces would lead to heavy fighting, and the Angolans introduced MiG-17s and MiG-21s.

Left: A FAP Alouette III supports a casualty evacuation during the fighting in Mozambique. The image may date from Operation Gordian Knot of June 1970, a major offensive involving paratroopers, commandos and African troops.

Angola, but the arrival of Cuban forces would lead to heavy fighting. The Angolans introduced MiG-17s and MiG-21s to the battle from 1976, and these were used to attack airfields, among other ground targets. In response, the South African-backed União Nacional para a Independência Total de Angola (UNITA) was armed with man-portable SAMs.

By 1976, overt US and South African support had effectively been withdrawn, but the local Marxist Movimento Popular de Libertação de Angola (MPLA) continued to be harassed by UNITA, which it in turn

Above: The bloody results of Operation Super, a South African cross-border raid into Namibia, in which a reported 201 guerrillas were killed, for the loss of three South African troops. Conducted on 13 March 1982, Super struck against a PLAN base at Cambeno.

Below: A SAAF Puma, of the type used during Operation Super. On this occasion, Pumas delivered 45 men from 32 Battalion plus a mortar group into Namibia, where they not only killed guerrillas but also destroyed a number of Mi-8 helicopters on the ground.

BACKGROUND TO THE BUSH WARS

Portugal's struggles in Guinea, Angola and Mozambique continued until the Portuguese revolution of 1974 effectively put an end to the country's military adventures in Africa. Guinea-Bissau was granted independence in the same year. Independence for Angola and Mozambique came in 1975, but did not bring a conclusion to conflict in these countries, and in the former the US became involved in an effort to counter Cuban influence. While Cuba provided military support for the ruling MPLA in Angola, the US backed the Frente Nacional de Libertação de Angola (FNLA), and South Africa the União Nacional para a Independência Total de Angola (UNITA). The first 'warplanes' available to the anti-MPLA factions were light aircraft including Piper Aztecs and various Cessnas, plus a pair of F.27 airliners, but these were supplemented by C-130s and DC-4s from Zaire, used to transport troops and materiel. Before long, South African Air Force (SAAF) C-130s were also bringing in arms and troops, backed up by Puma helicopters and Cessna 185s for liaison.

pursued with helicopters. Mi-8s arrived with the communists by 1978, and in the same year MiGs were back in action against ground targets.

Beginning in the early 1960s, the infiltration of modern-day Namibia by the South West Africa People's Organization (SWAPO) led to a military response by South Africa, which laid claim to the territory. The disputed area was scene for a major South African COIN campaign that gathered momentum in the early 1970s. As SWAPO launched incursions into South West Africa, South Africa responded with Alouette IIIs used to deliver troops against the insurgents. After Angola's independence, SWAPO began to establish bases here, from which to launch raids into South West Africa, supported by the MPLA. The result was South Africa launching

large-scale operations against Angola and Namibian insurgents from 1978 in what was known as the Bush War.

Over Angola, SAAF air power met with powerful opposition in the form of Angolan and Cuban-flown MiG-17s, MiG-21s and ultimately MiG-23s. In response, South Africa deployed Mirage III and Mirage F1 fighters, and Canberra and Buccaneer strike aircraft. The latter types allowed raids to be launched against MPLA and People's Liberation Army of Namibia (PLAN) guerrilla bases deep inside Angola. Meanwhile, the ground war saw South African troops transported and supplied by Alouette III, Puma and Super Frelon helicopters and large-scale deployment of paratroopers by SAAF C-130 and Transall transports.

In 1979, the campaign against PLAN was extended into Zambia,

Left: Alongside the SAAF's Buccaneers, the Mirage IIIEZ was used to mount strikes against Cuban forces in Angola, primarily using cannon fire and rockets, and notably during Operation Reindeer in May 1978, which saw a major South African incursion.

where SAAF Canberras, Buccaneers and Impalas were all involved in attacking ground targets.

MAJOR INCURSION
In 1980, South Africa launched Operation Sceptic, a combined-arms offensive against PLAN in Angola, and which involved widespread use of heliborne troops and Impalas. By 1981, the SAAF was confronted by medium-range SAMs in Angola and these, as well as the more prolific shoulder-launched SAMs, would remain a significant threat throughout the cross-border campaign.

In 1981, South Africa advanced deep into Angola to seek out PLAN bases, under the cover of air support

South Africa's fleet of Canberras (this is a T.Mk 4 trainer) was used to conduct strike missions into Zambia in August 1979. For these raids, known as Operation Safraan, the Canberra was operated in conjunction with SAAF Buccaneers and Impalas (licence-built MB.326s).

from Mirages, Buccaneers and Canberras, and MiG-21s clashed with Mirages in the air battles. Another major South African offensive began in 1982, with air power used to hit Angolan and PLAN targets while troops were inserted by Puma. A year later, the SAAF recorded a major success in claiming five MiG-21s and four helicopters destroyed in a single battle, although SAAF aircraft also fell to Angolan SAMs.

In 1980, South Africa launched Operation Sceptic, a combined-arms offensive against PLAN in Angola, and which involved widespread use of heliborne troops and Impalas.

Above: This B-26 was put to use by the Biafrans during the civil war. The type's most audacious mission was an attack on the destroyer *Nigeria*, with the aim of blocking off Port Harcourt. Some B-26 missions were flown by legendary Polish World War II ace Jan Zumbach.

THE TRAGEDY IN BIAFRA

The bloody civil wars that afflicted the former British colony of Nigeria and the former Belgian Congo may not have been classical colonial conflicts, but they nonetheless involved air power from western and other powers, as well as mercenaries. In the case of Nigeria, it was the state of Biafra that was declaring independence from federal rule, and the Nigerians responded by seizing objectives in Biafra in 1967. The Biafrans also went on the offensive, and were supported by a small air arm that at this time included a hijacked F.27 airliner adapted as a bomber, a pair of B-26 Invaders and a de Havilland Dove executive transport, among others. In order to counter the Biafrans, Nigeria acquired combat equipment in the shape of MiG-17s and Il-28s from the USSR, as well as mercenary pilots to fly them. With the MiGs operating in the ground-attack role and with Il-28s mounting a significant bombing campaign, the Nigerians had soon regained the initiative. With Biafran forces pinned back by 1968, external powers entered the fray with military and humanitarian support; the latter mission also presented hazards, and at least one aid aircraft was shot down by a MiG-17. In 1969 Biafra could begin a new offensive, in which Nigerian troops received supplies air-dropped by DC-3s. In the same year, Count Carl Gustav von Rosen began using his MFI-9B light aircraft in the ground-attack role, armed with rockets, in support of the Biafran cause. The MFI-9Bs damaged a number of Nigerian aircraft on the ground and attacked oil installations, but these aircraft – plus a delivery of AT-6 Texans – could not prevent ultimate Nigerian victory, which came after a final offensive in early 1970.

In 1984, anti-communist UNITA rebels claimed to have destroyed six MiGs and 12 helicopters during fighting over a six-week period, using anti-aircraft guns and lightweight SAMs. In 1985, SAAF Mirages and Impalas were in action in support of UNITA, and again claimed a number of helicopters and MiGs destroyed. By this stage, the Angolans and Cubans were deploying Mi-25 assault helicopters, while recently received Angolan equipment included Su-22 ground-attack aircraft.

The period 1983-84 saw a significant reduction in South African efforts against PLAN in Angola, and a partial withdrawal from the country; in the meantime, the anti-PLAN initiative was continued in Namibia itself by helicopters and Bosbok and Kudu utility aircraft.

Fighting flared again in Angola in 1985, with a renewed offensive by Angolan forces, and this time UNITA responded with claims for no less than 22 aircraft and helicopters destroyed; the SAAF again provided support for UNITA, and a number of MiGs and helicopters were destroyed on the ground and in the air.

In 1988 MiGs were undertaking a new wave of air strikes to counter UNITA, and the SAAF kept up cross-border raids despite ever more powerful Angolan air defences. By the end of the decade the situation on the

> The civil war that followed Congo's 1960 independence from Belgium also saw the use of mercenaries, but involved a more concerted use of modern air power, initially under UN auspices.

ground was effectively stalemate, and both the Cubans and South Africans agreed to withdraw from Angola. At the same time, Namibia won its independence and also saw a withdrawal of South African forces.

CRISIS IN THE CONGO

Like Biafra, the civil war that followed Congo's 1960 independence from Belgium saw the use of mercenaries, but also involved a more concerted use of modern air power, initially

under UN auspices. The newly independent Congo was gripped by violence and unrest from the outset, and as the Belgian community withdrew, a military presence – including 'weaponized' Magisters and T-6s – remained to maintain order.

The main flashpoint was the province of Katanga. Here, Belgian

Below: Mercenaries stationed at Kamina, Congo, line up to board a DC-4 to go into action for the Congolese against the rebels. This particular aircraft was chartered by the UN and was lost in a take-off accident at Leopoldville in November 1964.

CONTINUED FIGHTING IN THE CONGO

The UN withdrawal and return of Katanga to Congolese rule was not the end of violence in the Congo, and before the 1960s came to an end there would be further clashes and deployment of air power. Left-wing rebels were soon active in the country, and from 1964 these were put down with the aid of US-supplied B-26s and T-28s, and further T-6s, all flown by mercenaries. As white interests came under threat and European hostages were taken, the Belgian military returned to the Congo, with C-47s to transport troops. In a major operation, USAF C-130s dropped Belgian paratroopers at Stanleyville, and T-6s and T-28s saw widespread use in the close support of ground troops. The situation became increasingly chaotic when the Congolese then tried to eject the mercenary forces, one of which, under the renegade Jean Schramme, took up arms against its former client. Congolese T-6s and T-28s now turned on the mercenaries. By 1968 Moise Tshombe, the former Katangan leader, was expelled from the Congo, and in 1972 the country was renamed Zaire.

paratroopers were dropped in 1960, preceding a declaration of Katangan independence. UN forces were soon mobilized to return Katanga to Congolese rule, and RAF and USAF

transports brought troops to the region. Aircraft left by the Belgians were impressed by Katanga – including a handful of T-6s, later joined by mercenary-flown Magisters.

Against these were soon arranged the air forces of the UN, including Indian Canberras, Ethiopian F-86s and Swedish J 29 and S 29 jets.

The situation had become more confused by 1961 with the entry to the conflict of pro-communist forces in the Congo, and the province of South Kansai, which also declared independence, but the main UN objective remained bringing Katanga back into the fold. Katanga's Magisters attacked UN transports and troops on the ground, as well as Congolese forces, while UN aircraft hit back in return, aiming to destroy the Katangan air and ground forces on the ground – the Canberra proved most effective in this role – and even assisting the pro-communist Gizengist forces with trooplift. The UN looked to have the Katangan forces cornered, but the resistance did not end and Katanga obtained T-6s to make good earlier losses, and also put to use Doves and Piper Comanches in an offensive capacity. Deliveries of new aircraft allowed a new offensive to begin against the Congolese, with sustained attacks in late 1962.

In early 1963 the UN deployment received Iranian and Italian F-86s and UN troops began a renewed offensive against Katanga, which was contravening a previously agreed ceasefire, and a new wave of air strikes again destroyed much of the Katangan air arm. UN forces finally withdrew in mid-1964, having taken control of Katanga by late 1963.

Key British interests in Africa during the Cold War era were Kenya, where a savage COIN campaign

Left: Among the aircraft used in operations against the Mau Mau were the Vampire FB.Mk 9 fighter-bombers of No. 8 Squadron, RAF, detached from Aden to Eastleigh. From here they were used in sweeps around Nairobi during Operation Anvil in spring 1954.

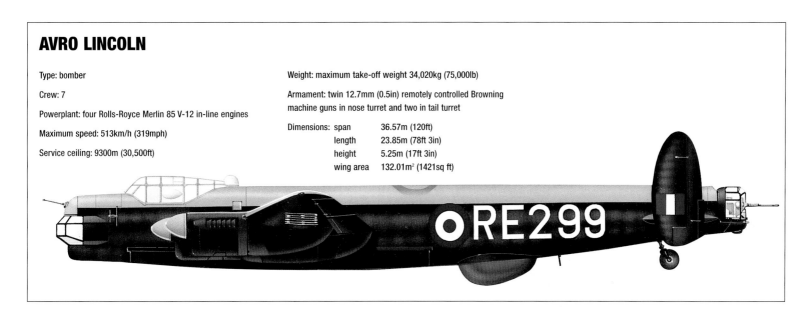

AVRO LINCOLN

Type: bomber

Crew: 7

Powerplant: four Rolls-Royce Merlin 85 V-12 in-line engines

Maximum speed: 513km/h (319mph)

Service ceiling: 9300m (30,500ft)

Weight: maximum take-off weight 34,020kg (75,000lb)

Armament: twin 12.7mm (0.5in) remotely controlled Browning machine guns in nose turret and two in tail turret

Dimensions:
span	36.57m (120ft)	
length	23.85m (78ft 3in)	
height	5.25m (17ft 3in)	
wing area	132.01m² (1421sq ft)	

against Mau Mau rebels between 1952 and 1956 saw a concerted use of RAF air power, and Rhodesia, which had emerged from the Central African Federation in 1963.

CONFRONTING THE MAU MAU

The Kenyan crisis erupted in 1952, when the Mau Mau began attacking white settlers. Troops were flown in and the limited air power on hand – RAF Dakotas and Harvards – was called to arms, with the Harvards being used for bombing. As the crisis

Before the end of the campaign in Kenya, the RAF had introduced Austers and Pembrokes fitted for psychological warfare operations and Sycamore medevac helicopters, while jets arrived in the form of Meteors and Vampires.

deepened in 1953, more troops were flown in and RAF Lincolns began their bombing campaign against the Mau Mau. Before the end of the conflict, the RAF had introduced Austers and Pembrokes fitted for psychological warfare operations and Sycamore medevac helicopters, while jets arrived in the

form of Meteor photo-reconnaissance aircraft and Vampires. By 1955 the Mau Mau was declared defeated, but

Flanked by a Zambia Air Force DHC-2 Beaver, these Javelin all-weather fighters from No. 29 Squadron, RAF, were despatched from their base in Cyprus to Zambia in order to police the airlift operation into the country. The Javelins were based at Ndola and Lusaka.

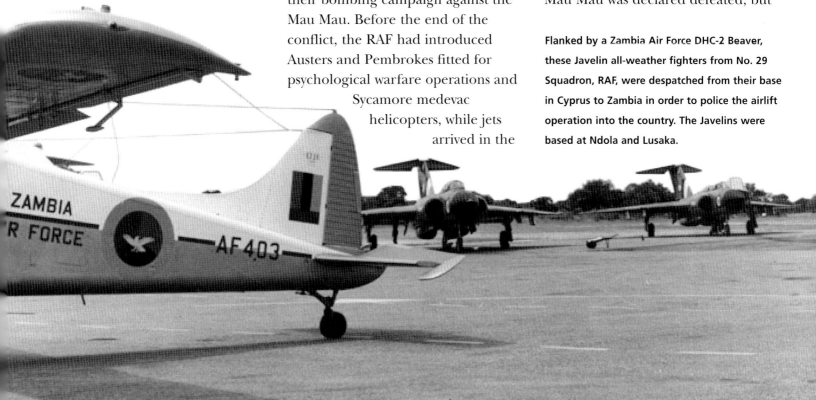

the bloody campaign had been won at a cost that included numerous human rights abuses and atrocities committed on both sides.

THE BEIRA PATROL

When the Rhodesian government – representing the minority white rule – proclaimed independence in 1965, the UK intervened with a blockade: the Beira Patrol. This was imposed together with an RAF airlift of oil from Mozambique to Zambia

(circumventing Rhodesia); these actions were covered by aircraft from Royal Navy carriers stationed in the Indian Ocean, and by land-based RAF assets including Javelin fighters and Shackleton maritime patrol aircraft. The 'Rhodesian problem' worsened towards the end of the 1960s, as guerrilla activity by nationalist Zimbabwean groups intensified.

The Rhodesian air arm was taking part in major anti-guerrilla actions from 1967, using piston-engined

An Alouette III disembarks troops during the war in Rhodesia. During the fighting, Rhodesian Alouette IIIs were adapted as gunships (known as 'K-Cars') as well as straight transports ('G-Cars') and a number fell to both AAA and SA-7 missiles.

Provosts, Hunter and Vampire jet fighter-bombers and Alouette II/IIIs. By the mid-1970s, guerrilla fighting had again intensified, and Rhodesia bolstered its air arm in response, acquiring Cessna 337 utility aircraft adapted for COIN work. The

---

ENGLISH ELECTRIC CANBERRA

Service ceiling: 14,630m (48,000ft)

Weights: maximum take-off weight 24,925kg (54,950lb)

Type: bomber

Crew: 3

Armament: up to 2727kg (6000lb) bombs internally, with provision for 907kg (2000lb) of external stores on underwing pylons

Powerplant: two 36kN (7400lb thrust) Rolls-Royce Avon Mk 109 turbojet engines

Maximum speed: 917km/h (570mph)

Dimensions: span 19.49m (63ft 11in)
length 19.96m (65ft 6in)
height 4.78m (15ft 8in)
wing area 89.19m² (960sq ft)

EARLY INDO–PAKISTAN CLASHES

In 1947, the UK granted independence to India and Pakistan, but some provinces were caught in between these two new powers. Kashmir, for example, refused to join Pakistan. After an insurrection by Kashmiri Muslims and an invasion by Pashtuns (Muslims from the border area with Afghanistan), India intervened, sending in troops in Dakota transports; the latter type was later used as a makeshift bomber. Indian Spitfires and Tempests were involved in attacking insurrectionists on the ground and providing close support for Indian troops, while Harvards were used for spotting. Pakistan also employed Tempest fighter-bombers for ground-attack duties during the conflict, and used World War II-era Halifax bombers for transport and night-bombing work, before a UN-backed ceasefire came into force in 1949.

Despite the attentions of Indian Air Force Vampires that harassed armoured columns, Pakistani ground forces made good progress, operating under cover provided by Pakistani Air Force F-86s and F-104s.

Rhodesians then started to take the war to guerrilla bases in neighbouring Angola, Mozambique and Zambia, including raids by Hunters and Canberras from 1976.

Starved of support as a result of sanctions, Rhodesia was left to confront guerrilla activity on four fronts. 'Fireforces' were assembled as mobile units that could deploy firepower as and when needed: these typically included armed Cessna 337s and Alouette IIIs, plus C-47 and Alouette troop transports. Rhodesia continued to pursue guerrillas from the air – with the most significant actions in the late 1970s involving combined Hunter and Canberra forces guided by Cessna 337 FACs – until the final collapse of minority white rule in 1979.

Fighting was to continue into the next decade and beyond, however,

and the newly established Zimbabwe put to use former Rhodesian aircraft to pursue its own campaign against anti-government groups.

1965 INDO–PAKISTAN WAR

In 1965, renewed fighting broke out between India and Pakistan in the disputed Kashmir region, which had by now become part of India. Pakistani-trained irregulars entered Kashmir in August 1965 before the Pakistani invasion proper, and Indian troops were quickly deployed in response. Despite the attentions of Indian Air Force (IAF) Vampires that

Gun camera film records the demise of a Pakistan Air Force F-86. The Sabre was the mainstay of the PAF during the 1965 Indo-Pakistan War, and remained in large-scale service in the 1971 conflict. In both cases, losses to Hunters and Gnats were significant.

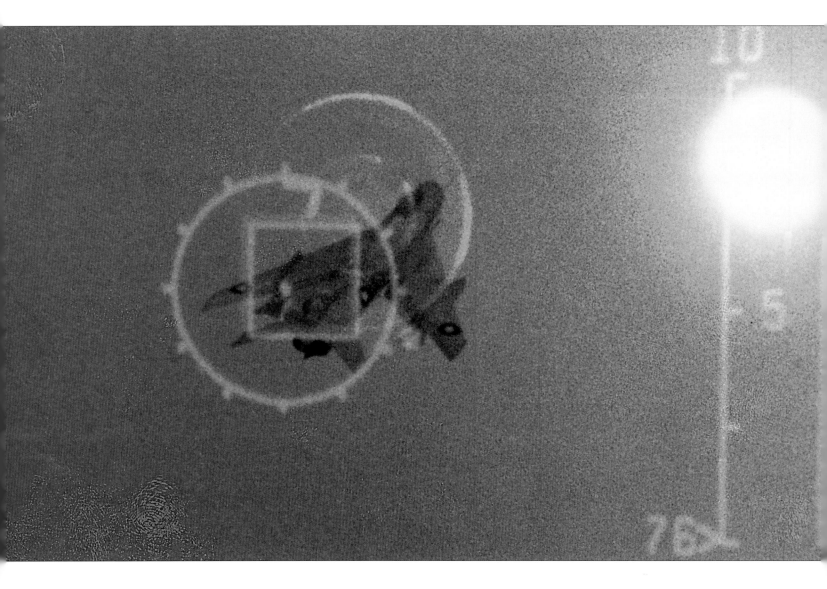

Above: An F-6 is caught in the sights of an Indian fighter during the 1971 Indo-Pakistan War. A Chinese-built version of the MiG-19, these aircraft had been acquired to make good losses incurred in the 1965 conflict and were flown by at least three squadrons.

harassed armoured columns, the Pakistani ground forces made good progress, operating under cover provided by Pakistani Air Force (PAF) F-86s and F-104s. Early Vampire losses saw the IAF pull both this and the

Ouragan from the front, while Pakistan made further progress, now with F-86s used in the CAS role. As the Pakistani advance slowed, the air battle expanded, and PAF F-104s and F-86s clashed with IAF Gnats and

HAWKER SEA FURY

Type: single-seat fighter

Powerplant: one Bristol Centaurus XVIIC 18-cylinder twin-row radial engine producing 1850kW (2480hp)

Maximum speed: 740km/h (460mph)

Service ceiling: 10,900m (35,800ft)

Weight: maximum take-off 5670kg (12,500lb)

Armament: four 20mm (0.79in) Hispano Mk V cannon; 12x76mm (3in) rockets or 908kg (2000lb) of bombs

Dimensions: span   11.7m (38ft 5in)
length   10.6m (34ft 8in)
height   4.9m (16ft 1in)
wing area   26m² (280sq ft)

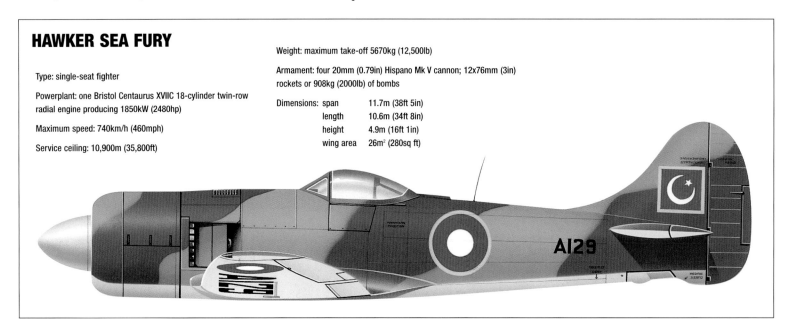

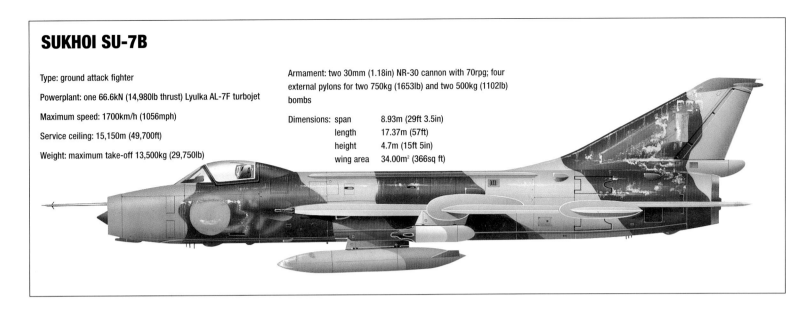

SUKHOI SU-7B

Type: ground attack fighter

Powerplant: one 66.6kN (14,980lb thrust) Lyulka AL-7F turbojet

Maximum speed: 1700km/h (1056mph)

Service ceiling: 15,150m (49,700ft)

Weight: maximum take-off 13,500kg (29,750lb)

Armament: two 30mm (1.18in) NR-30 cannon with 70rpg; four external pylons for two 750kg (1653lb) and two 500kg (1102lb) bombs

Dimensions: span   8.93m (29ft 3.5in)
           length   17.37m (57ft)
           height   4.7m (15ft 5in)
           wing area   34.00m² (366sq ft)

Hunters. As Indian forces moved across the Pakistani border, both sides deployed air assets in ground-attack roles – with mixed results – against airfields, armour and other targets.

AIRFIELDS ATTACKED

The PAF then turned its attentions to the IAF on the ground, which led to dogfights between F-86s and Hunters over IAF bases. With the exception of clashes between Taiwan and China in 1958, this was the first conflict in which large-scale use was made of air-to-air missiles (AAMs), in this case, AIM-9s fired by PAF F-86s and F-104s.

By night, PAF B-57s hit IAF bases, and the IAF soon returned the favour, sending Mystères, Hunters, and later night-flying Canberras, against PAF bases, where they were met by defending F-86s and F-104s. The Indians now pushed further into Pakistani territory, but were turned back in places and harassed by F-86s.

The PAF used C-130s to deliver paratroopers on IAF bases, without success. As new fronts opened, ground-attack and CAS became more important; the PAF used armed T-33s and F-86s – and even bomb-carrying C-130 transports – while the IAF used Hunters against enemy armour. At the same time, attacks on both sides' air bases and radars were maintained by

day and night, and continued air combats saw a number of encounters between Gnats, Hunters and F-86s. As ground fighting intensified, Indian tanks and artillery increasingly fell

prey to F-86s and T-33s, but both sides soon found themselves in a stalemate. The war lasted around five weeks, before arms embargoes put an end to fighting, and a ceasefire was declared.

1971 INDO–PAKISTAN WAR

In 1971, India and Pakistan went to war again, this time over East Pakistan, which declared independence as Bangladesh, leading to civil war. Indian forces entered East Pakistan in November and met Pakistani forces, and IAF Gnats were soon battling PAF F-86s. The PAF quickly put into action a pre-emptive attack on IAF air bases, led by B-57s and F-86s, but the IAF was able to respond in kind, using Hunters and Su-7 fighter-bombers escorted by MiG-21s, and indigenous HF-24 fighter-bombers. At the same time, an Indian naval blockade was put up in the Bay of Bengal, aided by Alizés and Sea Hawks from the carrier *Vikrant*, and these aircraft also hit targets on land. In common with the 1965 air war, this was a battle of airfields, and as Indian and Pakistani land forces geared up for their major offensives, raids on both sides' air bases continued, and there were numerous air-to-air confrontations, while PAF received additional F-104s from Jordan to boost its strength. In early December, the Indians looked to have the upper hand as they moved towards their major objective, the Bangladeshi capital Dhaka, and their Gnats, MiG-21s, Su-7s and Sea Hawks continued their destruction of air bases; a number of IAF An-12 airlifters were also adapted for bombing duties for use against enemy materiel and troops. Meanwhile, Mi-4 helicopters, supported by armed Alouettes, transported Indian troops, and before long the PAF was back on the offensive, directing Mirage III, F-86 and F-104 warplanes against IAF installations, where they were tackled by MiG-21s and Gnats. By mid-December, Indian forces had reached Dhaka, and a ceasefire was called. This signalled the full establishment of Bangladesh, but fighting briefly continued, with massed tank battles, airfield strikes and further clashes between MiG-21s and F-104s.

The Air War in Vietnam 1964–1973

When Vietnam was divided following the end of World War II in 1945, Nationalist China and the UK were set to take control of equal shares; but France asked for the UK's share, and duly assumed control.

Ho Chi Minh, Vietnam's Japanese-appointed leader, wanted neither France nor Nationalist China occupying his country, but of the two he most despised the Chinese Nationalists. France negotiated with China to allow it to control the north as well as the south in return for France relinquishing its concessions in China. With a deal struck and now able to assert control over all of Vietnam, France tried and failed to form a government of its liking, and ended up bombarding Ho Chi Minh's harbour city of Haiphong.

Minh fled to the hills and the Chinese communists, fresh from victory over the Nationalists, came to Minh's aid. France was about to get its nose bloodied as it became embroiled in a war that it could never win. By 1950 France had had enough, and four years later it called a ceasefire, granted independence to Vietnam and neighbouring Cambodia and Laos, and finally extricated itself from the quagmire of Southeast Asia after final collapse at Dien Bien Phu in 1954.

From an air combat perspective, the Vietnam War provided the US and the USSR, the world's two superpowers, with the opportunity to put their best technology and systems into the sky to battle it out.

On the ground, US troops began arriving in Vietnam in great numbers, and by 1964 the US Army

The UH-1 'Huey' helicopter opened a new era in battlefield mobility during the Vietnam War, making it possible for soldiers and their weapons to be delivered directly onto the battlefield.

A US adviser watches as South Vietnamese soldiers are put through weapons drill. At this early stage in the war, the South Vietnamese were mainly equipped with older weapons surplus to US requirements.

THE US ENTERS THE WAR

The Geneva Conference of 1954 partitioned Vietnam temporarily until national elections could take place in 1956. In the north, Ho Chi Minh went on his infamous killing spree, targeting those social classes and individuals likely to threaten communist rule. Meanwhile in the South, a supposedly democratic but brutal leadership was established that would take direction from the US. Over the course of the next decade, US interest in Vietnam increased drastically as communist China and the Soviet Union backed Minh's regime. US military advisors had been 'in country' since the First Indochina War – officially to advise, but actually covertly leading operations – and further escalation always seemed likely. All that was required was an ignition source.

The spark that started the Second Indochina War came in 1964, when the USS *Maddox*, a US Navy destroyer on an intelligence-gathering mission in the Gulf of Tonkin, was reportedly twice attacked by North Vietnamese torpedo boats. US President Lyndon Johnson authorized a retaliatory air strike, and with that the US war in Vietnam had started.

was operating more than 300 'Huey' gunships – armed UH-1 Iroquois – to escort Army and Marine transport helicopters. The 'Huey' had been in Vietnam since 1962, two years before the US officially entered the war, and was assigned a reactionary medical evacuation (medevac) role supporting the South Vietnamese Army.

ICONIC 'HUEY'

The distinctive-sounding 'whoop-whoop' of the UH-1's rotor blades would go on to become symbolic of the Vietnam War, and images of soldiers flying into landing zones in the 'Huey' would be equally iconic. The US Army learned quickly that helicopters offered them the ability to insert and extract troops into landing zones over great distances, and with a speed and efficacy that were superior to overland travel – airmobile warfare had been born.

At its peak in March 1970, the US military operated more than 3900 helicopters in the war in Vietnam, and two thirds of them were 'Hueys'.

In the months following the Gulf of Tonkin Incident, the United States

Air Force (USAF), Marine Corps (USMC) and Navy (USN) maintained a continuous bombing campaign against Ho Chi Minh's North Vietnam that was intended to escalate gradually, giving the North Vietnamese leadership time to come to the negotiating table before all-out war was waged. That campaign was known as Rolling Thunder.

ROLLING THUNDER STRIKES

Rolling Thunder presented the US military with the opportunity to test out a number of new or unproven technologies. The North Vietnamese Air Force (NVAF) had acquired some 60 Soviet-made MiG-17 fighter jets by 1965, and these were guided from the ground by controllers using ground control intercept (GCI) radars, also built and supplied by the USSR. But with a few notable exceptions, the North Vietnamese did little that was technologically groundbreaking, and this was no surprise since they were trained and supplied by a Soviet Union that had always placed an emphasis on quantity over quality.

For the US, the opposite was true.

As the Cold War had heated up, it had sunk its resources into miniaturization of electronics, computer technology and manufacturing techniques – all expensive investments that meant that fewer examples could be built with the budget that remained. What came out of this were sophisticated aircraft and weapons built in much smaller quantities. Whereas older-generation fighter jets like the USN's F-8 Crusader relied on the same simplicity

The Gulf of Tonkin Incident, in which North Vietnamese light naval craft were deemed to have attacked US Navy warships in international waters, was the trigger for the US move towards direct involvement – on an ever-increasing scale – in the Vietnam War.

that the Soviets subscribed to, newer fighters like the F-4 Phantom II carried a sophisticated radar and were essentially missile platforms. The Phantom carried weapons such as

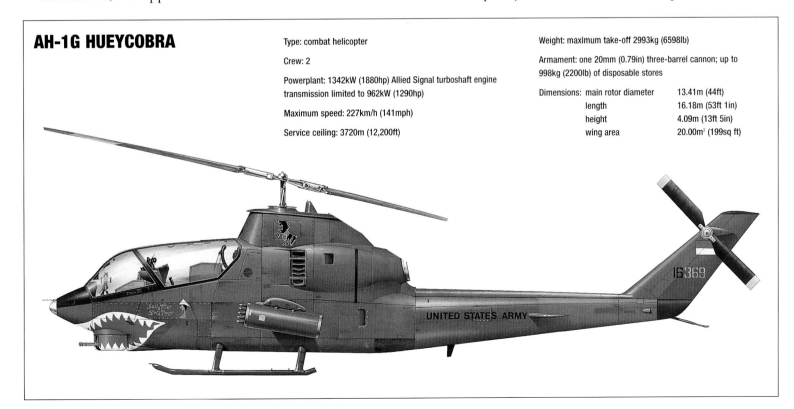

AH-1G HUEYCOBRA

Type: combat helicopter

Crew: 2

Powerplant: 1342kW (1880hp) Allied Signal turboshaft engine transmission limited to 962kW (1290hp)

Maximum speed: 227km/h (141mph)

Service ceiling: 3720m (12,200ft)

Weight: maximum take-off 2993kg (6598lb)

Armament: one 20mm (0.79in) three-barrel cannon; up to 998kg (2200lb) of disposable stores

Dimensions:		
main rotor diameter	13.41m (44ft)
length	16.18m (53ft 1in)
height	4.09m (13ft 5in)
wing area	20.00m² (199sq ft)

UNITED STATES ARMY

16369

Left: Formating on a B-66 Destroyer pathfinder, equipped with advanced navigation, attack and defensive electronics, four F-105 Thunderchief strike fighters of the US Air Force release their sticks of free-fall 'dumb' bombs onto a North Vietnamese target.

the radar-guided AIM-7 Sparrow medium-range air-to-air missile (AAM), in addition to the short-range AIM-9 Sidewinder and AIM-4D Falcon AAMs, both of which tracked the hot exhaust of the target aircraft. Vietnam would be the proving, or perhaps the *dis*proving ground, for them all.

AERIAL CLASHES

The first air-to-air encounters between the two sides occurred in the first days

UNRELIABLE ARSENAL

The AIM-7 Sparrow had a number of drawbacks: the rocket motor proved to be unreliable, the missile took more than two seconds to even come off the aircraft once the 'pickle' button had been pressed, it had a restrictive minimum range, and the radar lock needed to guide it to the target was often lost when the target manoeuvred aggressively or descended below the launch aircraft, resulting in the Phantom's radar set being bombarded with confusing radar echoes from the ground. The Sidewinder was simply too readily confused by other extraneous heat signatures – the sun and the ground being two of them, and would often transfer lock from the target to elsewhere. Neither missile was working as advertised.

of March 1965, and ended unhappily for the USAF and USN, which lost two F-105 Thunderchiefs and had an F-8 Crusader damaged, respectively, to the technologically inferior MiG-17. The MiGs had engaged with their heavy

The finest US warplane of the Vietnam War was the McDonnell Douglas F-4 Phantom II. Created for the US Navy as a fleet air defence fighter, the Phantom II matured as an exceptional multi-role warplane, and was later adopted by the US Air Force in a number of variants.

canon armament, under GCI control, starting a trend that would continue for the duration of the war: the MiGs would almost always attack only when the tactical situation gave them the best chances of success and survival.

April 1965 saw the first use of the Sparrow and Sidewinder missiles. Four USN F-4Bs fired eight AIM-7s and two AIM-9s at four MiG-17s. All but one of the missiles missed, with the final Sparrow claiming a MiG. Another trend had been started: the probability of kill (Pk) of the AAMs was poor, and fell well short of that which the manufacturers had claimed in their

sterile tests back in the US. While US fighter pilots grew increasingly frustrated at the low Pk of their missiles, the battlespace around them was about to take on a dangerous additional dimension.

'GUIDELINE' AND ECM

In 1965 the Soviet Union began supplying North Vietnam with more early warning radars and radar-directed anti-aircraft artillery (AAA). But that was only half the problem: there were also indications that the Soviets had supplied the SA-2 'Guideline' surface-to-air missile

(SAM), and in early April that year a USN RF-8 Crusader on a tactical reconnaissance mission photographed an SA-2 site under construction southeast of Hanoi.

The SA-2 operated like the AIM-7 Sparrow in that it locked onto the radar beam illuminating its victim, and literally 'rode the beam' of the system's 'Fan Song' radar until it came within lethal distance of the target. The 'Guideline' wasn't a particularly manoeuvrable missile, but it did have a range of 27km (16 miles), and could engage targets as low as 914m (3,000ft) and as high as 15,240m (50,000ft). The missile had already been used to down a U-2 spyplane flying over the Soviet Union in May 1960, and another over Cuba in 1962, and was now about to make its presence felt over Vietnam.

The US response was to send specialist electronic countermeasures (ECM) aircraft to the region in a bid to jam the 'Fan Song' radar, or confuse the missile's radar proximity fuze. The EB-66B Destroyer, based on the B-66 light bomber and reconnaissance aircraft, was sent by the USAF to Thailand in May 1965, and the EB-66C arrived later that year.

The EB-66Bs were also employed against the 'Fire Can' radars of the radar-directed AAA in North Vietnam, often to good effect. The EB-66C could jam these radars, but was also able to gather electronic intelligence (ELINT) on the frequencies and characteristics of the Soviet-built radars, allowing the US to refine the jamming techniques and tactics employed against them. The USN employed the carrier-based EA-3B

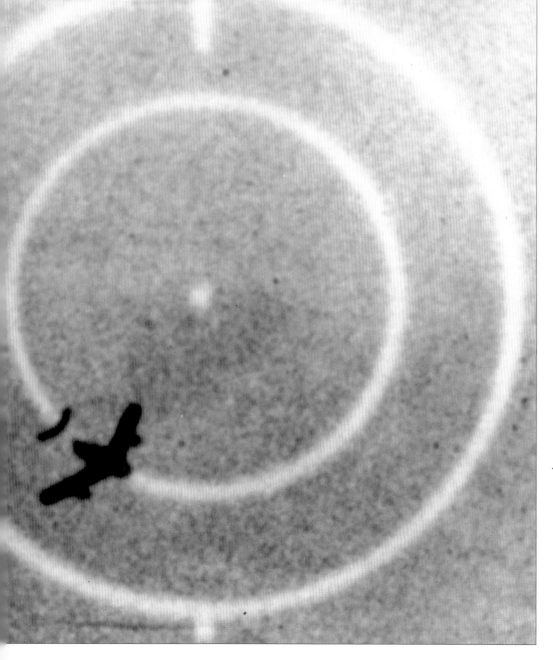

A North Vietnamese MiG-17 is caught in the sights of a US fighter. Starting from scratch, North Vietnam built up a small but capable air arm that caused the US air arms considerable problems as NVAF pilots learned to exploit the advantages offered by their agile fighters.

> From a tactical perspective, US aircraft were forced to operate below the SA-2's 914m (3,000ft) minimum engagement altitude, but this meant they were forced into the heart of the AAA envelope.

The US weapon of choice for medium-range air-to-air engagements was the AIM-7 Sparrow. North Vietnamese pilots tried to keep their aircraft inside the Sparrow's useful tactical envelope, but outside that of the short-range AIM-9 Sidewinder.

(based on the A-3 Skywarrior bomber) and EA-1F (based on the A-1 Skyraider), the former gathering ELINT, the latter jamming the radars.

INITIAL VICTIM
In late July 1965 the 'Guideline' claimed its first victory – a USAF F-4C – and within three weeks had claimed

13 more 'kills'. The Johnson administration, in its characteristic naivety and insistence on interfering in military matters, had not approved the destruction of the SAM sites, believing that the North Vietnamese would not dare to use them.

From a tactical perspective, US aircraft were forced to operate below

the SA-2's 914m (3,000ft) minimum engagement altitude, but this meant they were forced into the heart of the AAA envelope, which was precisely where the NVAF wanted them. US losses to AAA would far outweigh any other cause, including SAMs and MiGs, by the end of the war, and in this respect the rugged simplicity of the North Vietnamese air defence network overcame the highly evolved technological prowess that defined aspects of the US military arsenal.

A US air reconnaissance photograph reveals the details of a North Vietnamese 'Guideline' SAM site. The threat of this missile at higher altitudes sometimes persuaded US pilots to bring their aircraft to lower altitudes, but here they could often be tackled by radar-controlled AAA.

The low-altitude ingress that was required posed navigational challenges and also limited range because of the much higher fuel consumption at low altitude, and this was especially true of the USAF's F-105 Thunderchief, which was the most numerous fast jet in theatre and the workhorse of the fighter-bomber fleet. The 'Thud' was the first fighter to be fitted with a radar homing and warning (RHAW) receiver, however. The RHAW told the pilot when a 'Fan Song' radar was looking at him, and gave him time to evade the radar's scan pattern – it took around 75 seconds for a 'Fan Song' to find, lock on to a target and then fire a 'Guideline' missile, so the F-105 pilot had ample warning. When the hostile missile guidance signal came on line, a red 'launch' light in the F-105's cockpit glowed steadily, and it was then just him and the missile.

'WILD WEASELS'

The stand-off jammers like the EA-3 and EB-66 were vulnerable themselves to both MiGs and SAMs, and the US recognized the need to have dedicated tactical fighters that could accompany a strike package and ferret out the 'Fan Song' and SA-2 sites. The USN opted to use its A-4 Skyhawks, while the USAF selected the two-seat F-100F Super Sabre and, from early 1966, F-105F Thunderchiefs, because these could carry a dedicated electronic warfare officer (EWO) in the back seat. The USAF coined the name 'Wild Weasel' for its SAM suppression operations, but the official mission designator was actually Iron Hand. (Later, from 1972, single-seat F-105Gs would also perform 'Wild Weasel' attacks as part of a hunter-killer team with the new F-4E Phantom.) The F-105F became the quintessential SAM hunter of the war, carrying the AGM-45 Shrike missile in addition to conventional munitions such as unguided general-purpose bombs and cluster bombs. The Shrike took an AIM-7 Sparrow body and added a new seeker head that could

AVOIDING THE 'GUIDELINE'

Outmanoeuvring the SA-2 was perfectly possible, but it took nerves of steel and excellent timing. Since there was no training tool to allow pilots to learn, the training was 'on the job', and was therefore something of a steep learning curve. USAF General Robin Olds, a decorated World War II ace, led an F-4C wing in Vietnam and later recalled that no matter how often he was fired upon by a SAM, the sheer terror of the experience was always the same. He recalled that he had been the target of some 150 SA-2s.

home in on the transmissions of the 'Fan Song' and 'Fire Can' radars.

The Shrike was basic in nature, had a range of only 24km (15 miles), but was at least a 'fire and forget' missile that would autonomously home in on the radiating target following launch. However, it was much slower than the SA-2, and with the latter having a 27km (16 mile) engagement range, in a straight fight between the two, the SA-2 would hit the A-4 or F-105 before the Shrike hit the 'Fan Song'. Of course, the 'Wild Weasel' could turn around following a Shrike launch, but if it did that the 'Fan Song' operator could conclude that a missile was headed inbound, and might shut down the radar signal, leaving the Shrike without a source to home in on.

NEW-GENERATION MISSILE

The AGM-78 Standard anti-radiation missile (ARM) solved several of these problems, and was introduced in early 1968. Based on the RIM-66 naval SAM, it had a much larger warhead than the Shrike, a range of up to 90km (55 miles), and some variants even carried a phosphorous flare, helping the 'Wild Weasel' locate the now-disabled SA-2 site so that it could follow up with cluster bombs.

The USN complemented its Iron Hand A-4s with a derivative of the A-6 Intruder strike aircraft known as the EA-6A. This carried onboard jammers and actually entered the target area with the USN strikers, providing them with jamming protection as they ingressed and egressed the target.

By the summer of 1965, the USAF, without its own equivalent of the

Vietnam saw the first large-scale use of tactical air-to-surface missiles in warfare. Even in their initial and comparatively primitive forms, these 'smart' weapons were capable of destroying targets that had survived several attacks with conventional 'dumb', or unguided, ordnance.

The 'Thud' was the first fighter to be fitted with a radar homing and warning (RHAW) receiver. The RHAW told the pilot when a 'Fan Song' radar was looking at him.

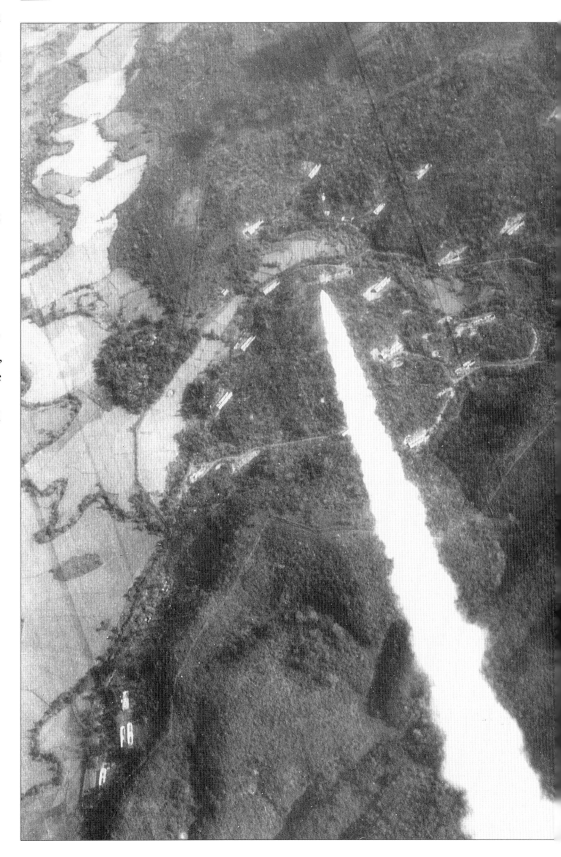

Left: An A-4 Skyhawk light-attack aircraft leaves the catapult as it is launched from a carrier of the US 7th Fleet in the waters off Vietnam. Light, agile and possessing good performance, the Skyhawk carried a modest but useful warload and it could deliver this with a good degree of accuracy.

Navy's EA-6A, had issued contracts to develop Quick Reaction Capability (QRC) jammer pods for its strikers. It took the ECM jamming equipment from strategic bombers and mounted them in pods that could be carried by tactical jets. The first pod was the QRC-160, and it first equipped the tactical reconnaissance RF-101 Voodoo and RF-4C Phantom. These tactical reconnaissance fighters carried cameras internally and were sent daily to photograph a range of targets across the length and breadth of Vietnam. They often went alone and because the information that they supplied was so critical, they routinely found themselves tasked to overfly the SA-2 sites without any form of self-defence. They were an ideal candidate for the QRC-160. The USN was one step ahead of the USAF, and by the end of 1965 its A-4s and A-6s were equipped with the internally mounted ALQ-51 jammer.

JAMMING TECHNIQUES

The QRC-160 was a 'noise' jamming pod that put out a very 'loud' signal that hid the radar echo that the 'Fan Song' radar needed in order to acquire a lock, whereas the ALQ-51 was a 'deception' jammer that sent out spurious radar echoes to confuse the 'Fan Song' operator as to which target on the scope was the real one. The USAF trialled the ALQ-51, but derided the USN's pod when it discovered that a confused 'Fan Song' or 'Fire Can' operator would simply barrage-fire as many SA-2s, or as much AAA, as he could at all of the targets.

STRATEGIC RECONNAISSANCE

The SR-71 – which cruised at Mach 3.3 at about 25,300m (83,000ft) – flew from the Japanese island of Okinawa and could directly overfly North Vietnam (and China) to bring back photographic and electronic intelligence (ELINT – including recording the electronic signals associated with the enemy's air defence network). The glider-like U-2 operating out of South Vietnam flew much more slowly and was therefore more vulnerable to the SA-2, but it too brought back valuable photographic intelligence from overflights of North Vietnam, and was particularly successful at photographing SA-2 sites in the early war years.

> Despite the introduction of the ALQ-51 and QRC-160 jammers, neither was particularly effective, and pilots were still unconvinced that modern fighters could survive in a SAM environment.

The USAF considered the USN's 'solution' to be self-defeating. Despite the introduction of the ALQ-51 and QRC-160, neither was particularly effective, and pilots were still unconvinced that modern fighters could survive in a SAM environment.

Throughout the war, the tactical reconnaissance platforms were underpinned by the strategic reconnaissance efforts of the manned SR-71 and U-2 spyplanes, and the unmanned AQM-34 Firebee drone.

The Firebee operated mostly at very low altitude, skimming over treetops and rooftops on autopilot, and following a pre-programmed route downloaded to it by its DC-130

The F-105 Thunderchief was conceived for the supersonic delivery of nuclear ordnance in a European environment, but in Vietnam was used to deliver conventional ordnance at subsonic speed, and also suffered severe maintenance problems in the heat and humidity of Vietnamese conditions.

Hercules 'mother ship'. The later Lightning Bug was an even more sophisticated version of the Firebee, and like its predecessor, was an excellent photographic platform. Lightning Bugs and Firebees were also used as decoys for SA-2 sites to engage, and as ELINT gatherers.

In December 1965, Lyndon Johnson called a halt to Rolling Thunder in the hope that the North Vietnamese were prepared to come to the negotiating table. The halt gave US military commanders and planners

The Firebee was one of the most important recce types available to US forces in Vietnam. Launched from specially equipped variants of the C-130 Hercules transport, the camera-equipped AQM-34 Firebee stood less chance of destruction than a larger, manned aircraft.

a chance to administratively divide Vietnam into seven separate areas known as Route Packs (RPs). These started with friendly South Vietnam as RP I and ascended in a northerly direction, meaning that Hanoi and the northern parts of North Vietnam were RP VIa (for the USAF) and RP VIb for the USN and USMC. In addition, RPs II and III were the primary responsibility of the USN and USMC. In essence, the further north a pilot was required to fly, the greater the threat of being shot down, because the North Vietnamese Army (NVA) and NVAF clustered most of their AAA and air bases around the industrial centres at the top of the elongated country. Thus, RP I and II missions were seen as low risk, RP III and IV as medium risk, and RP V and VI as the highest

risk. RP VI was divided into two zones: the USAF took the westerly RP VIa because the USN's aircraft carriers were operating from Yankee Station in the Gulf of Tonkin to the east, and could therefore fly over the shoreline and straight into the easterly RP VIb. This was a logical decision, but it had the added advantage of allowing the USN aircraft to approach their targets with little advance warning for the NVAF's growing network of air defence sites and GCI.

ENTER THE 'FISHBED'
The start of 1966 heralded the introduction to NVAF service of the supersonic MiG-21 'Fishbed' fighter. Once again, it was a tactical reconnaissance asset – an RF-8 – that first spotted the MiG-21, and it was

not long before the new fighter was on the prowl for prey. The MiG-21 was a real threat. It was one of the latest Soviet export fighters, and was expected to be superior in some respects to both the F-8 and F-4, and superior in all areas to the F-105.

By April 1966 the MiG-21s were being vectored by GCI to attack the EB-66 jammers, but without success. On their second attempt to down a Destroyer, the USAF's F-4C Phantom escorts downed two of the attacking MiGs with Sidewinder AAMs.

But US air-to-air missile woes had continued, and the Sparrow was averaging an unimpressive 8 per cent Pk and the Sidewinder a 28 per cent Pk. The Phantom had no internal cannon, so even if a pilot manoeuvred behind a MiG for a 'kill', he had no option but to disengage if his Sparrows and Sidewinders failed.

To further turn the tide in the NVAF pilot's favour, the GCI was improving and the Soviets had now supplied fixed-site 'Bar Lock' surveillance radars and truck-mounted 'Flat Face' radars to expand its coverage. Despite its best efforts, the US never managed to interfere with the NVAF's GCI, which would simply

The Firebee was launched from drone-carrier variants of the C-130 tactical transport operated by the US Navy (opposite) and US Air Force (above). The Firebee was much used in high-threat situations such as the photographing of SA-2 'Guideline' surface-to-air missile sites.

switch frequencies to a band that was not being jammed.

RED CROWN

The US also had its own GCI network made up of a number of agencies and platforms, although it lacked the coverage that the NVAF enjoyed. Three radar ships in the Gulf of Tonkin were known as Red Crown and could observe the east coast of North Vietnam, and the USN operated the E-1B Tracer, which carried an APS-82 radar that helped improve the quality of that coverage.

The USAF had the Big Eye Task Force, which consisted of the EC-121D Warning Stars (based on the Super

> The Phantom had no internal cannon, so even if a pilot manoeuvred behind a MiG for a 'kill', he had no option but to disengage if his missiles failed.

The most advanced fighter used by North Vietnam during the war was the MiG-21 'Fishbed' daylight interceptor supplied by the USSR. This lacked the advanced electronics of US fighters, but was fast, agile and armed with potent cannon armament.

Constellation airliner) that arrived in Thailand in 1965 and had a radar that could cover a sector of sky measuring around 120km either side of the aircraft. By bouncing the radar beam off the sea, that range could be extended to almost 240km. Neither Big Eye nor Red Crown attempted to guide US fighters to engage MiGs in the same 'close hold' manner that the Vietnamese did. Instead, they provided warnings and advice that helped the pilots create a mental picture of the battlespace and allowed them to chose where, when and how best to engage.

For USN pilots, the prospect of engaging MiGs improved in July 1966 with the introduction of the latest Sidewinder AAM, the AIM-9D, which the USAF had wanted no part of and which would prove to be a huge improvement over the earlier AIM-9B.

NORTH AMERICAN F-100D SUPER SABRE

Type: single-seat fighter-bomber

Powerplant: one 7711kW (17,000hp) Pratt & Whitney turbojet

Maximum speed: 1390km/h (864mph)

Service ceiling: 14,020m (46,000ft)

Weight: maximum take-off 9525kg (21,000lb)

Armament: four 20mm(0.79in) cannon; 2402kg (7500lb) bombs

Dimensions: span   11.82m (38ft 9.5in)
              length   14.36m (47ft 1.25in)
              height   4.95m (16ft 3in)
              wing area   35.77m² (385sq ft)

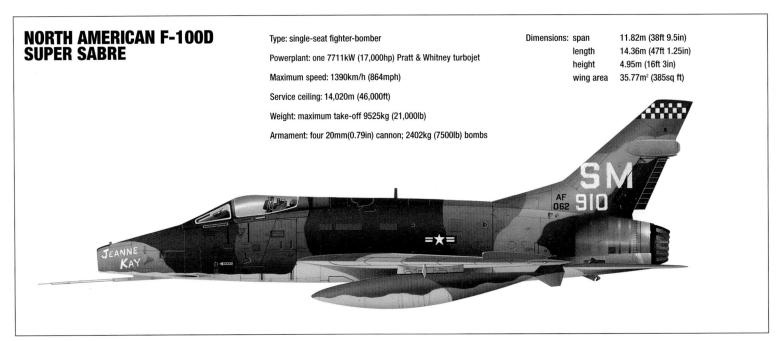

The new missile had a nitrogen-cooled seeker that made it more sensitive to a MiG's hot exhaust plume and less sensitive to the sun and clouds, and it also had an improved minimum range and a larger warhead.

IMPROVED ECM
On a positive note for the USAF, front-line F-105 wings were now beginning to receive an improved version of the QRC-160 ECM pod, and while the singleton tactical reconnaissance Voodoos and Phantoms had mixed results with the device, the 'Thud' community had strength in numbers and developed a 'pod formation'. This formation allowed a large number of F-105s to fly

a very precise formation that overlapped the coverage of all of their QRC-160s. The F-105s flew the formation at medium altitude, and although it took skill and discipline to execute, it paid off dramatically:

The US forces' standard short-range AAM was the AIM-9. Seen here on an F-8 Crusader of the US Navy, the Sidewinder had infra-red guidance to home on an enemy fighter's hot exhaust plume, and was thus a weapon with essentially rear-hemisphere engagement capability.

A SOVIET SIDEWINDER

The USSR had been busy developing its own short-range, infra-red-guided, air-to-air missile: the AA-2 'Atoll'. It appeared on the MiG-21 in the summer of 1966, but it was not until October that it claimed its first victim – a USAF F-4C. The 'Atoll' suited the 'Fishbed' and GCI combination perfectly: the pilot positioned the MiG behind his victim, made a Mach 1.4 supersonic slashing attack that saw two 'Atolls' ripple-fired in succession, and then pointed the aircraft's nose skyward to disengage from the fight. In many cases, the first indication a US pilot had that such an attack was taking place was the impact of the missile.

ALPHA STRIKES

By 1967, the US Navy had three carriers permanently on Yankee Station, each sustaining air operations for 12 hours to provide 24-hour coverage. The USN split its operations into two modes: cyclical operations, which saw 25 to 40 aircraft launched every hour and a half against targets in RP II, III and IV. These missions were ideal against the NVA's transport and logistics trails that threaded their way south below dense jungle canopy. Meanwhile, for RP VIb, the USN pooled its assets and flew large-scale Alpha strikes.

Alpha strikes took all the aircraft from a carrier wing and brought them together into a single strike package tasked with hitting a single target. This provided maximum mutual support and protection against NVA air defences and NVAF MiG-17, MiG-19 and MiG-21 fighters, and also concentrated the air wing's destructive power to improve the chances of being able to destroy the target.

In fact, the 5 August 1964 strike in response to the USS *Maddox* incident had been an Alpha strike involving 64 aircraft from the carriers USS *Constellation* and *Ticonderoga*.

Despite the difficulties it suffered in maintenance terms, the F-105 offered excellent range, speed and payload capabilities. Later in the war it was developed for the 'Wild Weasel' defence-suppression role with advanced electronics and the ability to tackle the radars associated with SAMs and AAA.

Right: In the twilight of its career by the time of Vietnam, the Falcon was the first AAM to enter full service anywhere in the world. The weapon was produced in many forms with two guidance types: semi-active radar and infra-red. These are AIM-4D missiles with infra-red guidance.

statistically, by 1968 it was taking more than 100 SA-2s to down a US fighter, whereas it had taken just 16 in 1965.

By now, the EC-121Ds in Thailand had been renamed College Eye and were using some of the most classified technology of the war to help keep US pilots' situational awareness of the battlespace as up to date and accurate as possible. Since March 1967 they had been equipped with the QRC-248, which could listen to the replies given by SRO-2 transponders on the MiGs. The NVAF GCI would send out a signal that 'interrogated' the SRO-2, and it would send a response

identifying it as friendly. In doing so, the SRO-2 allowed the NVAF GCI to keep track of its MiGs and steer them towards intercepts. Being able to pick up these signals was of huge benefit to the US, and soon fighter pilots in all three armed services were paying close attention to College Eye radio transmissions because, even though they didn't know why or how, they were invariably very accurate.

QRC-248 could also actively interrogate the MiGs' transponders, although the extreme sensitivity behind the technology meant that it was not until the summer of 1967 that the College Eye crews were permitted

to use the device in that mode of operation. At around the same time, the EC-121K Rivet Top also appeared in theatre. If anything, Rivet Top was even more classified than College Eye.

In addition to the QRC-248, Rivet Top carried custom-built electronics that allowed interrogation of a number of other Soviet-built IFF (identification friend or foe) transponders, but most importantly it carried a team of Rivet Gym linguists working for the National Security Agency (NSA) who could listen in on the NVAF GCI controllers' conversations with the MiGs, at the same time as actually monitoring the

Above: The USAF demanded a number of changes from naval standard for its version of the F-4 Phantom II multi-role fighter. One of the most important, and stemming from experience in the Vietnam War, was inbuilt and therefore more accurate rotary cannon armament.

MiGs' progress via their transponders. But in the ultimate paradox, Rivet Top's usefulness was limited because the NSA did not want anyone – including US fighter pilots who depended on GCI to help keep them alive – from knowing about it.

FALCON TRIALS

May 1967 had seen the arrival for evaluation of the AIM-4D Falcon AAM with USAF Phantom units, by now operating the air-to-ground optimized F-4D. It was hoped that it would improve on the AIM-9B, but the Falcon proved to be of little use in the dogfight scenario, where a convoluted

> Fifty-five MiGs had been shot down in the first half of 1967, and another 30 destroyed on the ground.

array of switches had to be flipped to arm it, following which its seeker head coolant ran for two minutes without any means for the pilot to temporarily halt the cooling. After the coolant ran out, the missile was effectively useless.

Characteristically intransigent, the USAF recognized the need to improve upon the AIM-9B, but instead of swallowing its pride and adopting the USN's successful AIM-9D, it commissioned the AIM-9E – basically an AIM-9B with a cooled seeker.

It was therefore fortunate indeed that the USAF's new F-4D Phantom had a lead-computing sight that could predict with good accuracy the impact point of 20mm rounds fired from the belly-mounted SUU-16/23 cannon pod. This gave the Phantom pilot a generally reliable weapon for the close-in fights that occasionally occurred between MiGs and US fighters and strike aircraft.

Such engagements were becoming few and far between as time moved on

and the NVAF consolidated. Fifty-five of its MiGs had been shot down in the first half of 1967, and another 30 destroyed on the ground: the majority of its air force had been eliminated. Even so, US performance in the air

The US Navy's finest attack warplane of the Vietnam War was the A-6 Intruder. This was firmly subsonic, but had long range, the ability to carry up to 8165kg (18,000lb) of ordnance, and advanced electronics allowing it to bomb with great accuracy under any weather conditions.

COMMANDO HUNT

Igloo White was an integral part of a USN-led covert operation against the Ho Chi Minh Trail conducted between late 1968 and mid-1972, and designated Operation Commando Hunt. This resulted in continuous round-the-clock bombing of the trail, with O-1 Bird Dog and OV-10 Bronco forward air controllers (FACs) directing attacks by F-100s, F-4s and F-105s, with B-52s conducting 'carpet-bombing' by day. Meanwhile, AC-119G Shadow and AC-119K Stinger, AC-47 Spooky and AC-130 Spectre gunships delivered streams of fire towards the ground by night. Between November 1968 and April 1969, Commando Hunt claimed 7322 enemy trucks destroyed. For the gunships in particular, policing the trail was hazardous, and of the six AC-130s lost between 1969 and 1972, all of them occurred while hunting for or engaging targets situated on the trails in Laos or South Vietnam. At the end of the Commando Hunt campaign in 1972 the USAF intelligence service claimed that 51,000 trucks and 3400 anti-aircraft guns had been destroyed.

fell short of what it had expected and the US was certainly nowhere near as dominant as it had been over Korea.

ECM pods for both F-105 and F-4 units had drastically increased survivability for the USAF, whose raids required air refuelling – which the NVAF monitored – and were therefore anything but a surprise when they arrived over North Vietnam. This

Below: F-105s refuel from a KC-135. This capability proved invaluable in Vietnam: aircraft could take off with a maximum warload and reduced fuel before topping up in the air, while damaged warplanes could take on the fuel they required to make it back to base.

made them vulnerable to an organized defence; by contrast, the USN strikes were far shorter in duration and therefore left the NVAF with less time to mount opposition, improving the USN's chances of survival accordingly.

Still the AIM-7 Sparrow problems persisted, however. USAF F-4s had fired 72 Sparrows for only eight hits,

and 59 AIM-9B Sidewinders for only 10 hits, making for respective Pks of only 11 per cent and 17 per cent when fired from the Phantom.

REFUELLING ASSETS

Key to any USAF missions flown over North Vietnam were the KC-135 Stratotanker refuelling aircraft. These orbited in a number of racetrack-

By 1972, most of the USAF F-4s flying out of bases in Thailand were of the F-4E variant, with fixed 20mm cannon in the nose. This example carries 500lb Mk 82 'dumb' bombs fitted with extended fuzes to ensure they exploded above ground for maximum effect.

patterned 'anchors', from where they topped up the fuel tanks of fighters about to enter North Vietnam to

Operating over very long ranges with huge bombloads, the B-52 heavy bombers were intended for the strategic role, but operated mainly in the tactical bombing role over Vietnam, saturating vast areas of jungle with concentrated patterns of conventional bombs.

bomb, and filled their exhausted fuel tanks as they made their way back home. Without them, the USAF could not have fought the war to anywhere near the same extent; tankers may not have made the headlines, but they were every bit as important as many of the more illustrious aircraft types.

By the end of 1968, President Johnson had already announced he would not be running for another

term in office, and had called a total halt to the bombing of North Vietnam. Rolling Thunder was over.

REFINED TACTICS

With time to reflect between bombing campaigns on the successes and failures of Rolling Thunder, it was clear that from a tactics perspective the USN was more progressive in its thinking than the USAF.

The USN used a formation that allowed two fighters known as a 'section' to support each other, with the lead jet engaging the enemy, and the 'free' second jet maintaining a loose formation that allowed it to monitor the fight, and check the

lead's vulnerable rear quarter (and his own). In case the lead jet had a problem or ran out of ammunition, the second jet could then become the 'engaged' fighter and begin shooting missiles and cannon.

Conversely, the USAF used a 'Fluid Four' or 'Fighting Wing' formation of four jets that saw numbers 2, 3 and 4 in a flight do little but stay in a rigid formation while the lead aircraft attempted to engage the enemy.

The USN's 'Loose Deuce' formation was flexible and provided mutual support, whereas the 'Fighting Wing' was difficult to fly and often left numbers 3 and 4 vulnerable to a surprise MiG-17 attack coming in from behind, or a MiG-21's supersonic slashing attack. There were occasions when these members of the flight could be shot down without the lead aircraft having any idea of their fate. The USAF knew by 1968 that USN tactics were superior, but for some reason or another decided to stick with its 'Fluid Four'.

USAF ADVANCES

The USAF looked to technology to help improve its performance. In 1968 it introduced the new F-4E Phantom with internal 20mm 'Gatling' gun; the new 'Dogfight Sparrow', the AIM-7E-2, which had a 475m minimum range and better capabilities against agile targets; and most impressively, the APX-80 Combat Tree interrogator modification for its F-4Ds, giving them the ability to interrogate the MiGs' IFFs in the same manner as both the EC-121D College Eye and EC-121K Rivet Top.

The USN used technology to complement its superior tactics and training. The improved F-4J arrived in

PRECISION WEAPONS

Linebacker was not only characterized by the contrasting performances of the USAF and USN against the MiGs, but also by the first large-scale use of precision-guided munitions (PGMs), which we now know today as 'smart bombs'. The television-guided AGM-62 Walleye sent a TV picture back to the launch aircraft, allowing it to monitor and control the weapon's targeting until the moment of impact. The Walleye was so precise that a bridge's individual spans could be targeted.

The Walleye was followed by the Paveway I laser-guided bomb (LGB), which took a standard general-purpose bomb and attached a laser seeker head, guidance fins at the front, and pop-out fins at the back to increase the bomb's glide distance. To guide the bomb to target, the backseater in the F-4 used a laser designator in his cockpit known as a 'Zot' to illuminate the target – the bomb tracked the reflected laser energy and guided down onto the target with great accuracy. Paveway had been evaluated in Vietnam in 1968, but the Rolling Thunder bombing halt had limited further combat trials of the weapon. Thereafter it was deployed in larger numbers, striking small AAA emplacements on the Ho Chi Minh Trail with great effect.

'Zot' was soon replaced with a pod-mounted laser target designator known as Pave Knife, which was gimbal-mounted so that the Phantom pilot could manoeuvre and the laser would remain centred on the target. Paveway became the most important weapon of Linebacker because it was reliable, accurate and cheap. It could also be used against targets that had traditionally been off limits, because previous bombing techniques and systems were not accurate enough to prevent civilian casualties.

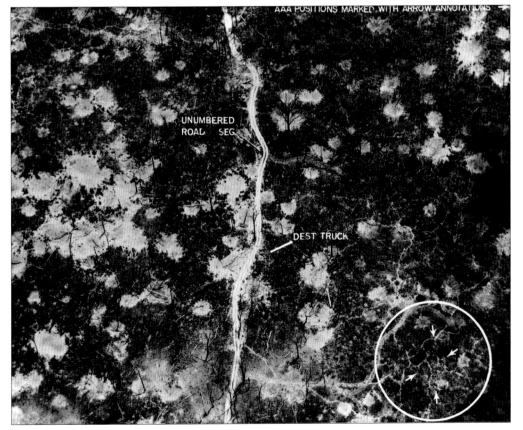

the summer of 1968, and the AIM-9G Sidewinder was set to improve on the already superior AIM-9D.

The NVAF was consolidating, too. The US political leadership halted bombing of the North for three and a half years, giving them ample chance to restock and re-evaluate their tactics. By May 1970 the NVAF had 265 MiGs on strength, and a new GCI network had been built to direct the MiGs as they went about their work.

With bombing of North Vietnam put on hold and MiG engagements

Saturation bombing by tightly controlled formations of aircraft such as the B-52, even from high altitude, was intense enough to flatten whole acres of the terrain below, destroying the jungle cover and shattering transport and communications networks.

therefore something of a rarity, the air war took on a form that consisted primarily of interdiction missions designed to stem the flow of supplies, ammunition and logistical support to NVA and Viet Cong (VC) militia making their way into South Vietnam.

Originating in North Vietnam and

Targeting the Ho Chi Minh Trail was a challenge because much of it was situated under jungle canopy, and because the NVA and VC moved predominantly at night.

One of the most hazardous but useful of all Vietnam missions was forward air control. The crews of aircraft such as the O-1 Bird Dog cruised slowly and at low altitude to call in attack aircraft and mark targets close to ground troops requiring close air support.

routing through neutral neighbouring Laos before entering South Vietnam, the communists' Ho Chi Minh Trail supply route was a spider's web of trails approximately 3000km in length. It carried the

supplies and war materiel required by the communist fighters. Targeting the trail was a challenge because much of it was situated under a dense jungle canopy, and because the NVA and VC moved predominantly at

night, when the chances of detection were slimmer.

The trail had long been an area of focus for the likes of the B-52 Stratofortress, whose 'carpet-bombing' Arc Light raids against the trail had been ongoing since 1965. B-52s flew 400 such missions between April and June 1966 alone. Between 1964 and the end of 1967 there were 103,148 tactical air sorties launched against the trail; these missions were supplemented by 1718 B-52 strikes.

The challenges posed by the Ho Chi Minh Trail prompted a wide array of technological innovations in an attempt to challenge them. The obvious answer to the jungle canopy was to spray a defoliant on the leaves, and so Agents Purple, Pink, Green and (most infamous of all) Orange were devised and used from 1961 to 1971. Sprayed variously from 'Hueys' and C-123 Provider airlifters, these herbicides/defoliants proved highly effective. Only later was it learned that they also increased the likelihood of genetic disorders and cancer.

With or without foliage, spotting or detecting enemy movements was made all the more difficult because the NVA and VC were masters of camouflage and deception. Initially, the US military used sensors mounted on 'Hueys' that could detect urine, but when a multitude of false alarms gave rise to the dawning realization that the elephants and water buffalo underneath the jungle canopy were also urinating, a different approach was sought!

IGLOO WHITE

That approach came in the form of the Igloo White programme, which used seismic sensors dropped in key locations from USN OP-2 Neptunes, and USAF HH-3 helicopters and Phantoms, to detect the passage of personnel nearby. Orbiting EC-121Rs

LINEBACKER II

When peace talks faltered once more in December 1972, President Richard Nixon ordered Operation Linebacker II into action. Linebacker II was a massive effort that targeted not the predominantly logistical and tactical targets of Rolling Thunder and the original Linebacker, but instead concentrated the tremendous destructive firepower of the B-52 on the cities of Haiphong and Hanoi. Finally, the administration in the US opened up a list of targets that had for the duration of the war been off limits, but which military commanders had always insisted should have been struck from the start of the war – this sort of political meddling in military matters was one of the defining characteristics of the war. But it was now all too little, too late.

collected the data transmitted by the sensors, which were then collated at a central Infiltration Surveillance Center in Thailand, and compared with traffic data supplied by other intelligence sources. From there, air strikes could be directed at key nodes of the trail.

The anti-infiltration effort was supported by MSQ-77 Combat Skyspot, a ground-based radar bombing system first introduced in 1966 to direct B-52 strikes in poor weather or at night. Skyspot directed a

quarter of all the strike missions conducted by the US during the conflict, and spawned the development of LORAN (long-range navigation): a series of radio transmitters that measured the time difference between signals from three

A US infantryman watches 'Huey' helicopters. Available in large numbers, the Bell UH-1 transformed the nature of ground warfare by providing much-enhanced tactical mobility to deliver troops, weapons and supplies, and to extract whole units or their casualties.

Seen here while delivering building equipment to a US fire base by means of LAPES (Low-Altitude Parachute Extraction System), the C-130 was the most capable tactical transport available to the US forces in Vietnam. Capacious and reliable, it offered semi-STOL performance.

or more transmitters to determine the position of an aircraft. Aircraft bombing with Skyspot or LORAN would be told when to release their weapons by a controller sitting on the ground, but the technique was really only useful against large area targets.

Skyspot and Igloo White were both tools that helped win the Battle of Khe Sanh between January and April 1968.

When the USMC found itself fighting off two division-sized elements of the NVA, Operation Niagara, a massive aerial bombardment campaign headed by the USAF (but with extensive USN and USMC involvement), was launched to support them. On an average day 350 strike assets, 60 B-52s, and 30 O-1 and OV-10 observation sorties would be flown. A total of 316 Igloo White sensors in 44 separate strings helped identify the covert night movements of the NVA forces.

The C-130 Hercules transport was one of the less likely heroes of Khe Sanh. The C-130s worked tirelessly

under AAA and small-arms fire to ferry supplies into the besieged airfield, itself heavily cratered following continuous NVA mortar fire.

SIEGE OF KHE SANH
The C-130 had established itself as a very valuable support tool for logistics and supply across the theatre, and Khe Sanh's requirements perfectly illustrated this: the base needed 60 tons per day in mid-January, later rising to 185 tons per day – 65 per cent of all supplies were delivered by C-130 parachute drops. USMC CH-46 Sea Knight twin-rotor helicopters, supported by A-4s providing AAA

> On the first day of Linebacker the Navy was rewarded with the honour of having the first US aces of the war when Randy Cunningham and William Driscoll claimed their fifth MiG 'kill' in their F-4J.

suppression, also ferried underslung loads into the base.

In May 1972 the USAF and USN commenced Operation Linebacker to interdict supplies and materials destined to support North Vietnam's planned invasion of South Vietnam. The targets included bridges, rail yards, and petroleum, oil and lubrication (POL) plants.

LINEBACKER UNLEASHED

On 10 May, the first day of the operation, a total of 414 sorties were flown, 120 by the USAF and 294 by the USN. There were more MiG engagements than on any other day of the war: four NVAF MiG-21s and seven MiG-17s were downed at a cost of two USAF F-4s. The USN lost two more aircraft when more than 100 SA-2s were launched into the approaching strike force; another 150 SAMs had been launched at various other points in the day without loss to US forces.

The USN, which had not been idle in the quiet period between bombing campaigns (and the concurrent air-to-air encounters with the NVAF), had formed the 'Top Gun' weapons school to further educate and train its pilots and radar intercept officers (RIOs).

US Navy A-6 Intruder attack aircraft unload their bombs over a communist target. Powered by two comparatively small turbojet engines, the Intruder was reliable and capable, and was flown by a two-man crew seated side-by-side in the spacious cockpit.

That investment was now paying off. On the first day of Linebacker the USN was rewarded with the honour of having the first US aces of the war when Randy Cunningham and William Driscoll claimed their fifth MiG 'kill' in their F-4J. The USAF, ever several steps behind, suffered miserably at the hands of the MiGs, and while the USN racked up a 6:1 'kill' ratio between May and June, it struggled to maintain a diabolical 1:1 even footing with the NVAF. Poor weapons, poor training and the antiquated 'Fighting Wing' formation all conspired to leave the USAF battered and bruised.

Between May and June B-52s, strike aircraft and gunships flew 18,000 sorties for a loss of 29 aircraft. Later in the operation, USN A-7 Corsair IIs and A-6s mined Haiphong harbour, effectively limiting the ability of China and the USSR to re-supply North Vietnam by sea. The pressure of the bombing campaign continued unabated, and almost 29,000 sorties were eventually flown between April and June. By now the effect was being felt, and the North Vietnamese's own official history recalls that only 30 per cent of its supplies now actually reached the front-line units.

In August, the GCI agencies Disco (College Eye) and Red Crown were routed through a central GCI centre called Tea Ball. Tea Ball took the 'take' of Disco and Red Crown and melded it with that of other sensitive intelligence-gathering platforms, including USAF RC-135 Combat Apple platforms, USN EC-121 Big Look aircraft and ground-based intercept stations manned by linguists. But, as with Rivet Gym, the security classification of some of the information Tea Ball received meant that a debate existed as to what information could actually be passed to the crews airborne over Vietnam.

Tea Ball did little to improve one of the US military's weakest areas – radio communications. With so many aircraft airborne and so many transmissions on a single frequency, the radios were often jammed with personnel talking over one another. When

communications broke down like this, everyone became more vulnerable to attack, and less effective altogether.

In September 1972, less than a month before the end of Linebacker, the new AIM-9J Sidewinder debuted with great success on Combat Tree-equipped F-4Ds and the newer gun-toting F-4E. The AIM-9J scored two

'kills' during two launches, both of which had been fired at the extremes of the missile's envelope. Weeks later, in another encounter, the missile scored only one hit out of eight firings, and the J-model Sidewinder started to look little better than the AIM-9B and AIM-9E weapons that it had superseded.

On 8 October the North Vietnamese agreed to negotiate a peace settlement, and on 23 October Operation Linebacker drew to a close (although bombing of the NVA and VC in South Vietnam and Laos continued unabated). The US administration had had enough and had been steadily withdrawing its forces from Vietnam even before the cessation of Linebacker, but the prospect of peace further fuelled the withdrawal.

RIVET HASTE

As the US military handed over its air bases in South Vietnam to the South Vietnamese Air Force from November 1972, the USAF's F-4E was being retrofitted with leading edge slats that drooped at low speeds and almost eradicated an aerodynamic phenomenon known as adverse yaw. Adverse yaw caused the aircraft to depart from controlled flight and could occur during dogfights if the pilot did not apply rudder instead of aileron to roll the big jet left and right when he was low on speed. The introduction of the so-called 'soft wing' slatted jets came under the codename Rivet Haste, which also saw the Phantoms equipped with Combat Tree and a Target Identification System Electro Optical (TISEO) camera mounted in a pod just outboard of the port wing root.

TISEO addressed an issue that had dogged US fighter pilots throughout the war and further impacted on the effectiveness of the AIM-7 Sparrow: the rules of engagement (RoE) by which every fighter pilot had to abide required each target to be visually

Operating from bases as distant as Andersen AFB on Guam – part of the Marianas group deep in the Pacific – the USAF's B-52 Stratofortress heavy bomber made extensive use of inflight refuelling to reach, attack and return from its various targets in Vietnam.

CESSNA O-2A

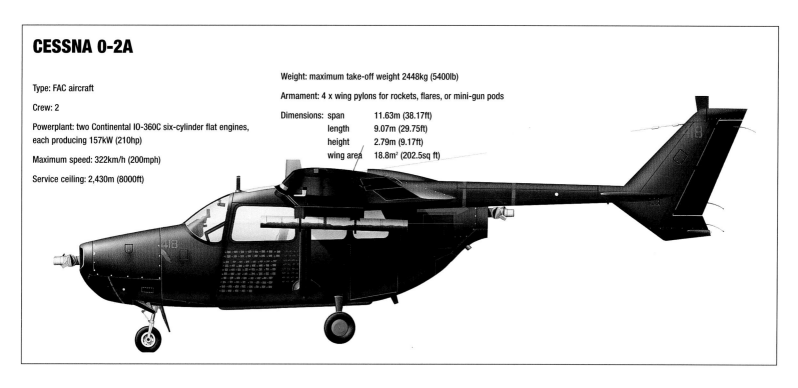

Type: FAC aircraft

Crew: 2

Powerplant: two Continental IO-360C six-cylinder flat engines, each producing 157kW (210hp)

Maximum speed: 322km/h (200mph)

Service ceiling: 2,430m (8000ft)

Weight: maximum take-off weight 2448kg (5400lb)

Armament: 4 x wing pylons for rockets, flares, or mini-gun pods

Dimensions:
span	11.63m	(38.17ft)
length	9.07m	(29.75ft)
height	2.79m	(9.17ft)
wing area	18.8m²	(202.5sq ft)

identified (VID) before it was fired upon. Throughout the war there were only a handful of occasions when this RoE could be broken – when Red Crown or Disco permitted it, and in a handful of Combat Tree engagements – and for the most part it meant that the Sparrow could not be fired at anything like its optimum range. Also, because the MiGs were very small and

difficult to see head-on, the US fighter pilot often found himself at dogfight range by the time he could VID the 'bogey' as a 'bandit'. By electronically slaving TISEO to the F-4E's radar, the TV set could display its picture in the Phantom's rear cockpit so that an early VID could be made.

The collapse of the next round of peace talks in December 1972 saw a

return to large-scale bombing operations, with Linebacker II now directed at the North Vietnamese

The B-52's weight-carrying capability was not fully exploited by the capacity of its internal bomb bay, designed primarily for the carriage of modest numbers of nuclear weapons. Many older aircraft were therefore adapted as 'bomb trucks' by the addition of external bomb racks.

cities of Haiphong and the capital, Hanoi. For 72 hours B-52s pounded the two cities. A few NVAF MiG-21s attempted to intercept the bombers, but the latter were protected by

Combat Tree-equipped Phantoms that thwarted them at every turn, and the B-52s proceeded to bomb the MiGs' airfields, which had previously been off target.

On the first night, 129 B-52s were launched, 87 of them from the Pacific island of Guam, and these were supported by EA-6A, EB-66 and F-105 'Wild Weasel' aircraft. The B-52s struck airfields, railroads, warehouses and powerplants, losing two B-52Ds

and a B-52G to SAMs. Meanwhile, F-4s were used to sow chaff corridors, dropping millions of strips of tin foil in a strip 10km wide and 50km long, giving the B-52 bombers a 32-minute 'window' in which the blooming chaff hid them from the search and acquisition radars of the SA-2s. These chaff corridors had first been introduced in the original Linebacker operation, but they were now more refined and much more effective.

The end in Vietnam was characterized by widespread confusion as the last Americans and many South Vietnamese tried to escape. Here, a 'Huey', perhaps only slightly damaged, is pushed over the edge of the deck of a US Navy vessel to make room for another refugee-filled helicopter.

On the second night of Linebacker II, the big bombers suffered not a single loss, although several were damaged. But the third night was to be the bloodiest. Firing an estimated 300 SAMs, the North Vietnamese had monitored the B-52s' tracks and jamming patterns and were better prepared. They downed four B-52Gs and three B-52Ds (a fourth B-52D was damaged and crashed in Laos as it attempted to limp back to Thailand).

THE FINAL PUSH

Following a brief stand-down over Christmas, the B-52s were once again bombing on 26 December. No less than 120 of the bombers clawed their way into the air that evening, and protected by 113 tactical support aircraft (jammers, escort and 'Wild Weasel' aircraft), they overwhelmed the tired and frayed North Vietnamese air defence network, suffering only one loss.

A similar cycle, to include 200 B-52 missions against targets in South Vietnam, continued for three more days until 29 December, when Linebacker II was halted. The two Linebacker operations ended with the

Troops rush to board a CH-53 helicopter. Larger and more powerful than the UH-1, the CH-53 offered a much greater payload but, like all other aircraft used to effect rescues as South Vietnam succumbed to defeat, it generally operated at weights far greater than those for which it had been intended.

USAF claiming an air-to-air 'kill' ratio of 2:1 and the USN a more respectable 6:1.

In mid-January 1973, President Nixon announced the cessation of offensive operations in Vietnam. The Paris Peace Accords were signed soon thereafter, officially ending US involvement in the war.

Middle East Wars

1945–1973

In the years after World War II and into the 21st century, the skies of the eastern Mediterranean – an area encompassing Egypt, Israel, Jordan, Lebanon, Palestine and Syria – have more often than not served as a proving ground for the latest airborne weapons, technology and tactics. The complex politics of these territories ensured that as early as 1945, aircraft were involved in diverse conflicts in the region.

At the close of World War II, the UK occupied Palestine, where they faced insurrection by the local Jewish militia; as early as 1945, the RAF was using Halifaxes, Warwick (and later Lancaster) maritime patrol aircraft and Austers to prevent further immigration by Jewish settlers. When militia violence escalated in 1946, RAF Spitfires were on hand to fly patrols. Meanwhile, the progenitor of the later Israeli Defence Force Air Force (IDF/AF) was active with a few light aircraft, a number of which were lost to ground fire. On the back of a UN vote, the UK left Palestine in 1948. Israel was created, and was, in fact, so quickly at war with its Arab neighbours that Egyptian Spitfires attacked Israeli airfields while they were still occupied by RAF Spitfires – UK forces claimed several invaders shot down.

Newly independent Israel was initially without genuine combat aircraft, with a small air arm of mainly light aircraft. Egyptian aircraft immediately began attacking Jewish territory as Arab forces advanced.

Israel began to receive the powerful F-4 Phantom II in 1969 and in the 15 years that followed the type was widely used in combat. Seen over Jerusalem, these F-4Es belong to No. 119 'Bat' Sqn, which began to take on the Phantom in 1970 and flew the type in the 1973 war.

These war-weary Boeing B-17s were among the first combat aircraft to be used by Israel and arrived during the war that followed the Jewish state's independence. As such, they were used to bomb Egyptian targets, including Cairo, from July 1948.

Egypt's Spitfires and Harvards flew unopposed until Israel acquired Czech-built S.199 fighters, which were followed into action by Spitfires, Beaufighters and P-51s. On the Arab side, Egypt was using both the C-47 and Harvards for bombing, before Israel acquired B-17 bombers that could take the war to Egypt. Rearming during periodic truces, the Israelis succeeded in maintaining their territorial integrity. Before an armistice came into force in January 1949, Israel had also managed to penetrate Egyptian territory, in a pointer towards future operations.

WAR IN THE SINAI

By 1956, Israeli and Arab air arms in the region had re-equipped: primarily with advanced French- and Soviet-supplied warplanes respectively. The Suez Crisis of that year provided Israel with an opportunity to stake its territorial claims, with an invasion into the Egyptian-controlled Sinai.

The Israelis received extra firepower from the French, in the form of Armée de l'Air F-84Fs, Mystère IVAs and Noratlas that arrived at IDF/AF bases. The Israeli action began on 29 October as P-51s attacked Egyptian positions, and paratroopers were dropped by C-47s with Meteor and Ouragan escorts. IDF/AF Mystères were on hand to maintain air superiority, and a drop of weapons was made by French Noratlas transports.

The first response to the invasion force was put up by Egyptian Air Force (EAF) MiG-15s, followed by Meteors and Vampires. The latter British-made types typically attacked ground forces, while the MiGs flew patrols and fought with Mystères. The Israelis advanced towards the Suez Canal, despite attacks by Egyptian aircraft and armour. The latter was blunted by the attentions of IDF/AF ground-attack sorties.

By the time that the RAF entered the fray on 31 October, IDF/AF dominance was effectively ensured, their final push to the Canal being covered by Mosquitoes, Ouragans and P-51s, while Israeli Mystères scored 'kills' against EAF MiGs. The

SELF-PRESERVATION FOR ISRAEL?

In April 1967, the IDF/AF's French-supplied Mystère fighters clashed with Syrian MiG-21s over Syrian territory in the Golan Heights. As Arab forces were redeployed and reinforced, Israel feared a large-scale Arab attack and in turn built up its forces along the Syrian border in May, before invading and holding territory in the Golan Heights, the Sinai and West Jordan. Israel declared their 1967 operation to be an act of self-defence, the prime minister later stating that 'the threat of destruction that hung over Israel since its establishment and which was about to be implemented has been removed.'

conclusion to the warfare saw rocket and napalm attacks along the Canal Zone by Mystères, Ouragans and P-51s and further use of paratroopers, while C-47s and Noratlas brought troops and materiel to the front.

IDF/AF B-17s also made a raid against the southern Sinai. Israeli occupation of the Sinai was achieved successfully by 5 November, but in the fallout of the wider Suez operation (see Chapter 7), these territorial gains would have to be given up.

THE SIX-DAY WAR

After 1956 there was relative peace in the Middle East, but by 1965, Israel was facing increasing border attacks by Palestinian guerrilla groups sponsored by Egypt and Syria. The Six-Day War that began on 5 June 1967 with an attack by Israel against neighbouring Arab states was a classic example of pre-emptive warfare, and the IDF/AF's destruction of Arab air forces on the ground – Operation

Although obsolete, Egypt's Vampire FB.Mk 52 fighter-bombers (this is a two-seat trainer version) were active over the Sinai in 1956. At least four examples were confirmed destroyed by IDF/AF Mystère IVAs during the October campaign fought over the Sinai.

Moked (Focus) – would have massive implications for Cold War air commanders worldwide.

On the morning of 5 June the first wave of IDF/AF strikes was launched and saw around 170 fighters and fighter-bombers directed against no less than 10 Egyptian air bases, achieving a considerable level of surprise. IDF/AF aircraft involved were Ouragans and Mystères flying from southern Israel to attack bases in the Sinai, while Super Mystères and Mirage IIIs attacked their objectives in the Canal Zone after flying in from the west. Although the Mirage III was designed as an interceptor, the aircraft was also well suited to the offensive role, and, serving with three squadrons, these fast-flying warplanes were typically tasked with attacking the more difficult objectives. The first wave succeeded in catching the EAF by surprise, arriving over its targets between 0745 and 0900, although a number of Egyptian MiG-21s did scramble and clash with Mirages over the airfield at Abu Sawayr.

Around 10 Israeli aircraft were lost in the first wave of strikes, but the damage they caused accounted for as many as 140 Egyptian aircraft, both on the ground and in the air. Further disruption was wrought by Israeli airborne ECM (electronic countermeasures) assets, including specially adapted Vautour IIN night-fighters. The Israelis would go on to benefit greatly from their 'head start' in the field of electronic warfare, and would later deploy a range of

Below: Israeli soldiers examine the remains of an Egyptian MiG-17 fighter at Al Arish in the Sinai. The MiG-17 was the most advanced Arab fighter in service during the fighting over the Sinai in 1956 and the type was still in large-scale Arab service at the time of the 1967 Six-Day War.

Above: Immediately prior to the Suez Crisis, Israel had re-equipped with a quantity of French-supplied jets, like this Dassault Ouragan fighter-bomber. The type was also used in an air defence role, scoring at least one confirmed air-to-air victory – an EAF Vampire – in 1956.

Around 10 Israeli aircraft were lost in the first wave of strikes, but the damage they caused accounted for as many as 140 Egyptian aircraft.

sophisticated ECM tactics and equipment in the Middle East conflicts that followed.

FOLLOW-UP RAID

A second wave of attacks was launched by the IDF/AF against airfield targets along the Nile, aircraft arriving over their targets from 10:00, and such raids continued throughout the day, involving the aircraft from the earlier strikes, plus Vautours. The second wave was slightly smaller in terms of overall aircraft numbers involved, but also hit 10 bases, and this time claimed in excess of 100 Arab aircraft

destroyed, for minimal Israeli losses. In order to gain an impression of the level of damage achieved on the EAF bases, the IDF/AF operated a pair of Mirage IIIs with specially adapted camera noses, for post-strike reconnaissance. The two waves completed their objective of disabling the EAF, but Egypt's Jordanian and Syrian allies were in a position to enter the air war, which they did on the same day, employing Jordanian Hunters and Syrian MiG-17s and MiG-21s for strikes on Israeli targets.

The IDF/AF responded in kind with a third wave of strikes that now attacked air bases in Jordan and Syria, with Mirages, Mystères, Ouragans and Vautours again involved. Once more, the IDF/AF threw around 100

ISRAELI EQUIPMENT IN 1967

At the time of the Six-Day War, the IDF/AF was operating a front line that was primarily equipped with French-supplied fighters and fighter-bombers; in addition to the straight-wing, first-generation Ouragan; the second-generation Vautour and Mystère IVA; and the supersonic Super Mystère B2, the Israelis were flying the most capable interceptor fighter in the region: the delta-wing Mirage IIICJ with air-to-air missile (AAM) armament. Some of these aircraft were, in fact, also involved in incidents of air combat in the run-up to the war, with Jordanian Hunters, Egyptian MiG-19s and Syrian MiG-21s all falling to the Israelis in 1966.

Above: Israel had a total of 16 Mystère IVAs in use at the outbreak of the 1956 Sinai conflict, with No. 101 Sqn based at Hatzor. The fighters put in a good performance in 1956, achieving at least eight confirmed aerial victories with their fixed armament of 30mm cannon.

warplanes into the fray for the third wave, striking another 10 airfields and destroying around 60 enemy aircraft.

THE GROUND CAMPAIGN

With the Egyptians deprived of adequate air cover in the Sinai, the Israeli ground forces made their move. Before the day was out, the IDF/AF had prosecuted a fourth wave of air strikes – the smallest of the day in terms of aircraft numbers – this time directed against five targets – mainly air bases – in Egypt and Syria, and including Cairo West (home to Tu-16 bombers) and an air base outside Damascus, the Syrian capital. Israeli armour moved west in three directions, with close support provided by armed Magister trainers.

The sixth of June saw Israeli air power deployed in support of the troops on the ground, and paratroopers were also landed by Super Frelon and S-58 helicopters. The EAF made attempts to harass

Israeli forces on the ground, using MiG-21s and Su-7 fighter-bombers, while IDF/AF aircraft continued to pummel Arab armour and interdict materiel heading to the front. At the same time, Israel attacked Jordan, driving towards Jerusalem. As they had against Egyptian armour, IDF/AF aircraft were charged with taking out

Below: The French-supplied Vautour was delivered to Israel in three subtypes: IIA for long-range strike (illustrated here), the IIN all-weather interceptor, and the IIB pathfinder and reconnaissance aircraft. The twin-jet warplane saw extensive use in the 1967 war.

RE-EQUIPMENT AFTER THE SIX-DAY WAR

Both Israel and the Arab forces became involved in a massive campaign of re-equipment after 1967, extending to their air forces, and this led to the arrival in the theatre of the RF/F-4 Phantom II (the fighter version introducing an important beyond visual range missile capability to the Middle East), A-4 Skyhawk light-attack aircraft and new versions of the MiG-21, among others. Arguably more significant was the arrival of more capable SAMs on the Arab side – large numbers of Soviet-supplied SA-2 and SA-3 high/medium-altitude, SA-6 medium-altitude and SA-7 shoulder-launched missiles would have a major impact on the coming confrontations in the Middle East and would, to a large extent, dictate tactics in the air. The Egyptians' new fighter equipment was based around increasingly advanced versions of the MiG-21 – the MiG-21PF and the MiG-21PFM – as well as Su-7 fighter-bombers from the USSR.

PALESTINIAN RAIDS

March 1968 saw Palestinian guerrillas launch a number of raids against Israeli troops from bases in Jordan. In order to counter the guerrillas, the Israelis launched a raid on terrorist bases, flying in troops in helicopters, but taking heavy losses in the process. In September 1968 there was another artillery bombardment in the Canal Zone, during which Egyptian MiG-17 fighter-bombers attacked targets in the Sinai and took losses to IDF/AF Mirages. In response to the Egyptian offensive, the Israelis launched a commando raid, in which S-58 helicopters were used to insert troops to attack strategic targets in Egypt.

Below: The remains of a Syrian fighter that was downed and crashed near an Israeli settlement in the Golan Heights. The aircraft, a Soviet-supplied MiG-21 'Fishbed', was apparently on a ground-attack or close-support mission, evidenced by the 57mm rocket pod visible among the wreckage.

Jordanian tanks and artillery in a push towards the River Jordan; again, the Magisters were called into action for CAS duties. Of concern for the Israelis was a mission launched by a single Iraqi Tu-16 bomber against an IDF/AF air base, but the intruder was shot down on its return flight to Egypt. In response, IDF/AF Mirages attacked the Iraqi bomber's base in Iraq, over which they fought with defending Iraqi Hunters.

On 7 June the IDF/AF found itself called upon to support the ground forces' drive towards Suez, during which large quantities of Arab armour were knocked out by the IDF/AF in the Mitla Pass. As the Israelis raced forward, paratroopers were deployed to the front by Noratlas, and others

Above: Designed as a primary trainer, the Fouga Magister gave good service in the light-attack role in a number of post-war conflicts. With the IDF/AF in 1967, the type was particularly active against armour on the Jordanian front, after it had been withdrawn from the Sinai.

delivered by helicopter. Jerusalem and bridges over the Jordan were captured, and the UN now engineered a ceasefire, with West Jordan now occupied by the Israelis. With the Jordan front silenced, 8 June saw the Israelis continue their objectives between the Sinai – scene of massed tank battles – and the Suez Canal, despite the attentions of EAF MiG-21s against their ground forces.

GOLAN FIGHTING

By 9 June, Egypt had agreed to a ceasefire, and Israeli attentions could now turn to the Syrian front and the Golan Heights. An armoured thrust into Syrian territory was bolstered by air power, but, despite support from

heliborne troops, the Israeli advance was relatively slow, and fighting continued into 10 June.

By the end of the day the Syrians too had signed a ceasefire agreement, as IDF/AF air power increased its tempo of attacks against

Syrian troops that were now left without effective air cover. On 10 October fighting came to an end, when Israel also agreed to the terms of a UN-brokered ceasefire, ending its forces' advance into Syria. Israel's territorial wins included the Sinai

MIG VERSUS MIRAGE

During air combats in the War of Attrition, Mirages clashed with MiG-21s and air-to-air confrontations continued for several months from early 1969. On a number of occasions the Israelis lured Egyptian MiGs into traps in which they were either ambushed by Mirages or engaged by Israeli HAWK surface-to-air missiles. Although the MiG's infra-red guided AAMs proved to be generally unreliable, on several occasions Mirages were claimed. In reality, the Soviet-supplied AA-2 missiles that armed the MiG-21 were little worse than the comparable AIM-9B, and Israel's Shafrir AAM also experienced serious reliability problems. July 1970 witnessed large-scale aerial battles, as the IDF/AF launched an entrapment ploy in which EAF fighters were to be lured into a 'kill box' in the Suez area, outside of Egyptian radar coverage. The tactic was successful, and the IDF/AF's Mirages claimed as many as nine MiG-21s destroyed, for just one loss. At the same time, the Mirages were scoring equally well on the Syrian front, and on one day claimed seven MiG-21s destroyed over Syria.

Peninsula, taken from Egypt in the south, and the vital Golan Heights taken from Syria in the north. At the same time, Jordan was thrown out of the West Bank and, as a result, Jerusalem, last occupied in 1948, was back in Israeli hands.

After the end of the Six-Day War, Egypt would launch the War of Attrition: an attempt to overcome Israel by a process of sustained bombardment and penetration into Israeli territory by land and air forces.

ARTILLERY EXCHANGE

As early as July 1967, the IDF/AF was in action, when an artillery exchange across the Suez Canal escalated and Israeli warplanes fought EAF MiG-17s and MiG-21s overhead; in the same month, EAF aircraft attempted to both attack and reconnoitre Israeli positions in the Sinai, losing a number of MiG-17s, MiG-21s and Su-7s in the process to Israeli air defences, including Mirage IIIs. In October 1967 Syrian MiG-19s penetrated into

Above: An oil refinery on the Suez Canal burns after an attack by Israel during the 1969 War of Attrition. A static conflict, much of the war was conducted through artillery barrages from either side, but also saw the use of commando raids and air strikes by both combatants.

Right: A pair of IDF troops hunkers down in the desert as an S-58 passes overhead. During the 1967 war, the Israelis made good use of both the S-58 and the Super Frelon for the commando assault role, on a number of occasions delivering troops behind Egyptian lines.

IDF/AF FIGHTERS ON THE OFFENSIVE

A key event in October 1969 was the first large-scale use of the IDF/AF's F-4E Phantom II, which was initially used on a mission against Egyptian SAM sites. Key targets for the IDF/AF in this period were air defence sites (as well as artillery), with the result that Israeli aircraft could penetrate into Egyptian airspace in order to fulfil their ground-attack objectives; indeed, in this year the IDF/AF even succeeded in flying Mirages over Cairo in 'show of force' missions that took place in June.

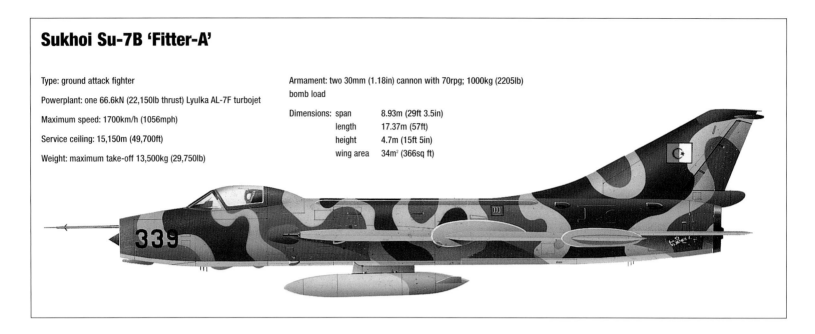

Sukhoi Su-7B 'Fitter-A'

Type: ground attack fighter

Powerplant: one 66.6kN (22,150lb thrust) Lyulka AL-7F turbojet

Maximum speed: 1700km/h (1056mph)

Service ceiling: 15,150m (49,700ft)

Weight: maximum take-off 13,500kg (29,750lb)

Armament: two 30mm (1.18in) cannon with 70rpg; 1000kg (2205lb) bomb load

Dimensions: span   8.93m (29ft 3.5in)
            length   17.37m (57ft)
            height   4.7m (15ft 5in)
            wing area   34m² (366sq ft)

Israeli territory, suffering losses to Mirages in the process, and the same month saw renewed artillery bombardment from either side of the Suez Canal lead to a commando raid launched by the Israelis – this was followed by construction of Israeli defences along the Canal. (By now, the IDF/AF had established forward bases from where Mirages and other fighters could be scrambled to challenge incoming attack aircraft at short notice, and it was Mirages from such bases that claimed the MiG-19s in October.)

In the course of 1968, a further commando raid was launched by Israel, this time using newly received Bell 205 helicopters. The objective was a number of bridges, all of which were put out of use. A more ambitious heliborne assault was made in December, when Bell 205s and Super Frelons flew commandos into Beirut airport, destroying airliners in reprisal for Lebanon's sponsorship of Palestinian guerrillas. In the continued effort to extinguish guerrilla groups, the IDF/AF also undertook a raid into Jordan in December, using Super Mystères.

THE WAR OF ATTRITION

The continued construction of Israeli defences along the Suez Canal – and in particular the so-called Bar-Lev Line – was ultimately the signal for Egypt to declare its War of Attrition in early 1969; this was to be spearheaded by artillery, a field in which the Egyptians enjoyed a degree of supremacy over their enemy. This in turn led to a response in kind from the IDF/AF, which sent aircraft to attack artillery and air defence installations on the other side of the Canal. In February 1969, the IDF/AF attacked targets in Syria and their fighter-bombers fought off the attentions of Syrian MiGs.

In March, the Egyptians launched a new offensive, with artillery and air power striking over the Canal, targeting Israeli command posts and other military objectives.

In the course of 1969 the IDF/AF began to make good their losses through the acquisition of the Mirage 5 – acquired by illicit means and named Nesher in Israeli service. A major new IDF/AF offensive began in July under the codename Boxer. This saw large-scale air strikes against Egyptian SAM sites and artillery positions, and these attacks escalated such that in one week the IDF/AF flew as many as 700 missions. The July attacks were countered by the EAF's air power, which in turn led to a series of raids against Israeli targets.

The IDF/AF offensive reached a new peak of activity in October 1969, with an attack on Egyptian targets that included air strikes against Suez SAM sites – up to 200 Israeli aircraft were involved; these were primarily A-4s escorted by Vautour ECM aircraft. In the same month, the Egyptians made a commando raid on an Israeli base – the Egyptian troops were transported to their objective by Mi-8 helicopters.

SYRIAN ASSAULT

On the Golan Heights, the Syrians began their attack at almost the same time as Egypt, on the afternoon of 6 October 1973. Again, tanks led the charge, with support provided by Su-7s and MiG-17s operating in a CAS role, and in common with the Egyptians, the Syrians deployed airborne troops using Mi-8 helicopters. Such was the pace of the Syrian advance, that operations were soon being conducted without SAM protection.

In early 1970 the IDF/AF ventured further into Egypt, attacking targets around Cairo as part of a large-scale campaign. In return, the EAF began to receive additional aid from the USSR, including the latest MiG-21MF fighters and crews. In April 1970 it was the turn of the EAF to make air raids on targets near the Canal, using Su-7s and other Soviet-supplied equipment. In May, the IDF/AF was back on the offensive, but was taking significant losses at the hands of SAMs. A major air battle was recorded in July, when IDF/AF A-4s, F-4s and Mirages clashed with MiG-21s, some of which were Soviet-flown. The War of Attrition came to a conclusion with a ceasefire of August 1970, by which time Arab losses in air combat were far outnumbering those of the IDF/AF.

THE YOM KIPPUR WAR

Following the end of the War of Attrition, the Egyptians continued to bolster their defences along their side of the Suez Canal, including additional SAM sites. During a period

In the course of 1969 the IDF/AF began to make good their losses through the acquisition of the Mirage 5 – acquired by illicit means and named Nesher in Israeli service.

of planning, the major Arab powers in the region – Egypt and Syria – agreed to launch an offensive against Israel, with the aim of recapturing territory lost in the 1967 war.

On 6 October 1973 – the holiest day in the Jewish calendar – Egypt and Syria invaded Israel. While Egyptian forces invaded from the south, with an armoured thrust across the eastern bank of the Suez Canal, Syria invaded from the north, with tanks and troops contesting the Golan Heights. The two fronts were to be spearheaded by armoured formations that would receive close support from warplanes.

The Arab invasion marked the

beginning of a two-week conflict – the Yom Kippur War – in which air power would again play a critical role; at the time of the outbreak of fighting, the Arab powers' air forces possessed numerical superiority over the IDF/AF. Also in Egypt and Syria's advantage was the availability of additional units drawn from the Algerian, Iraqi and Libyan air arms.

The IDF/AF's Nesher (Mirage 5) fighters were assembled locally using French-built components and served with four squadrons. Of the 61 aircraft delivered, many were later sold to Argentina and South Africa, the former seeing service as Daggers in the Falklands War.

A pair of IDF/AF Vautours of the type used by No. 110 'Knights of the North' Squadron during the opening phase of the Six-Day War, which focused on the destruction of the Egyptian Air Force on the ground. Vautours also provided ECM support for the raids.

The campaign began on the afternoon of 6 October with an Egyptian artillery barrage over the Suez Canal, before ground forces crossed the Canal at numerous points along its length. A major bridgehead was soon established, under the cover of the EAF, allowing heavy armour to roll into Israeli-controlled territory, but losses in the Canal Zone were heavy, and advanced landings of paratroopers by Egyptian Mi-8 helicopters proved very costly.

BOMBER RAIDS

Attempts by the IDF/AF to disrupt the Egyptian assault were countered by SAM belts located on the western bank of the Canal. In order to keep the IDF/AF on the ground, the EAF launched counter-air missions against Israeli air bases in the Sinai, while EAF Tu-16 bombers attempted to hit Israeli cities with cruise missiles.

The same afternoon the IDF/AF began to make counterattacks and record some air-to-air success against the EAF, making claims on aircraft that were flying outside of the defensive 'umbrella' over the western bank of the Canal. However, by the

end of the first day, the Egyptians had control of their objectives.

On 7 October the IDF/AF began its response in earnest, launching a

major campaign against EAF airfields, although protective measures ensured that the results were not as effective as those made during the Six-Day War. The next targets for the IDF/AF were the bridge crossing points assembled by the Egyptians over the Canal. As the Israelis gathered their ground forces to launch a sustained counteroffensive, they were subjected to harassment from EAF MiG-17s and Su-7s and Iraqi Hunters. The Syrian forces, meanwhile, were making further progress and succeeded in driving the Israelis to the outer perimeter of the Golan Heights.

SUPERPOWER SUPPORT

With attrition impacting on the air forces of both sides during the 1973 war, re-equipment was pursued with the aid of the US and USSR, among others. While the USSR supplied additional MiG-21s – including examples of the advanced MiG-21MF model and crews – the US supplied the IDF/AF with more A-4s and F-4s, as well as additional CH-53 helicopters. Another aspect in the IDF/AF's favour was the supply of more advanced electronic warfare self-protection equipment and other countermeasures from the US, which would help to reduce losses against Arab air defences.

In an effort to master the SAMs and radar-directed anti-aircraft artillery (AAA) before these caught up with the advancing ground forces in the Syrian sector, the IDF/AF deployed Super Mystères and F-4s against air defence sites, the latter type being equipped with AGM-45 Shrike anti-radiation missiles (ARMs).

On 8 October a major armoured battle saw Egyptian and Israeli tanks clash during an Israeli counterattack launched in the Canal Zone and, although air power was available to support the ground forces, the major losses were sustained to ground-launched anti-tank guided weapons.

While the IDF/AF again attempted to strike crossing points on the Canal, the Israelis' own ground forces came under attack from EAF and Iraqi aircraft, and the Egyptian advance into the territory on the eastern side of the Canal continued. Better results were achieved by the Israelis on the Syrian front, where the IDF/AF played a key role in gaining an upper hand against Syrian tanks through the use of close support. With much of the IDF/AF's strength tied up on the Syrian front, the Egyptians took the opportunity to try and make yet further advances, but their forces now

TUPOLEV TU-16 'Badger-A'

Type: medium bomber

Powerplant: two 93.2kN (20,900lb thrust) Mikulin RD-3M turbojets

Maximum speed: 960km/h (597mph)

Service ceiling: 15,000m (49,200ft)

Weight: maximum take-off 75,800kg (167,110lb)

Armament: two fixed forward-firing .303in Vickers machine-guns

Dimensions: span 32.99m (108ft 3in)
length 34.80m (114ft 2in)
height 10.36m (34ft 2in)
wing area 164.65m² (1772sq ft)

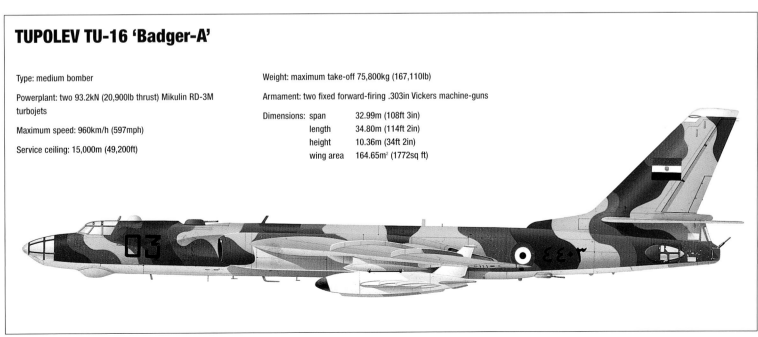

extended beyond the protection afforded by the SAMs, which made their aircraft more vulnerable to interception by the IDF/AF.

The appearance of the SA-6 SAM in combat then turned the tables once more in the favour of the Egyptians, and F-4s and – especially – A-4s proved vulnerable to this weapon when flying ground-attack sorties. On 10 October the Israelis made further efforts on the Syrian front, and they succeeded in driving the Syrian ground forces back to their original positions. In

concert with ground operations, the IDF/AF also attacked Syrian air bases.

By 11 October the situation had stabilized somewhat in the Sinai, while on the Syrian front, the Israelis launched their biggest operation of the war to date: a full-scale invasion of Syrian territory, preceded by a further wave of strikes against Syrian airfields.

On 12 October there was a resumption of fighting on the Egyptian front, as both Egyptian and Israeli ground forces, including armour, came under air attack. However, Israel was still putting the focus of its attention on the Syrian

> On 10 October the Israelis made further efforts on the Syrian front, and they succeeded in driving the Syrian ground forces back to their original positions.

IDF/AF Super Mystère B2s, with the nearest aircraft's cockpit protected against the desert heat by an improvised sunshade. This type suffered among the highest losses of the 1967 war on the Israeli side, partly a reflection of the hazardous close-support missions assigned to the Super Mystère fleet.

front, where the superiority of IDF/AF air power was beginning to tell over the battlefields of the desert.

The successful Israeli drive into Syria employed armoured thrusts together with air strikes and commando assaults launched by helicopters. Such were the advances made on the Syrian front that the Arab command now switched its priorities to the Egyptian front, and threw Jordanian ground forces into the fray. A huge armoured battle took place in the Sinai on 14 October and the Israelis emerged victorious, with a key role played by IDF/AF assets in the destruction of Egyptian tank formations.

ANTI-AIRFIELD RAIDS

In order to ensure that the Egyptian armoured columns would be denied air support – that could in turn harass the Israeli forces – the IDF/AF was sent against airfields in both Egypt

McDONNELL DOUGLAS F-4E PHANTOM II

Type: two-seat all weather fighter/attack aircraft

Powerplant: two 79.6kN (17,845lb thrust) General Electric J-79 turbojets

Maximum speed: 2390km/h (1485mph)

Service ceiling: 19,685m (60,000ft)

Weight: maximum take-off 26,308kg (58,000lb)

Armament: one 20mm (0.79in) cannon and four other weapons up to 1370kg (3020lb) on centreline pylon; 5888kg (12,980lb) bombload

Dimensions: span 11.7m (38ft 5in)
length 17.76m (58ft 3in)
height 4.96m (16ft 3in)
wing area 49.24m² (530sq ft)

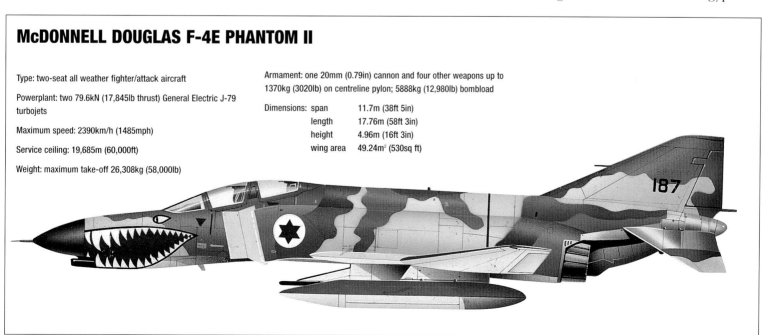

Left: The end of an Egyptian MiG-17 downed by the Israelis in 1973. The MiG-17 was no match for the Mirage III during the 1967 war and the type also suffered badly in the 1973 conflict, by which time it was totally outclassed by the missile-armed Phantom II and Nesher.

and Syria. On 15 October the Arab forces launched one final major offensive of the war, with brief gains made before the Israelis succeeded in retaking the territory in the Golan Heights. Meanwhile, on the Syrian front, the Israeli forces pushed towards Damascus.

With the Egyptian forces split on the Suez Canal front, the Israelis were able to drive into the gap and make a break across the Canal. Despite Egyptian counterattacks – which included air strikes by the EAF – the Israelis continued their push through the Canal Zone and were able to capture some of the prized SAM sites on the western side.

While the EAF continued to launch air raids on the Israeli ground forces, the IDF/AF in turn attacked Egyptian armour and SAM sites, and continued to deplete the EAF's fighting capacity with strikes against airfields. With another bridgehead established by the Israelis over the Canal, territorial gains now included a number of EAF airfields, such that supplies could be flown in direct to the combat zone from 20 October. By this stage the EAF was stretched to the limit – despite the arrival of reinforcements in the form of Libyan Mirage 5s, a handful of claims for which were made by the IDF/AF –

and losses were mounting. As well as attacking Israeli crossings of the Canal, the EAF was attempting to mount ground-attack sorties against the Israeli forward positions and to regain some degree of air superiority.

FINAL GAINS

On 22 October, with Israeli forces now within a few miles of Cairo, a UN-advised ceasefire was called, but not before Israel had made a few last territorial claims, assisted by heliborne commandos and paratroopers.

Fighting continued on 23 October, as Israel made further gains around

With its unit marking on the tail obscured by the Israeli censor, this A-4E Skyhawk was one of those available for service during the War of Attrition, the aircraft being part of a batch of ex-US Navy airframes delivered from 1969. The type proved vulnerable to SAMs in 1973.

the Canal Zone, extending its campaign against Egyptian air bases and air defence objectives. The EAF was still on call, however, and attempted to provide some relief for Egyptian forces that had been cut off in the eastern Canal Zone. In order to try and blunt the last Syrian air force resistance, the IDF/AF was also tackling Syrian warplanes both on the ground and in the air over the Golan Heights and deeper into Syria itself.

With a renewed UN ceasefire looming, the IDF/AF made concerted efforts to destroy as much of the Arab air forces' fighting potential as it could, but on 24 October, with US assistance, the ceasefire was finally agreed.

> With Israeli forces now within a few miles of Cairo, a UN-advised ceasefire was called, but not before Israel had made a few last territorial claims.

The Falklands and Lebanon 1982

The Falklands War was fought in 1982 between Argentina and the UK. Conflict was sparked when Argentine armed forces occupied the historically contested territory on 2 April to claim Argentina's sovereignty over the islands. The initial invasion was considered by Argentina as the re-occupation of its own territory, and by the UK as an invasion of an overseas territory, but war was never actually declared by either side.

The Argentine military government used the Falklands as a means of averting the attention of the general public from pressing domestic problems, and it did so on the ill-conceived idea that the UK would not respond in kind. Of course, the UK did respond, sending a Royal Navy (RN) Task Force to engage the Argentine navy and air force, with the aim of retaking the islands by amphibious assault.

As the Task Force headed south, Argentine Boeing 707 reconnaissance aircraft monitored its progress, but the first encounter between UK and Argentine forces occurred in late April, when the Argentine submarine, *Santa Fe*, was spotted by a Wessex HAS.Mk 3 anti-submarine warfare (ASW) helicopter, which promptly engaged it with depth charges. Wasp HAS.Mk 1 and Lynx HAS.Mk 2 helicopters scrambled from the fantails of other RN ships, with a Lynx launching a torpedo and strafing the surfaced submarine with machine-gun fire. Yet more Wasps became airborne and engaged the exposed submarine with AS.12 lightweight anti-ship missiles. Ultimately, *Santa Fe* was damaged badly enough to prevent her from submerging and her crew abandoned ship.

Most of Argentina's small fleet of IA-58A Pucara light-attack/COIN aircraft, based at Port Stanley airfield on the Falkland Islands, were disabled or destroyed by a daring Special Air Service (SAS) raid.

With Argentine Mirage IIIEA fighters restricted to operating from the mainland, Argentina was greatly hampered in its ability to protect its own troops on the islands from air attack, and in its desire to engage the RN Task Force located close to the coast. The Mirages lacked the range of the less numerous, Israeli-supplied Daggers (Israeli-assembled Mirage 5s), further limiting their use.

The biggest headache for the Argentine soldier and airman was the RN Fleet Air Arm's Sea Harrier FRS.Mk 1s. These 'jump jets' were stationed on the aircraft carriers HMS *Hermes* and *Invincible*: they began flying air-to-ground missions in support of UK forces on the ground, but it was in the air that they were most potent, and the US had secretly supplied the Fleet Air Arm (FAA) with the latest version of the Sidewinder missile, the AIM-9L. There was yet to be an air-to-air encounter in the war,

> The biggest headache for the Argentine soldier and airman was the RN Fleet Air Arm's Sea Harrier FRS.Mk 1 'jump jets'.

THE RAF AT WIDEAWAKE

By mid-April 1982, the Royal Air Force (RAF) had re-established itself at Wideawake airfield on the mid-Atlantic island of Ascension, from where it had once conducted free-fall, air-launched nuclear weapons trials. Sent to Wideawake were a force of Avro Vulcan B.Mk 2 bombers and Handley Page Victor K.Mk 2 refuelling aircraft, as well as Phantom FGR.Mk 2 all-weather interceptor fighters to escort them. The Victors would also undertake reconnaissance missions to help map the Falkland Islands prior to the arrival of the naval Task Force.

Left: The effectiveness of the RAF's Vulcan raids remains contested, even today. What is undeniable, however, is that the raids restricted the use of aircraft at Port Stanley, and served notice to the Argentine government that the UK had the capability to strike targets at will.

but when it came Argentina would be in for a shock – the AIM-9L was going to be pivotal in the FAA's ability to secure air superiority.

STRIKE FORCES

The first major Argentine strike force was comprised of a mixed force of 36 aircraft: A-4 Skyhawks, Daggers, Canberras, and Mirage III escorts, but only the Daggers found the Task Force and the engagement ended in stalemate. However, marauding Sea Harriers from *Invincible* intercepted a Dagger and a Canberra, shooting down both. Then the Harriers engaged two Mirage IIIs, shooting

down one (the other escaped to Stanley, only to be shot down by trigger-happy Argentine defenders).

From the first encounter onwards the Sea Harrier dominated the air-to-air fight, recording a total of 21 'kills', the majority with the AIM-9L, throughout the 74-day conflict. Although the Argentine fighters were often operating at the edge of their maximum range, meaning they had little fuel for dogfights, this was largely academic. The Sea Harrier pilots were the better dogfighters, and adding the excellent Blue Fox radar and AIM-9L to the mix put matters beyond doubt.

But the air war was far from being all one-sided. Argentina had acquired the air-launched AM.39 Exocet anti-ship missile from France, and an Argentine navy P-2 Neptune patrol aircraft spotted three RN radar picket ships on 2 May. Two Argentine Super Étendards were scrambled, each

HAWKER SIDDELEY NIMROD

Type: Maritime Patrol aircraft

Powerplant: 4 x 54.09kN (12,160lbf) Rolls-Royce Spey turbofans

Maximum speed: 923km/h (575mph)

Service ceiling: 13,411m (44,000ft)

Weights: maximum take-off weight: 105,376kg (232,315lb)

Armament: various bombs, laser-guided bombs, air-to-surface missiles, torpedoes and mines

Dimensions: span 35.00m (114ft 10in)
length 38.6m (126ft 9in)
height 9.45m (31ft)
wing area 197.05m² (2,121 sq ft)

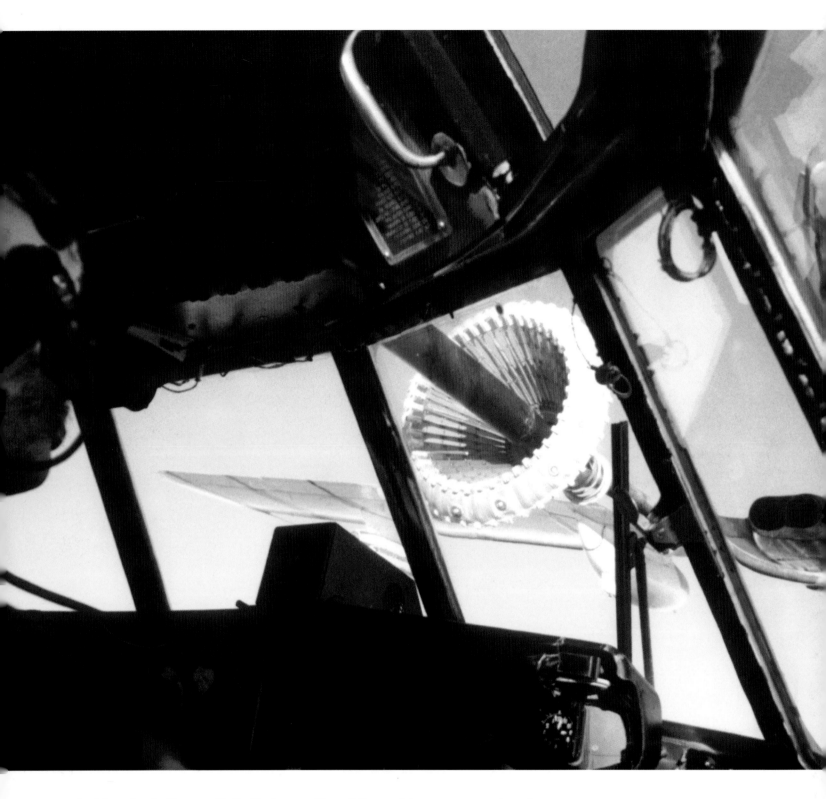

armed with a single Exocet. Refuelled by an Argentine KC-130H Hercules after launch, they went in at low altitude and fired their missiles as far as 48km (30 miles) from their targets. HMS *Sheffield*, a Type 42 destroyer, was hit by one of the missiles and eventually sank. Later, an Exocet sank the support ship *Atlantic Conveyor*, and another of the missiles struck and damaged the 'County'-class destroyer HMS *Glamorgan*.

Free-fall munitions were employed by the RAF's Harrier GR.Mk 3s (operating off the RN's aircraft carriers) as they supported UK troops, and to an even greater effect by Argentina's A-4s, which sunk the Type 21 frigate HMS *Ardent*, the Type 42 destroyer HMS *Coventry*, and the troop landing ships *Sir Galahad* and *Sir Tristram*. All of these ships were sunk with unguided bombs. On June 14 the Argentine garrison at Stanley

Above: Key to the UK's ability to launch long-range missions from Wideawake was the inflight refuelling provided by Victor tankers, this example being photographed from a C-130. These tankers also provided air refuelling for aircraft on their way from the UK to Ascension.

Right: The RAF also deployed a number of Harriers onboard the RN's two carriers. They assumed ground-attack and reconnaissance duties, while the Sea Harriers were responsible for combat air patrol (CAP) and escort missions.

OPERATION BLACK BUCK

Based at Wideawake, the RAF's Vulcans were prepared for a series of raids on the Falklands' main airport at Port Stanley. The codename for the raids was Black Buck, and although their effectiveness remains a subject of debate, it is certain that the Argentine air force and naval air arm were limited in their ability to use the airfield – and that had been the aim of the main Black Buck missions. Other Black Buck missions employed US-supplied AGM-45 Shrike ARMs to target threat radars on the islands. It required 11 Victor tankers to get two Vulcans to their target, which ultimately amounted to an unsustainable logistical effort for the contingent on Wideawake.

surrendered, and the UK declared that hostilities were over on June 20. The Falklands were in British hands once more.

Below: The Argentine air force had a small number of MB.339 light-attack aircraft based at Port Stanley. Many of these were destroyed or damaged on the ground by the strafing runs of Sea Harriers and RAF Harriers. Some were also damaged in an SAS raid.

1982 LEBANON WAR

In June 1982, Israeli ground forces invaded neighbouring Lebanon. They did so in a bid to put a halt to cross-border terror attacks by Palestine Liberation Organization (PLO) militants based in southern Lebanon.

The 1982 Lebanon War was waged by Israel under the codename Operation Peace for Galilee.

The standing of the Israeli Defence Force Air Force (IDF/AF) as the pre-eminent air arm in the Middle East was in some doubt by 1982. The IDF/AF had dominated the Six-Day War of June 1967, and over the course of 3300 sorties had bloodied the noses of the Soviet-equipped air forces of Egypt, Syria and Jordan. Combined, 400 of its neighbours' aircraft had been shot down in the sky, or destroyed on the ground by Israel.

FACING THE SAM THREAT

But it wasn't the Arab air arms' aircraft that most concerned Israel as it contemplated Operation Peace for Galilee. It was their surface-to-air missiles (SAMs). Between 1969 and 1970, Israel had battled Egypt in what became known as the War of Attrition, and it was then that a new range of SAMs had been employed against

From a 'stick' of unguided bombs rippled at an angle across the runway by a Black Buck Vulcan, only a single bomb impacted Port Stanley's runway itself. The bomb ruptured the surface of the runway, but the physical damage was soon repaired by the Argentine occupiers.

them. Although the Egyptian SAM sites were attacked sporadically, there had been no concerted effort to take down the Egyptian air defence system in its entirety and IDF/AF loss statistics reflected this; at the height of the War of Attrition, Israel's aircraft were coming off worse against the SAMs. Whereas the IDF/AF had enjoyed a 40:1 'kill' to loss ratio against Arab jet fighters, it was experiencing a 2:1 loss ratio against the SAMs.

While Israel initially underestimated Egyptian SAMs, another part of the problem was that Egypt had applied pressure on Moscow and secured the latest battlefield SAM at the time, the SA-6. Israeli pilots knew the SA-6 as 'three fingers of death', on account of the appearance of the triple launcher configuration, and the SAM featured a number of tracked armoured vehicles each carrying components of the system: 'Straight Flush' tracking radar, a missile-loading crane, missile transporter-erector launchers (TELs), and spare missiles. As such, the SA-6 was very mobile and difficult to locate. The SA-6 was also a much more potent weapon than the SA-2 or SA-3 that preceded it. As a medium-range SAM, it was particularly well suited to

AGUSTA A109

Type: helicopter

Powerplant: Two 426kW (567hp) Turbomeca Arrius 2K1 turboshafts

Maximum speed: 285km/h (154 knots, 177mph)

Service ceiling: 5974m (19,600ft)

Weights: maximum take-off weight: 2850kg (6283lb)

Armament (options): 12.7mm machine-gun (250 rounds) in pod, pintle mounted 7.62mm machine-gun, door gunner post 12.7mm machine-gun; 2 TOW missile launchers (2 or 4 missiles each); unguided rockets in pods (2.75in or 81mm rockets with 7 or 12 tubes per pod)

Dimensions: Rotor diameter 11.00m (36ft 2in)
length   13.04m (42ft 9in)
height   3.50m (11ft 6in)

A CH-53 helicopter helps the Israeli Defence Force (IDF) prepare for the battle ahead. One of the IDF/AF's key remits was to provide close air support to the Israeli forces on the ground, and that required the destruction of Syria's 'umbrella' of SAMs and AAA that had been moved in to protect airspace over Lebanon.

defending infantry and armour. Its radar could reach out and track a jet fighter from as far away as 75km (47 miles) and begin illumination and guidance at 28km (17 miles). Because Israeli radar warning receiver (RWR) equipment at that time was not programmed to detect the SA-6, the first thing many Israeli pilots knew about it was when they saw the smoking missile headed their way, or worse, when the warhead detonated close by.

OPPOSITION NUMBERS

Israel reacted, reprogramming its RWR equipment accordingly, but by the time of the Yom Kippur War its losses against a myriad of Egyptian SAMs (20 SA-6s, 70 SA-2s, 65 SA-3s, 2500 AAA pieces, and as many as 3000 shoulder-launched SA-7s) were still

ISRAEL'S SAM HUNTERS

When the IDF/AF launched its first sorties of the war on 9 June 1982, the question of who would emerge victorious, the SAM or the jet fighter, was soon answered. In the first 24 hours, Israel claims it destroyed 17 of Syria's 19 SAM sites for not a single loss in combat. It was a stunning and incontrovertible victory, and it came in no small part because of solid preparation by Israel and the intelligent use of what were then called remotely piloted vehicles, or RPVs.

unsustainable. In the first three days, the IDF/AF lost 50 aircraft, and later lost 53 of its 170 A-4 Skyhawks and 33 of its 177 F-4 Phantoms.

The lesson, that the SAM and AAA threat was one that required specific and decisive attention, had been written in blood. Come 1982, it was a lesson that had not been forgotten, but equally it had also generated few definitive solutions.

As tensions and hostilities between Israel and the Palestinians and

Lebanon intensified in 1981, Syria began to deploy its first SAM brigades to the Beka'a Valley of Lebanon. The move followed the shoot-down by the IDF/AF of two Syrian helicopters that had been participating in operations against Lebanese Christians in southern Lebanon.

PEACE FOR GALILEE

Israeli planners were already drafting plans and drawing up target lists for an Israeli invasion of Lebanon, but

the Syrian move raised the stakes. The real question was whether modern jet fighters could prevail against modern SAMs, and there were already senior figures in the world's air forces, including the

Below: Israel became the first international customer for the F-15 Eagle when it purchased its first batch in 1977. The Eagle provided a quantum leap in capability compared to previous jet fighters, as the Syrians were soon to discover.

IDF/AF, who thought that the SAM would reign supreme and that the jet fighter had had its day. The answer would be pivotal to the development and future of air warfare.

SAMs were more than just a deadly threat to aircraft and their pilots, they were also a lynchpin in the complex strategic relationship between different missions and objectives of the war: the IDF/AF would be required to bomb the massed artillery and SAM sites that posed a great threat to the Israeli war machine and that had been building up in southern Lebanon for almost a year. Israel would also have to guard its advancing army from air attack as well as provide close air support (CAS) when their troops came into contact with the enemy. If the SAMs were allowed to remain active, then the IDF/AF's ability to achieve any of these aims would be severely hampered, and losses would be unsustainable.

In addition, the Arab pilots rapidly realized that operating outside of their own SAM 'umbrella' would lead to massive losses at the hands of the IDF/AF. When operating within the 'umbrella', they would be at a distinct advantage. As such, destroying the SAMs' protective coverage would also expose any MiGs to the IDF/AF's own fighters. The Vietnam War, the War of Attrition and the Yom Kippur War were all testament to these realities.

DRONES AT WAR
For several months before Peace for Galilee, Israeli remotely piloted vehicles (RPVs) had 'fingerprinted' the Syrian SAMs by gathering the electronic frequencies of their radars. This allowed Israel to both plot the position of the radars, and allowed specific frequencies to be programmed into Israel's air-launched AGM-45 Shrike and AGM-78 Standard anti-radiation missiles (ARMs) that

Israel used its F-4E Phantom IIs as hunter-killers against Syrian air defences. The Phantom was beginning to show its age, but was still considered a versatile strike-fighter that could inflict significant damage – on the ground and in the air – when used carefully.

were to be employed for defence suppression on the first day of the war.

The Syrian SAM operators had failed to maintain a level of emission control that kept the Israelis guessing. Even so, Israeli RPVs were also responsible for spotting and tracking the movements of five more SA-6 systems that arrived at the last minute on the day before Israel attacked. Up until that point, the target list for attack comprised 14 SAM batteries that already constituted a thick defensive belt along the southern Lebanon border.

When the attack came on 9 June, the RPVs were the first aircraft to be sent over the battlefield, emitting false

> Syria had made several errors in the course of the first few hours of fighting. Perhaps the worst was ordering its MiGs home when the SAMs started to detect the false signals being generated by the RPVs.

target returns to the waiting Syrian SAM batteries, to give the radar operators the impression that a massive Israeli air raid was inbound. The Syrians responded with full commitment, bringing most of their SAM radars online and firing volleys of missiles at the drones. With their TELs exhausted, the Syrian batteries scrambled to load replacement missiles into place, but as they did so the real

IDF/AF strike force was already inbound, having followed the drones at a safe distance. The real attack – F-15 Eagles and F-16 Fighting Falcons to intercept Syrian MiGs, and F-4E Phantoms to shoot ARMs at the SAMs – made light work of the Syrian radars, and Israeli artillery also pounded those SAM sites that fell within its arc of fire.

Apart from electronically signalling to the Israelis where their fixed SAMs

were, both before and during the first day, and allowing Israel to track their mobile SA-6s, Syria had made several errors in the course of the first few hours of fighting. Perhaps the worst was ordering its combat air patrol (CAP) MiGs home when the SAMs started to detect the false signals being generated by the RPVs.

They had done so not only because they had been humbled by the IDF/AF in air combat before, but also because there existed the distinct possibility that the MiGs would be shot down by their own forces if they

Below: Some of the aerial 'kills' of the war were scored at low altitude, where Syrian fighters had descended to make good either their attack or their escape. Invariably, they were run down by marauding Israeli fighters, which stayed high and used diving tactics to help close the gap.

remained under the SAM 'umbrella' when it became saturated by Israeli aircraft – it was a major chink in the air defence system's suit of armour. But had the MiGs simply stayed close, the dynamics of the whole engagement would have changed. Israel would have had a more

complicated equation to solve that may have resulted in some SAM sites surviving the first wave of attacks.

With the fixed SAMs now largely neutralized, and the SA-6s on the move, the IDF/AF's fighters and fighter-bombers started flying over southern Lebanon in great numbers.

ISRAEL'S EYES OVER THE BATTLEFIELD

Israel's exceptionally well coordinated attacks were possible because its pilots had been practising the timings and choreography of their run-in for months, and because they dominated command, control, and intelligence over the battlefield. Information came from a number of sources, but in the air it was the IDF/AF's E-2 Hawkeye, supplied by the US, that provided the most comprehensive picture. Inside a large rotating dome mounted above the fuselage, the Hawkeye's radar penetrated deep into Lebanese and Syrian airspace and provided a comprehensive picture of the battlespace. This radar picture was transmitted via a radio datalink to a central command post at which many other sources of real-time intelligence and data were also assimilated and assessed. These other sources included video streaming from electro-optical cameras mounted on the RPVs that buzzed tirelessly throughout the day and kept tabs on the remaining mobile SA-6s.

The IDF/AF used a 'hi-lo' mix of fighters: high-technology interceptors like the F-15; and low-technology Kfirs, which lacked radar-guided missiles, but could close to short range and employ infra-red-guided missiles and cannon.

The job of keeping them all informed on enemy MiGs and SAMs, and providing deconfliction to one another, fell to the radar operators in E-2 Hawkeyes, who sometimes had more than 100 Israeli aircraft on their radar scopes at any one time.

PHANTOMS IN ACTION
The IDF/AF F-4s went about their SAM-killing business and then turned their attention to other fixed targets, striking methodically but quickly. They opted to use conventional unguided 'dumb' bombs rather than the laser-guided bombs (LGBs) sourced from the US because the former could be delivered expeditiously from a broad flight envelope, while the latter took time to

Key to Israel's dominance of the air war over Lebanon was the E-2 Hawkeye. Instrumental in the destruction of the Syrian air force's capability in 1982, IDF/AF Hawkeyes like this were used to vector F-15 and F-16 fighters against the Syrian MiG-21s and MiG-23s.

set-up and had a restrictive envelope. This left the Phantom pilots and weapons systems officers (WSOs) vulnerable to the remaining SAMs and the radar-directed fire of the feared ZSU-23-4 radar-guided, self-propelled AAA system. Once the ARMs neutralized the SAMs' radars, bombs were used to mop up the remaining SAM components, with the missile launchers taking priority.

While SAMs may have caused the IDF/AF headaches in 1973, the opposition MiGs had not, and Israel claimed to have downed some 277 enemy aircraft. IDF/AF claims for Operation Peace for Galilee which, at the time, represented the largest engagement of fighter jets in history, would prove to be equally as successful, if a little less emphatic: 86 Syrian aircraft were claimed destroyed for no Israeli combat losses.

The Syrian demise had occurred in predictable fashion. It had taken Syrian commanders 20 minutes to reverse their decision to send their CAP fighters back to base at the sign of the first attack, so by the time the

order had been given to scramble newly fuelled fighters to the border, the Israeli F-16s and F-15s were ready and lying in wait.

EARLY WARNING ASSETS

The IDF/AF E-2s provided ample warning that the Syrians had scrambled their fighters, and kept the command posts informed of their progress via datalink, and the F-15s via VHF (very high frequency) radio.

IDF/AF tactics were not unlike those developed by the US Navy during the Vietnam War: a four-ship formation of F-15 Eagles would fly together in two 'sections' of two aircraft. They would use their far-reaching AN/APG-63 radars to 'see' the Syrian fighters while still well beyond visual range (or use the Hawkeye controller to vector them towards the enemy until they were sighted on radar or visually). More often than not, the engagement would be over in a matter of minutes.

As the Eagles pressed home their interceptions, Israel's electronic warfare systems were used to jam the

Syrians' communication channels, effectively cutting their MiG-21 and MiG-23 fighters off from the outside world. Since the Syrians were Soviet-equipped and trained, they generally operated the 'close hold' system that relied on a ground control intercept (GCI) officer sat at radar screen to direct them to the enemy. The GCI officer would tell the pilots where and when to make basic 'slashing' attacks, and it was the GCI controller and not the pilot that controlled the engagement. As such, the Syrian pilots were severely lacking in situational awareness when they could no longer talk to or hear their GCI officer. To exacerbate this problem, the Syrians also lacked dogfighting skills, since this was a form of combat they had rarely trained for.

In common with most western fighter pilots, the Israeli pilots were proficient in dogfighting and were encouraged to operate independently; they used GCI officers and the Hawkeyes to get them the best situational awareness they could attain, but the tactical decisions about how, where, and when to engage were the responsibility of the pilots themselves.

The Syrian fighter pilots largely entered the fight without a proper game plan and reportedly often did little more than freeze in sheer terror. It was a turkey shoot, and one claim puts the result at as many as 26 MiGs downed by the IDF/AF fighters in the first 30 minutes.

The stage had been set: Israel had air superiority and Syrian forces on the ground in southern Lebanon were

TANK KILLERS OVER GALILEE

Bell AH-1 Cobra helicopter gunships used BGM-71 TOW (Tube-launched, Optically-tracked, Wire-guided) missiles against Syrian armour and were credited with destroying dozens of Syrian fighting vehicles, including the modern Soviet-built T-72 main battle tank. The Cobra was the first dedicated US helicopter gunship, and was actually an amalgamation of a new fuselage design with the UH-1's tail boom and powerplant (engine and transmission). It has a co-pilot/gunner (CPG) who sits up front and aims the TOW with a telescopic sight housed in a turret in the nose, and aims the M197 three-barrelled 20mm 'Gatling' gun in a corresponding turret underneath the nose. It is an excellent gunship, and although it was combat-proven in Vietnam, Operation Peace for Galilee was the first large-scale employment of the very successful air-launched TOW missile.

forces had entered Lebanon. The main brunt of the war was over and Syria's air arm had ceased to put up any meaningful resistance. The IDF/AF had dominated the fighting in the air from start to finish.

While the political benefits of the war were questionable, it became an example in the classrooms of military academies and war colleges around the world of the fact that good planning, command and control, and real-time communications could bring about total destruction of the enemy's capability to defend itself.

now open to both land and air attack. The F-4 Phantoms duly obliged, now employing more guided weaponry against enemy tanks and armoured personnel carriers, as well as a great many AAA positions.

Having achieved its objective and neutralized the PLO inside a 40km (25 mile) swathe of southern Lebanon, Israel called a halt to its military advance just five days after the Israeli Defence Force (IDF) ground

One of the best close-support platforms used by Israel was the AH-1S. The Cobra could shadow IDF troops, or roam ahead to neutralize Lebanese and Syrian infantry and armoured vehicles using either its 20mm gun, unguided rockets, or TOW anti-armour missiles.

Desert Storm and the Balkans
1990–1999

On 2 August 1990, Iraq acted upon its historical claim to the small, oil-rich country of Kuwait. The Iraqi dictator, Saddam Hussein, ordered a large invasion force to take control of Iraq's Arab neighbour. The international community's initial military response was defensive in nature and was titled Operation Desert Shield. Desert Shield allowed Coalition forces to amass while diplomacy took its course. The military build-up was massive by any definition.

First to arrive were US Air Force (USAF) F-15C Eagles and F-15E Strike Eagles, whose responsibility it was to patrol the skies of Saudi Arabia to dissuade Saddam Hussein from making a further claim on any Saudi oilfields. Twenty-seven F-15s arrived fully armed at Dhahran Air Base (AB), Saudi Arabia, on 7 August. The next day, an additional 25 F-15s followed, completing the arrival of 52 Eagles in just two days.

On 9 August F-15Es arrived at Thumrait AB, Oman, via Dhahran AB, Saudi Arabia. Thumrait had stockpiles of weapons that had been stored by the US for just such an eventuality, and while the exact orders to the F-15Es were unclear, the reality of the situation was stark; nine of Saddam Hussein's elite Republican Guard units stood at the Kuwaiti border ready to drive south into Saudi Arabia. It quickly became evident that

In Iraq the A-10 struck Iraqi armour and infantry with alacrity, incurring remarkably few losses in the process. In the Balkans, it did much the same, but this time without any losses.

The most successful fighter of the war was the F-15C Eagle. This example belongs to the highest scoring unit, the USAF's 58th TFS and carries a full load of Sidewinder and Sparrow missiles.

the F-15Es were the only force that could delay or harass such an advance, although the price they might pay in the process did not bear thinking about. By 11 August, there were 12 F-15Es on alert, most carrying Mk 20 Rockeye 'area munitions' that released hundreds of cricket-ball-size bomblets over an area as large as a football field, and were therefore highly effective in destroying lightly armoured troop formations. Two aircraft also stood ready to defend the base, or a strike package, from enemy attack, and were loaded with AIM-9 Sidewinder and AIM-7 Sparrow air-to-air missiles (AAMs). Luckily, the

feared Iraqi Republican Guard units never moved south.

MASSIVE DEPLOYMENTS

While Operation Granby, the UK commitment to Operation Desert Shield was impressive in its scale, it was dwarfed by that of the US. The US sent more than 50 different types

of aircraft to the region, almost half of which were engaged in combat operations of one type or another. Many of these missions were at the sharp end, and actually engaged the enemy: A-10 Thunderbolt II 'tank-busters', B-52 Stratofortress bombers, AC-130 Spectre gunships, various other special forces C-130s, F-16

OPERATION GRANBY

As part of the build-up in the Gulf, the Royal Air Force's (RAF) Tornado F.Mk 3 interceptors arrived in Saudi Arabia, as did Jaguar GR.Mk 1/1A ground-attack and reconnaissance aircraft, these being co-located at Thumrait with USAF F-15Es. The RAF operation was known as Operation Granby, and it also included the deployment of the interdictor/strike variant of the Tornado, the GR.Mk 1, which would play a crucial role in the first days of the war, but pay a high price as a result. Supporting operations and the deployment was the RAF's fleet of C-130 Hercules transports and Tristar, VC10 and Victor 'hose-and-drogue' refuellers.

Fighting Falcons, F-4G Phantom 'Wild Weasels', F-111 Aardvark strike aircraft, EF-111 Raven jammers, F-117 Nighthawk 'stealth fighters', MH-53J Pave Low special forces helicopters, RF-4C Phantom reconnaissance aircraft, U-2R and TR-1A strategic reconnaissance aircraft, OH-58 Kiowa reconnaissance helicopters, AH-64 Apache helicopter gunships and RV-1 and OV-1 Mohawk battlefield reconnaissance aircraft. Meanwhile, carrier and assault ship decks in the Persian Gulf and Mediterranean supported A-6 Intruders, A-7 Corsair IIs, F-14 Tomcats, F/A-18 Hornets, E-2

Below: The Royal Saudi Air Force operated a mixed fighter fleet of Tornado Air Defence Variants (pictured) and F-15 Eagles.

The UK commitment to Operation Desert Shield was impressive in its scale, but it was dwarfed by that of the US. The US sent more than 50 different types of aircraft to the region, almost half of which were engaged in combat operations.

Hawkeyes, EA-6B Prowlers, AV-8B Harriers, AH-1 Cobras and various USMC assault helicopters. The list was as exhaustive as the numbers were bewildering.

Other countries were also adding to the mass of military equipment

and firepower that would soon be unleashed on Saddam Hussein's forces. France's Operation *Daguet* (Deer) saw it send a range of helicopters and transports as well as its Mirage 2000, Jaguar and Mirage F1 warplanes. Italy, under Operation

Locusta (Locust), sent three squadrons of Tornado IDS strike aircraft, Bahrain deployed F-5E and F-16 aircraft, Qatar sent Mirage F1s; and the United Arab Emirates its Mirage 2000s. New Zealand and South Korea both supplied C-130 transports. Even Kuwait made a contribution through its exiled Free Kuwaiti Air Force, which had managed to escape to Saudi Arabia with a number of A-4 Skyhawk and Mirage F1 jet fighters, and a single Gazelle helicopter.

Its European camouflage scheme incongruous against the sandy terrain below, an A-10 scouts high above the desert. Up here, its twin turbofan engines were inaudible to the enemy.

The numbers of aircraft involved were astronomical, to say nothing of the land forces that gathered on the Saudi border with Iraq. The USAF had sent 1238 aircraft to the region, of which 210 were F-16s; the US Navy (USN) 421 aircraft, most of which were onboard six aircraft carriers sent to the Gulf; the US Marine Corps (USMC) 368 aircraft; and the US Army 1587 aircraft.

THE SUPPORT EFFORT

Much of this gargantuan build-up would have been impossible without the extensive efforts of US strategic airlifters. Within six months of Iraq's invasion of Kuwait, there were more than 500,000 US personnel, 2000 main battle tanks, six carrier battle groups and a dozen fighter wings dotted around 120 locations in the Gulf. USAF C-141 StarLifters and C-5 Galaxys had conducted the bulk of the strategic airlift, taking materiel, men and vehicles from the Continental US and US bases in Germany, and moving them to the Middle East. Once there, the C-130 was crucial in ferrying these supplies to the places that needed them, and in doing so was the most important tactical airlift asset in theatre. In all, 542,000 tons of cargo was hauled by all three types in the course of more than 20,000 missions. It was a huge success for the US airlifters, whose work is often overlooked, but without whom the battle would not have even begun.

In the air, the Coalition's opponents were the men and machines of the Iraqi Air Force (IrAF). The IrAF air threat was significant; mostly because the air force was a source of pride to Saddam Hussein and he had therefore seen to it that it was powerfully equipped. It comprised a mixed array of aircraft capable of fighting for air supremacy, repelling ground-based assaults and attacking strategic targets, and some of its pilots had even been trained in the UK by the RAF.

The IrAF had eight squadrons of French-built Mirage F1EQs equipped with modern AAMs. For attacking Coalition troops, 10 IrAF air brigades were equipped with variable-geometry MiG-23BNs and Su-20/22s, plus

Hunters. Three Tu-22 squadrons, a Tu-16/II-6D squadron and two Su-24 squadrons completed the air to-ground contingent. The Su-24 was comparable to the F-111 and had the capability to mount devastating attacks against ground and sea targets.

But the biggest threat to Coalition aircraft came from five brigades of

Operation Desert Storm's air war was a truly multinational effort, as this photograph of (front to back) Qatari (Alpha Jet and Mirage F1), French (Mirage F1), US (F-16) and Canadian (CF-188 Hornet) participants demonstrates.

MiG-21, MiG-23 and MiG-25 fighters, and the highly regarded MiG-29. The MiG-25s were operated as part of a

The Iraqi Air Force (IrAF) air threat was significant; mostly because the air force was a source of pride to Saddam Hussein and he had therefore seen to it that it was powerfully equipped.

Above: Without the strategic airlifters, like this USAF C-141 StarLifter, the Coalition war effort in the Gulf would have been impossible.

IRAQI AIR FORCE POWER

The Iraqi Air Force (IrAF) was distributed across four sector commands, each of which was linked to an extensive GCI and IADS network. As in certain other Middle Eastern countries whose principal supplier had been the USSR, the IrAF operated using the central 'close hold' GCI control philosophy to orchestrate and control its pilots during their interceptions. Iraq's IADS was called Kari, which was the French spelling 'Irak' written in reverse, and was a reflection of the fact that France had been responsible for helping create it. It was very sophisticated, even going as far as utilizing high-bandwidth fibre-optic cables (cutting-edge technology at the time) buried deep beneath the desert to relay information and data between nodes. There was, however, never any doubt that the Coalition would be able to overcome the IrAF and its IADS, even if on paper the Iraqi air defences were well equipped and staffed by battle-hardened pilots and GCI controllers who had already spent almost 10 years fighting the Iranians to the east.

composite interceptor-reconnaissance wing. These could fly higher and faster than the F-15 and posed a considerable threat, especially to 'high-value asset' aircraft such as the E-2 Hawkeye and E-3 Sentry AWACS (Airborne Warning And Control System), and air refuelling tankers operating close to the Iraqi border.

Although much vaunted in the run-up to war, the IrAF's MiG-29 posed only a limited beyond-visual-range (BVR) threat. While it could employ the semi-active radar-homing (SARH)

AA-10 medium-range missile, its radar was not optimized for a long-range fight and had a poor 'look-down/shoot-down' capability. Once at the merge and into the dogfight, however, the tables could turn. The MiG-29 was highly manoeuvrable, could fire its short-range missiles off-boresight with the aid of a helmet-mounted monocle sight, and featured a passive infra-red search and track sensor with which to stealthily pick out targets without tipping off their electronic radar warning equipment.

TACTICAL AIR CONTROL CENTRE
Building on the lessons learned by Israel in Operation Peace for Galilee in 1982, in which command and control had proven critical, as well as its own experiences at the end of the Vietnam War, the USAF established the Tactical Air Control Centre (TACC) with its Coalition partners. The TACC planned the air war, as defined by a 600-page document called the Air Tasking Order (ATO), which in itself was a route map that showed every single sortie to be flown in the air campaign against Iraq.

The ATO, or 'Frag', outlined that the initial impetus of the first few hours would focus primarily on destroying the integrated air defence system (IADS) that protected Iraq. It also concentrated on taking out airfields, hardened aircraft shelters (HAS) and aircraft. With this achieved, Iraqi armour, logistics supplies, and command, control and communications (C3) facilities could then be struck, leading to the rapid weakening of the enemy prior to a Coalition ground assault. The first three days of the ATO were as scripted as possible, with changes occurring only to accommodate a fickle weather system that could generate blankets of cloud cover for days on end.

The original ATO saw all F-15Cs providing escort and combat air patrols (CAPs) from the south, but the decision to deploy more F-15s to Iraq's northern neighbour, Turkey, allowed planners to pin down the IrAF by attacking it from the north as well. The latest F-15E Strike Eagle was to fly

> The USAF's latest F-15E Strike Eagle was to fly sorties in unison with F-4G 'Wild Weasels' and EF-111A jamming aircraft against surface-to-air missile (SAM) sites and key airfield complexes.

sorties in unison with F-4G 'Wild Weasels' and EF-111A jamming aircraft against surface-to-air missile (SAM) sites and key airfield complexes. The F-15E was a new, all-weather, precision-strike version of the air-to-air F-15 Eagle. It was instantly distinguishable from the air superiority Eagle not only by its dark grey paint, but also by the two conformal fuel tanks nestled flush with the fuselage beneath each wing.

The F-15E was intended to replace the ageing F-111, and was equipped with state-of-the-art avionics to make it a truly multi-role fighter. In the air-to-air mission it lost some of the Eagle's manoeuvrability since it was somewhat heavier, but it lacked none of its punch when fighting opponents beyond visual range.

In the air-to-ground arena it had a sensor package housed in two pods –

MIKOYAN-GUREVICH MiG-21MF

Type: single-seat fighter

Powerplant: one 41.55kN (9,340lb st) Tumansky R-13-300 turbojet

Maximum speed: Mach 2.1. 2230km/h (1385mph) above 1100m (36,000ft)

Service ceiling: 19,000m (62,300ft)

Weights: maximum take-off weight 9398kg (20,723lb)

Armament: one 23mm twin-barrel GSh-23 cannon; various air-to-air and air-to-ground stores

Dimensions: span 8.1m (26ft 7in)
length 6.3m (20ft 8in)
height 2.35m (7ft 8in)
wing area 20.00m² (199sq ft)

The TR-1/U-2R was flying its usual very high-altitude profiles and listening for Iraqi radar and communications transmissions.

a navigation pod and a target pod – known collectively as LANTIRN (Low Altitude Navigation and Targeting Infra-red for Night). LANTIRN let the F-15E see in the dark and designate and lase targets for its own, or another aircraft's, laser-guided bombs (LGBs). Finally, the AN/APG-70 radar carried by the Strike Eagle was an excellent performer against other aircraft, but was so sophisticated that it could actually produce a radar map of the terrain ahead. This map could be 'frozen' on the cockpit display, allowing the rear-seat weapons systems officer (WSO) to analyze it (it resembled a fuzzy overhead satellite picture) and designate a target based on what was shown.

The F-15E's AN/APG-70 was a synthetic aperture radar (SAR) and, while this concept had existed for a few years, it required vast processing power that had until now been exclusive to huge computers that required large aircraft to carry them aloft. The F-15E was the first fighter-size aircraft to boast this capability.

ELECTRONIC ORDER OF BATTLE

Other state-of-the-art aircraft arriving in the region, albeit far more discretely, were the USAF's RC-135 Rivet Joint, the RAF's Nimrod R.Mk 1 and the French C.160G Gabriel. All three were extremely secretive in their operations and were there to help gather electronic and signals

Fresh from achieving initial operational capability at their base in North Carolina, the US Air Force's latest F-15E Strike Eagles played a dominant role in the air war.

intelligence on the Iraqi leadership and military. The RC-135 was based on the commercial Boeing 707 airliner, while the Nimrod used the well-known Comet airliner as the basis of its design. All three aircraft carried linguists and electronic specialists who monitored Iraqi voice and data communications, and noted the frequencies and locations of all electronic transmissions emanating from specific areas of interest.

These aircraft were essential in creating an electronic order of battle (EOB). The EOB told the Coalition's pilots what type of SAM systems were present in a given area of battle, how many there were and on which operating frequencies they relied. It also told them which IrAF aircraft were based at any given location.

The electronic and communications eavesdropping carried out by these aircraft also provided an additional layer of intelligence on the enemy's capabilities: how quickly they scrambled their fighters, what tactics they were using, at what range their ground control intercept (GCI) officers told them to fire their missiles, and what an Iraqi pilot would do if he was targeted by a Coalition aircraft – run away, press home his attack, or execute a good defence.

Above: The Iraqi Air Force was well equipped, if not well trained. Here, a two-seat Mirage F1 taxis to the runway. The Mirage was a respected opponent in the close-in, visual dogfight arena.

All of this was very important in building an accurate and up-to-date picture of what the Iraqis were doing, what systems they had, and how they were likely to behave when the war started. Of course, these aircraft also pinned down the locations of the major 'nodes' in Iraq's IADS and C3 information networks, all of which would be systematically attacked when the war began.

Other aircraft were also in on the game when it came to creating an EOB and snooping on the enemy. The TR-1/U-2R, which had first seen operational use with the Central

Intelligence Agency in complete secrecy, was flying its usual very high-altitude profiles and listening for Iraqi radar and communications transmissions, which it recorded for later analysis. The USN's EP-3E Aries

IIs, carrying an array of aerials and antennas that made them visually distinct from the P-3 Orion, were also on hand and were joined by the Vietnam-era EA-3B Skywarriors. Later, when the ground war started, the US

APACHE HELICOPTER GUNSHIP SENSORS

The AH-64A's Target Acquisition and Designation Sight (TADS) was used to find, identify and target the enemy. Magnets in each cockpit sensed an electrical field created by the crews' flight helmets, and this let either the pilot or co-pilot/gunner (CPG) cue the TADS sensors by simply turning their heads and looking where the target was. In doing so, they brought to bear the TV camera, infra-red (IR) sensor, high-power telescope, laser spot tracker, and laser designator/rangefinder that made up TADS. In 1991 this was an incredible capability that no other attack helicopter could match. The Pilot Night Vision Sensor (PNVS), mounted in a small fairing on the top of the nose turret, followed the head movements of the pilot and employed an IR sensor to let the pilot see in the dark or in dusty and smoky battlefield conditions.

Electronic listening posts roamed the skies intercepting Iraqi communications, plotting the location of radars and transmitters, and creating an electronic order of battle. This USAF RC-135 Rivet Joint was among them.

Army's RC-12 Guardrail and RV-1D Mohawk aircraft and EH-60A Quick Look helicopters would be very important in providing continuous electronic coverage of the battlespace as ground units below them

prosecuted their plans at great pace.

On 17 January 1991, the order for the first strikes was given by President George H.W. Bush. Operation Desert Storm had begun, and the largest military-build up since 1945 was ready to spring into action.

It all happened under the watchful eyes of the E-2 Hawkeye and E-3 Sentry AWACS, but the lead component in the attack came as something of a surprise to many: it

comprised eight AH-64A Apaches and a single MH-53J Pave Low of the US Army's Task Force Normandy. Their mission was to destroy or otherwise incapacitate two key early warning radar nodes in the Kari IADS. Shutting down these sites would effectively open the floodgates for all of the Coalition's other aircraft to penetrate Iraq and its IADS with the minimum of advanced warning and thus the greatest degree of surprise.

APACHE HELICOPTER GUNSHIP

At the time, the Apache was by far the most advanced helicopter gunship in the world. It could practically turn night into day for its pilot and co-pilot/gunner (CPG), thanks to two main infra-red sensors. Firstly, the AN/ASQ-170 Target Acquisition and Designation Sight (TADS) is what

The most enigmatic US warplanes, the F-117 Nighthawk 'stealth fighters' took off in blacked out conditions and began their solitary journeys north.

allowed the Apache to reach out into the battlefield and kill with great accuracy and speed; secondly, the AN/AAQ-11 Pilot Night Vision Sensor (PNVS) provided the pilot with night vision. TADS and PNVS were housed on separate sides of a rotating turret on the nose of the Apache.

Despite these excellent devices, navigation in the barren, featureless desert was hard enough by day, and very difficult by night. As a result, the eight Apaches were reliant on the MH-53J Pave Low, which carried very accurate navigational equipment, a reflection of its primary role of flying behind enemy lines and picking up downed aviators.

The importance of taking down the radar site could not be overestimated, and with great skill the Pave Low navigated the Apaches to a point where they could sight it visually with TADS, but remain in a hover far enough away so that the site's occupants could not hear the sound of their rotor blades.

'STEALTH FIGHTER' IN ACTION

As all this occurred in the early hours of 17 January, USAF KC-135 Stratotankers began to take-off from their Saudi airfields in great numbers and head towards the Saudi border with Iraq. Meanwhile, the most enigmatic US warplanes, the F-117 Nighthawk 'stealth fighters' took off in blacked out conditions and began their solitary journeys north, conducting one silent air refuelling before they entered Iraqi airspace.

At 0237 that morning, the US television network CNN showed live pictures of Tomahawk cruise missiles raining down on Iraqi political and military targets in the heart of Baghdad. Tracer fire weaved its way into the sky and missiles zoomed up into a scattered cloud base as the Iraqi gunners and SAM operators panicked. They couldn't see anything on their radar screens, and when they did detect a Tomahawk cruise missile it was already too late.

Most of the Tomahawks fired that night came from USN ships and submarines located in the Gulf, but 35 of these weapons came from the seven

The USAF's U-2R/TR-1A provided the battle commanders with electronic intelligence, as well as radar maps and detailed optical imagery of Iraq's defences.

STEALTH GOES TO WAR

To the general public, 'stealth' was still a new concept in 1991, and while most thought it made an aircraft invisible to radar, the truth is that it simply made it harder to spot. One of the reasons that stealth was so novel to most people at the time was that the USAF had been operating the F-117 in absolute secrecy at a remote airstrip in Nevada for many years, and had even sent it to war in Panama in 1989, but had only allowed the public to actually see the aircraft in the flesh as late as 1990. Reducing the radar (and visual, aural and infra-red) signature of an aircraft means that its survivability improves, and not that it becomes invincible. While some radar operators did briefly glimpse the F-117 on their scopes, it was always far too late to do anything about it and the blip on their screen seemed to disappear as quickly as it had arrived.

Right: Seen here hauling M117 'dumb' bombs, the B-52 Stratofortress undertook daring low-level missions against troops during the opening stages of the Desert Storm air war. Saddam Hussein's elite Republican Guard troop formations were among its targets.

USAF B-52G Stratofortress bombers that had flown all the way from

An AH-64 Apache helicopter is refuelled during Operation Desert Storm. It is armed with AGM-114 Hellfire air-to-surface missiles.

Barksdale Air Force Base (AFB), Louisiana. Their sorties lasted more than 35 hours and covered a distance of some 22,530km (14,000 miles).

The use of the B-52 as a cruise missile platform in this war was a

surprise, because up until this point the existence of the non-nuclear AGM-86C Conventional Air-Launched Cruise Missile (CALCM) had been a closely guarded secret. Usually, a cruise missile launched by the B-52 carried a nuclear warhead. The basic AGM-86 was an intelligent 'fire-and-forget' missile (it was totally autonomous after launch) that followed a pre-programmed route to the target. The AGM-86C CALCM was developed from the nuclear-tipped AGM-86B, a number of which had, from 1986, been converted in complete secrecy to carry a high-

The F-117A Nighthawk was among the first manned aircraft to enter Iraqi airspace on the night of 17 January 1991. It penetrated thick, overlapping defences, but suffered no losses.

explosive blast/fragmentation warhead and an internal global positioning system (GPS) for more accurate navigation.

'Showtime in five, four, three, two, one!' called the lead Apache pilot, and at 0238 precisely a barrage of 27 AGM-114 Hellfire missiles was on its way to the radar site just a few kilometres away. The Apache crews had split into two groups of four to attack the two sites, and were now following up with more than 4000 rounds of 30mm high-explosive incendiary fire from their turret-mounted M230 cannon, and 100 unguided 70mm (2.75in) rockets.

First they had struck the electrical generators that powered the sites, then they had destroyed the communications trailers, and finally they had wrecked the radar dishes themselves. Nothing survived, and in C3 centres around Iraq, senior officers asked why their gatekeepers had just dropped off the network. They were about to find out.

LGB STRIKES

Following the Tomahawks at exactly 0300, the 2000lb (907kg) GBU-10 LGBs launched by the F-117s began impacting key C3 targets in the heart of Baghdad – the telephone exchange went first, its destruction coinciding with the loss of communication with the world's press as it reported events live from the city. Before dawn, the USAF's F-117 fleet would attack

> 'Showtime in five, four, three, two, one!' called the lead Apache pilot, and at 0238 precisely a barrage of 27 AGM-114 Hellfire missiles was on its way to the radar site just a few kilometres away.

another 37 targets in downtown Baghdad, and not a single example would be shot down.

The F-117's success was in part down to the fact that it was coated with radar absorbent materials that converted the radar energy that struck the aircraft's skin into undetectable amounts of heat. But the ungainly shape of the aircraft gave away the most obvious reason for its low radar signature: 'faceting'. Faceting used sharp angles to deflect radar energy away from the transmitter, and used a myriad of carefully arranged flat surfaces to do so. Optimized to be

most stealthy when viewed head-on, as it approached its target, the F-117 had been extensively tested in the US against real Soviet early warning radars and SAM radars that had been captured, stolen, traded or otherwise acquired, but no one expected the Nighthawks to make it into the heart of Baghdad without a loss.

DEFENCE OF THE CAPITAL
The Baghdad Missile Engagement Zone (MEZ) was the name for the SAM rings that encircled the capital, and which defined Iraq's densest and most potent SAM threat. The MEZ

included Roland self-propelled SAMs and I-HAWK missiles captured from Kuwait, as well as SA-2, SA-3 and SA-6 missile systems. For each SAM system there was a multitude of AAA of all calibres, including 100mm (3.94in). The Baghdad MEZ had seemed for all the world to be impenetrable, but it was now clear that it was not.

The ATO had directed the three main F-15 wings to each patrol their

The US Army's UH-60 Blackhawk helicopter family became the workhorse of the airborne infantry force, replacing the venerable UH-1 Iroquois of Vietnam fame.

THE 'SCUD' THREAT

Iraq operated four 'Scud' types, all based on the original Soviet SS-1b 'Scud', which was a surface-launched missile with a range of over 300km (186 miles), albeit not a particularly accurate one. Iraq had adapted the 'Scud' warhead to carry chemical or biological loads, and showed no hesitation in using missiles against neighbouring countries. If Iraq drew Israel into the war with its 'Scud' attacks, then there was every chance that other Arab nations in the region would also interfere. And if that happened, the short, sharp operation that the Coalition was planning to rid Kuwait of Iraqi forces could turn into a drawn-out regional conflict.

own discrete area of responsibility, as defined by lines of longitude or recognizable geographical features. Eight Eagles pointed their powerful AN/APG-63 radars into the western sector of Iraq; eight more patrolled a central zone; and four aircraft were sent to cover the very east of Iraq. Their plan was simple: to push into the centre of each area and wipe out the

IrAF. The group of eight aircraft assigned to take care of the western sector had noted the density of IrAF fighter bases in their region, and had checked the Iraqi airfields H1, H2, Mudaysis, Al Assad and Al Taqaddum on their flight planning materials as areas where they would have to cue their radars particularly often. The timings were critical if the plan was to

work: with the F-117s over Baghdad and F-15Es over H2 and H3 airfields and engaging in 'Scud'-hunting activities from 0300 local time onwards, a 'wall' of eight F-15s was to mow down whatever took off from Iraqi airfields as the F-15Es and F-117s returned to Saudi Arabia. In essence, there was to be a surprise attack by the F-15Es and F-117s, then three 'walls' of Eagles whose radar coverage would act as a net to entrap the IrAF. Following them all would be the next wave of attacks by the rest of the Coalition's aerial strike force.

While AWACS would be scanning all of Iraq's airfields, and the RC-135 Rivet Joint would be listening in to detect any air traffic control radio

Below: Iraq's well-appointed military airfields were struck on the first night of the war and, with total air superiority, the Coalition continued to hit Iraq's runways and hardened shelters.

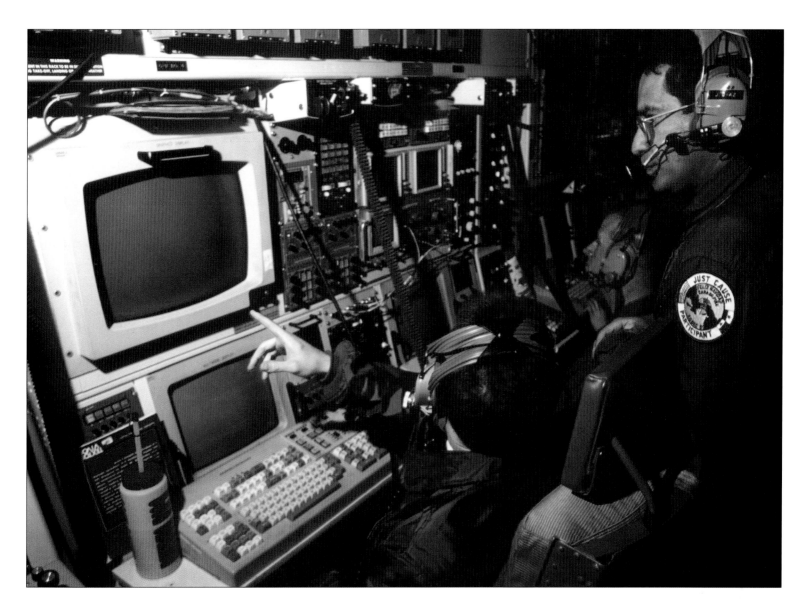

transmissions or GCI traffic that might give away a scramble by Iraqi fighters, the Eagles' other tool for detecting Iraqi combat patrols was its powerful radar. The AN/APG-63 pulse-Doppler radar held numerous advantages over the previous generation of radar, such as that used by the F-4 Phantom. While the Phantom's radar used low pulse repetition frequency (PRF), the AN/APG-63 employed high PRF to locate and track targets in ground clutter using Doppler shift, and medium PRF to 'fine tune' range data for weapons employment. This meant that the Eagle could track targets at different ranges, closing speeds and altitudes relative to itself. It could also interrogate a contact, using its built-in IFF (identification

friend or foe) interrogator to determine whether it was hostile or not.

Whereas the F-4's radar historically had a 74km (46-mile) search and a 19km (12-mile) lock-on range and could not 'look down' to find aircraft below it, the AN/APG-63 allowed the Eagle pilot to detect fighter-size targets in a 'look-up' environment at around 150km (93 miles), with a 'look-down' capability about half that. Overall, the Eagle's radar search volume was more than four times larger than that of the Phantom.

DEFEATING THE 'CLUTTER'

All this was useful, but what made the AN/APG-63's capability something that the pilot could really take advantage of was the 'clean' synthetic

Advanced technology, 'stealth' and 'smart' weapons were seen by the public as being at the heart of the air war over Iraq, but in truth much of the destruction that rained down on Iraq's military had changed little since the final months of the Vietnam air war.

image that the radar presented to the pilot. Whereas the Phantom WSO or pilot had had to look at the raw echoes detected by his radar, the Eagle used computers to do the radar interpretation and to then generate clear and easily interpreted symbols on the pilot's radar screen. Furthermore, software filters eliminated the 'clutter' reflected by the ground so that the pilot only saw symbols relating to the echoes coming from other aircraft (and not 'false' targets created by ground clutter).

The EF-111A provided stand-off and close-in electronic jamming of Iraqi radars. Flying unarmed deep into Iraqi airspace, one EF-111 claimed a manoeuvre 'kill' against a Mirage.

While the radar did all this, the Eagle's central computer, the aircraft's 'brain', was busy working out the engagement zone information for the weapon selected (either AIM-7 Sparrow or AIM-9 Sidewinder) and computing a myriad of details useful to the pilot for prosecuting the attack. These included the target's altitude, heading, airspeed, closure rate, aspect angle and *g*-loading.

So, with the Eagle's radar looking further ahead, with greater discrimination between real and false targets, and with this data presented as symbols that the pilot could interpret instantly, the Eagle held a massive advantage over his adversary. The Eagle pilot could now spend more time 'heads-up', looking outside the aircraft visually checking for threats, terrain and wingman, and gone were the days when fighter pilots and WSOs spent hours practising how to attain the correct radar gains and set-up in order to get the most from their air-to-air radars.

FOLLOW-ON WAVES

With great media attention focused on Baghdad, waves of RAF Tornado GR.Mk 1s, F-111Fs, EF-111s, F-16s, F/A-18s, F-14s, A-6s, A-7s, F-4Gs and even B-52s were to follow the Eagles. Not only were they targeting the IADS, but they were attacking the airfields, HASs and IrAF aircraft, too. If these strikes were successful, then air superiority could be attained and the ground war could be launched sooner rather than later. Other strikes called for by the ATO included those against key Iraqi armoured forces, C3 sites and logistics supplies, all of which would pave the way for a less protracted ground war.

With all the F-15E's advanced avionics and its ability to fight its way into and out of the target, it was hardly surprising that the TACC had

The view at night through the head-up display (HUD) in a USAF F-15E – the forward-looking infra-red picture gave the Strike Eagle a true night-attack capability.

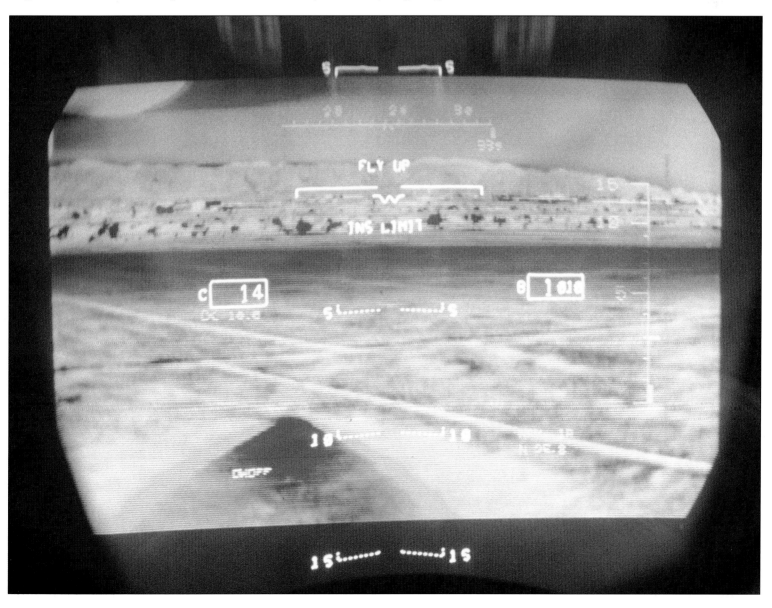

tasked its pilots and WSOs with the challenge of going after one of the war's most notorious targets: fixed and mobile 'Scud' missiles.

Fixed 'Scud' sites in western Iraq were attacked by the F-15E on the first night. A total of five sites were hit by 24 aircraft that were divided into three-ship or four-ship packages, each carrying two external fuel tanks, 12 Mk 20 Rockeye cluster bombs, and two AIM-9M missiles. There was one exception, and this flight attacked 'Scud' sites at H2, an Iraqi airfield, using 12 Mk 82 500lb (227kg) 'dumb' bombs.

'SCUD'-HUNTERS

The fixed 'Scud' sites were simple to strike, and the F-15Es ingressed the target areas at low level. Climbing briefly to altitude as they neared the target, they 'patch mapped' the area with their SAR radar mode before descending once again to the relative sanctuary of 91m (300ft).

AWACS called several unidentified aircraft in their vicinity, but none came closer than 48km (30 miles),

and the pilots used the steering cues in their wide-field-of-view head-up displays (HUDs) to precisely position for bomb release. Like the Apache crew, the F-15E pilot could see at night thanks to the LANTIRN pods, one of which looked straight ahead and transmitted an infra-red picture onto the pilot's HUD. Combined with the SAR and LANTIRN's targeting pod, this made the F-15E the most lethal and precise night-strike fighter available. LANTIRN's terrain-following radar (TFR) function gave the pilots pitch commands that helped them fly at an altitude of around 61m (200ft) in radio silence – the pilots were hand-flying with the TFR while concentrating on the FLIR picture in the HUD and maintaining their formation position. The WSOs in the Eagles' rear seats were monitoring the TFR scope and the radar, and keeping the navigation systems updated.

Nearing the target, the F-15Es executed either a sudden climb followed by a dive (called a 'pop-up' manoeuvre) or simply flew level

deliveries straight over their targets. At 0305 local time, five minutes after the F-117s' bombs had started to impact Baghdad, the first of the F-15Es' cluster bombs scattered their lethal payloads of submunitions.

Attacking the 'Scud' sites was not without risk as they were well defended, and several pilots exceeded the airframe g-limits as they hauled their aircraft into jinks and evasive turns to avoid seemingly impenetrable streams of AAA. In the haste to avoid the threats at least one aircraft came within 27m (90ft) of flying into the ground, saved only as a result of an aggressive pull prompted by the panicked scream of the WSO who had noted the pilot's error.

The F-15E flight tasked to attack the 'Scud' missile facility at H2 airfield was the only one that did not try and

Below: A small contingent of Kuwaiti Air Force aircraft, like this A-4 Skyhawk ground-attack aircraft (left), managed to escape the Iraqi invaders and flew missions throughout the war from Saudi Arabia.

Above: Iraq's use of 'Scud' missiles threatened to bring Israel into the war. As a result, the 'Scud' became a priority target for the Coalition.

duck under the cover of Iraq's SAMs that first night. Instead, the flight flew into Iraq at medium level and was greeted by the sight of more than 100 AAA pieces firing together. As the flight had crossed the border with Iraq the crews had noted fires burning at the observation posts and radar facilities that the Apaches and special forces troops had taken out. The flights had initially gone into Iraq at 152m (500ft) above the desert floor, with a plan to attack from low altitude if the AAA allowed. If there were too much ground fire then they would climb above it and drop their bombs from the relative safety of 6096m

NON-COOPERATIVE TARGET RECOGNITION

In basic terms, Non-Cooperative Target Recognition (NCTR) compared radar returns from the target's engine fan and turbine blades with those stored in an F-15's onboard library. As radar waves bounced off these blades they carried with them a signature that could be compared to those stored in the library, allowing the aircraft type to be identified. Once the radar had identified the aircraft type, it displayed the information on the radar screen for the pilot to see – 'MiG-21', 'MiG-25', 'MiG-29', 'Mirage'. Just like their predecessors flying Phantoms in Vietnam, the Eagle pilots going to war over Iraq had rules of engagement (RoE) that governed whether they could take a long-range missile shot – the difference now was that a lack of a friendly IFF response and an 'Enhanced ID' (EID) indication (either an organic NCTR indication from the AN/APG-63, or one from an AWACS' NCTR; or an EID from an RC-135 Rivet Joint, which could identify the presence of a MiG from its transmissions) was enough to allow the Eagle pilot to shoot.

(20,000ft). As they approached the target they watched as AAA snaked into the sky like a curtain from the ground. The squadron commander, who was leading the six-ship package, made a one-word radio transmission, 'climb', and all six happily climbed up to medium altitude from where each dropped their 12 Mk 82 bombs.

While the strikers began to systematically take apart the enemy's electronic eyes and ears, the IrAF itself was soon to be humiliated and the USAF was to claim six 'kills' on this night alone, all at the hands of F-15Cs. What was less obvious, but of greater overall importance about these victories, and those that lay ahead, was the way in which technology played a crucial part in the ability to score them. Vietnam had showed the US that missile technology – and in particular, the ability to electronically discriminate between friend or foe – required more time to mature before it could live up to even the most basic of expectations.

AIR-TO-AIR SUCCESS

While the excellent AN/APG-63 had its own built-in IFF interrogator and reply evaluator, it was not enough on

The F-15E (pictured) and A-10A spearheaded the Coalition's anti-'Scud' missile operations. The two types worked in concert to locate, identify and destroy the mobile launchers, but their overall effect was ultimately limited.

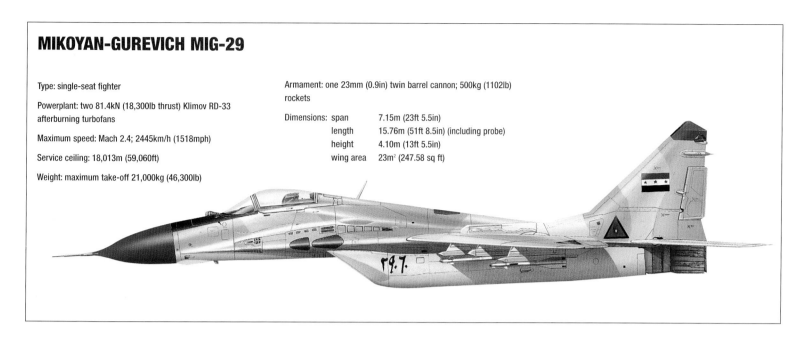

MIKOYAN-GUREVICH MIG-29

Type: single-seat fighter

Powerplant: two 81.4kN (18,300lb thrust) Klimov RD-33 afterburning turbofans

Maximum speed: Mach 2.4; 2445km/h (1518mph)

Service ceiling: 18,013m (59,060ft)

Weight: maximum take-off 21,000kg (46,300lb)

Armament: one 23mm (0.9in) twin barrel cannon; 500kg (1102lb) rockets

Dimensions:		
span	7.15m (23ft 5.5in)	
length	15.76m (51ft 8.5in) (including probe)	
height	4.10m (13ft 5.5in)	
wing area	23m² (247.58 sq ft)	

its own to permit the Eagle pilot to shoot missiles at a beyond-visual-range target. Vietnam had showed that the inability to identify the enemy at long range would lead to the advantages of missiles like the AIM-7 Sparrow being eroded as it became necessary to close within visual range to visually ID (VID) the target. With this in mind, the F-15 was built with a variety of systems that permitted electronic identification of the target from long range, including one based on the Vietnam-era Combat Tree. Another system built into the aircraft was Non-Cooperative Target Recognition (NCTR), which underpinned nearly all of the F-15 'kills' of the war (see box feature on page 290).

Notwithstanding horrendous weather conditions that presented some of the toughest air-to-air refuelling conditions the crews had ever experienced – towering cumulo nimbus up to 9144m (30,000ft) on a pitch black, turbulent night and without any external lights – the IrAF learned of the F-15Es' 'surprise attack' through some fairly rudimentary intelligence assets: physical listening posts along the Iraqi border with Saudi Arabia, where Iraqi conscripts and Republican Guard members listened for the sound of aircraft.

Although the Apaches had expertly taken out the two radar sites, it wasn't difficult to tell an attack was on its way when a flight of 18 F-15Es flew over at 91m (300ft) above the ground.

For the F-15C Eagle pilots, shooting down a friendly aircraft was a mortifying thought, and although NCTR, the AN/APG-63, AWACS and the precise Coalition planning gave them great confidence, technology was not infallible. In an ideal world the Eagle pilots would have kept the Coalition aircraft apart from the Iraqis trying to shoot them down.

Originally, the F-117s and F-15Es were going to have cleared out of Iraq when the F-15C Eagles steamrollered across the border. That way, when they went north into Iraq they would know that anything in front of them was an enemy. However, at around 0305, AWACS called that Iraq had scrambled aircraft. With four of the

first eight-ship of F-15Cs now 161km (100 miles) south of the border refuelling, the remaining four headed north into Iraq far earlier than had been planned, and with the F-15Es and F-117s still somewhere out there in front of them.

The four F-15Cs assumed a lateral separation of around 8km (5 miles), with each wingman laterally displaced from his lead by approximately another 3km (2 miles), creating a 14km (9-mile) 'wall' formation. It was just minutes away from initiating the first IrAF contact of the war.

BATTLESPACE CONTROLLERS
AWACS called two of the F-15Cs to engage one group of 'bandits' (aircraft identified as hostile) located southeast of Mudaysis airfield, but when the pilots pointed their AN/APG-63 radars towards Mudaysis and hit the IFF button on their

While the strikers began to systematically take apart the enemy's electronic eyes and ears, the USAF was to claim six 'kills' on the first night, all at the hands of the F-15C.

Iraq's SAM 'umbrella' was known as the Missile Engagement Zone (MEZ), and it was the job of the USAF's F-4G 'Wild Weasels' to systematically take this network down.

throttles, they were shocked to see as many as 40 friendly IFF returns.

One of the pilots, Capt. Jon Kelk, picked up an enemy contact on his own radar at the same time as his radar warning receiver (RWR) buzzed in his ears to inform him that he was being locked on to by the radar of a MiG-29. With the MiG on his radar showing at some 56km (35-miles) distant, Kelk relied on his own 'Enhanced ID' (EID) and that of the AWACS to identify the contact as a bandit. As the range closed, the MiG climbed from about 2134 to 5182m (7000 to 17,000ft) and started to manoeuvre in relation to Kelk. But the MiG-29 pilot was already at a disadvantage, not only because he was a single-ship facing a two-ship of USAF F-15Cs, but also because Kelk had almost double the altitude and airspeed of the MiG, and his AIM-7 Sparrows therefore had an increased engagement envelope against his opponent.

As Kelk hurtled towards the MiG at a combined speed of more than 2250km/h (1400mph), he closed his eyes to protect his night vision and pressed the 'pickle' button on his

control stick – unleashing one of his four AIM-7M Sparrow AAMs. Moments later, the MiG-29 erupted in the night sky into a purple smudge of flame. Kelk had become the first US airman to score a 'kill' in the F-15, and air combat in the beyond-visual-range arena had finally come of age.

PHANTOM 'WEASELS'

While the F-117s and F-15Es had flown into Iraq unescorted, the follow-on strikers included the F-4G 'Wild Weasels'. The F-4G had taken over the SAM-hunting role undertaken by the F-105F/G in Vietnam and, even after its retirement, it is still regarded as the most capable 'Wild Weasel' ever deployed. The F-4G was an uncompromised variant dedicated to sniffing out SAMs, AAA and early warning radars and was flown by pilots and electronic warfare officers (EWOs) whose sole objective was to thwart the enemy's air defences.

As Israel had in Lebanon in 1982, the US made extensive use of drones to cause Kari to come on line and betray the locations of Iraq's radars and SAM sites. These drones, some launched from sites secretly located by US forces within Iraq itself, were timed to coincide with the pre-emptive AGM-88 High-speed Anti-Radiation Missile (HARM) shots that would be made by

Drones were timed to coincide with the pre-emptive AGM-88 High-speed Anti-Radiation Missile (HARM) shots.

the F-4Gs, and the USN's F/A-18s, A-7s and EA-6Bs. With the HARMs rocketing upwards to seek the thinner air of very high altitude, the drones approached Iraq from multiple directions, each transmitting back numerous signals that flooded the Iraqi radar screens with blips that made them effectively unusable. For the most part, the Iraqis fell for this trick, and as even more radars came on line, the HARM rocket motors burned out and their seeker heads started looking for targets – by now there were plenty.

Other suppression of enemy air defence (SEAD) strikers were also by now inbound to their targets. These assets included the RAF's Tornado GR.Mk 1s tasked to fire their Air Launched Anti-Radiation Missiles (ALARMs) at defences protecting several Iraqi airfields that other RAF Tornados were to strike at 0350 local time. These latter Tornados were

A number of nations provided indirect support to the war effort. Here, a Qatari UH-60 provides additional transport capacity in the Persian Gulf.

weighed down with JP233 runway denial weapons, which required a straight and level pass over the runway while they discharged their submunitions, and therefore made delivering aircraft very vulnerable to ground fire.

Some Tornados lofted 1000lb (454kg) bombs at runways instead, but as they popped up and reached the apex of their climb with the speed rapidly bleeding away, they suddenly became vulnerable to AAA as well. In fact, it was during one of these loft manoeuvres that the first Tornado, and first Coalition aircraft, was shot down that night as it attacked Shaibah airfield; the second Tornado loss followed later that day, after being hit by a SAM while delivering its JP233.

In 1991, Iraq possessed biological and chemical weapons that it had used against both its own people and its neighbours. Finding the production sites for these weapons became a priority for Coalition forces.

The RAF maintained its low-level tactics until its losses mounted and pressure from the US to pursue medium-altitude tactics prevailed.

DIFFERING TACTICS

The RAF maintained its low-level tactics until its losses mounted and pressure from the US to pursue medium-altitude tactics prevailed.

With the Iraqi IADS somewhat incapacitated after the first few days, the US had opted with success to pursue the medium-altitude option, but the UK had not. The new tactics instantly stemmed the losses, but it certainly didn't mean that the

Right: USAF F-15C Eagles dominated the skies over Iraq from the first night, and by the end of the first week they had the Iraqi Air Force running for cover. This Eagle carries an Iraqi 'kill' marking below the cockpit and the name of 'MiG-killer' Capt. Tom 'Vegas' Dietz.

missions suddenly became risk-free. SA-2s were dotted around Iraqi targets, and despite the largely successful SEAD effort to disable Kari, several isolated SAM sites remained active throughout the war.

In fact, another Tornado loss (the sixth and final RAF Tornado loss) occurred when one jet was hit by two missiles simultaneously as it dropped LGBs on Al Taqaddum airfield. Then, of course, there was the many thousands of AAA pieces that returning crews described as being so intense that they would light up the night sky sufficiently to illuminate the low-altitude aircraft. Pilots said it was like flying through a tunnel of AAA.

MANPADS THREAT

For the likes of the UH-60 Blackhawk, OH-58 Kiowa, A-10 Thunderbolt II, Jaguar, AV-8B Harrier II and OV-10 Bronco, all of which spent a considerable amount of time at low level, the man-portable air defence system (MANPADS) and AAA threat persisted throughout the war and accounted for many of the Coalition's losses. The MANPADS threat came principally from the same SA-7 shoulder-launched IR-guided missile that US aviators had had to contend with at the end of the Vietnam War. Certain aircraft, notably some Army and USMC helicopters, sported 'disco lights', which sent out spurious IR signals in a bid to jam the homing mechanisms of these missiles. The USMC Harriers even carried a missile warning system that incorporated a laser that would fire at the seeker head of the missile in a bid to disable it, but the losses still came.

END GAME

The war went on for another 41 days before Saddam Hussein pulled all his forces back out of Kuwait and a ceasefire was announced. Northern and Southern No-Fly Zones (NFZs) were soon established to prevent Iraqi fixed-wing aircraft from posing any further threat to the Coalition.

The E-8C JSTARS (Joint Surveillance Target Attack Radar System) was rushed into theatre before it had even finished acceptance testing in the US. JSTARS allowed ground commanders to peer into Iraq and observe, in real-time, Iraqi armour movements and locations.

Saddam Hussein made full use of a loophole that allowed helicopters into the NFZs, and ordered Mi-24 assault helicopters to strike Kurdish refugees in Northern Iraq. Operation Provide Comfort was launched following the US-encouraged Kurdish uprising against Iraq's dictator in the northern territories. Saddam Hussein's response had been to overpower the rebel fighters, and to embark upon a policy of ethnic cleansing. Unable to stand by and watch any longer, the United Nations (UN) passed Resolution 688 to allow UN-sanctioned intervention. Provide Comfort sought to achieve two goals: to provide relief to the refugees, and to enforce the security of the refugees and the humanitarian effort.

Right: A US Marine Corps CH-53E Super Stallion lifts a fuel bowser during a maritime support mission. During Desert Storm, the Marine Corps were involved in amphibious assault, as well as close-in fighting further inland.

These two goals were maintained from April to September 1991 by a US-led Combined Task Force. Over 40,000 aerial sorties were flown, relocating over 700,000 refugees, and restoring 70-80 per cent of the villages destroyed by the Iraqis. However, at the same time that all of this was happening, Turkey was launching its own attacks, using air power against the Kurds with complete impunity.

Establishing these No-Fly Zones was the precursor to what would eventually

MONITORING THE GROUND WAR

Despite some losses to air defences, the war was going well and the scale of the losses the Coalition had calculated in computer simulations prior to the start of hostilities was turning out to be wholly over-estimated. One problem area that did return time and again was that of the elusive search for mobile 'Scuds'. A-10s and F-15Es were often diverted from their primary missions to engage suspected 'Scuds', but they failed to have much of an impact on their continued launches. Unknown to the TACC at the time, the Iraqis were hiding their mobile 'Scuds' in specially adapted buses and underneath road bridges, and they were being highly inventive and skilled in the art of deception and camouflage.

To help find the 'Scuds', and to assist in persecuting the Iraqi Republican Guard units that by now were making a quick getaway from Kuwait, the US introduced the E-8 JSTARS (Joint Surveillance Target Attack Radar System), which had prematurely finished its operational test and evaluation programme and had been rushed to the region. It carried a massive SAR and GMT (Ground Moving Target) radar in a canoe-shaped fairing under the lower fuselage, and was able to see many miles into Iraq and Kuwait. Every night, the TACC in Riyadh assigned F-15Es and A-10s to work 'Scud boxes' (patches of desert where 'Scud' launches might be possible) with the E-8. If a suspected 'Scud' was picked up on radar, the E-8 would pass the coordinates and the striker would put the bombs on the target. F-15Es would patrol their 'Scud box' for four to six hours, after which they would be relieved by another flight, and would then move on to drop their ordnance on secondary targets – anything from armour to artillery pieces or known fixed 'Scud' sites.

become known as Operations Northern Watch (Northern NFZ) and Southern Watch (Southern NFZ), which would last until 2003, and the start of Operation Iraqi Freedom.

YUGOSLAVIAN AIR WARS

In 1993 the USAF started deploying combat aircraft to Aviano AB, Italy, as part of Operation Deny Flight. Operation Deny Flight was centred around a No-Fly Zone that had been placed over the Balkan state of Bosnia-Herzegovina, when relations between the different ethnic groups in the region reached a new low.

UN peacekeeping troops moved in to instill peace, while the UN Security Council Resolution 781, which created the NFZ, was intended to prevent the Federal Republic of Yugoslavia air force from mounting air attacks over

Below: The cavernous bomb bay of the B-52 had once been intended to carry a payload of nuclear weapons, but as with Vietnam, Operation Desert Storm saw B-52s used for 'carpet bombing' with conventional munitions.

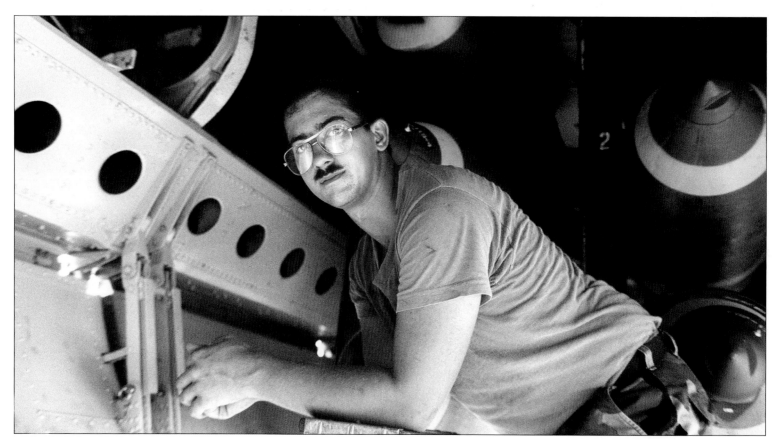

Bosnia-Herzegovina. On 31 March 1993, the UN Security Council passed Resolution 816, which extended the ban to cover flights by all Yugoslavian fixed-wing and rotary-wing aircraft except those authorized by UNPROFOR (the UN Protection Force). In the event of further violations, it authorized UN member states to take all necessary measures to ensure compliance.

Operation Deny Flight, the enforcement operation over the former Yugoslavia, began on 12 April 1993. It initially involved some 50 fighter and reconnaissance aircraft (later increased to over 100) from various North Atlantic Treaty Organization (NATO) nations, flying from airfields in Italy and from aircraft carriers in the Adriatic. By the end of December 1994, over 47,000 sorties had been flown by fighter and supporting aircraft. By now matters had worsened and NATO authorized a limited strike against Serbian-held targets in Croatia, and in particular Udbina airfield. A 30-aircraft strike package bombed the airfield, and shortly after two F-15Es destroyed two SA-2 sites that had fired upon two Royal Navy Sea Harriers. In early 1994, F-16s of the USAF downed four Serbian Super Galeb light-attack aircraft as they penetrated and contravened the NFZ.

DELIBERATE FORCE

Operation Deliberate Force commenced in August 1995, following a Serbian mortar attack on a market square in Sarajevo, the capital of Bosnia-Herzegovina. Five punitive NATO strikes hit Serbian armour and supplies positioned around Sarajevo on 30 August. A day later, three more strikes were flown. Four days later, nine GBU-15 precision-guided glide bombs were dropped against Bosnian-Serb ground forces and air defence

In 1991 the A-10 struck Iraqi armour and infantry with alacrity, incurring remarkably few losses in the process. In the Balkans, as here, it did much the same, but this time without any losses.

targets around Banja Luca.

Operation Deliberate Guard followed in 1997. This was another UN-mandated NFZ in the airspace over Bosnia-Herzegovina.

Months later Operation Allied Force was launched following the displacement of some 300,000 refugees from the enclave of Kosovo. Following repeated NATO warnings to Serbian President Slobodan Milosevic to remove his armed forces from Kosovo, the first Balkan Air Expeditionary Force of US warplanes arrived in Italy. A five-phase plan was put into effect – initially the NATO flights would act as a deterrent, becoming more aggressive if NATO's demands were not met. Despite some gains made at the Rambouillet talks in

GBU-15 GLIDE BOMB

The GBU-15 had started life in 1974 as a solution to the requirement for a stand-off precision-guided bomb, and had been cleared for carriage on the USAF's F-4E Phantom II, F-111F Aardvark and the F-15E Strike Eagle. It combined either an electro-optical seeker head, or one of two IR seeker heads, with a 2000lb (907kg) BLU-109 penetrator or Mk 84 general-purpose bomb body. A 'direct' mode allowed the bomb to be locked on to the target prior to launch, and once it was released it would be guided autonomously to the target. 'Indirect' mode used a datalink pod to allow the WSO to steer the weapon to the target after launch.

The GBU-15 differed from an LGB in that once launched, the bomb could be steered in flight. This allowed the pilot to turn the aircraft away from the enemy and to skirt around threats and enemy interceptors. It was also simple to use: the bomb could be cued from the radar, HUD or target pod, and once in flight its seeker-head picture was transmitted back to the launch aircraft so that the WSO could see the target and provide steering corrections. An enhanced version of the bomb, the EGBU-15, uses GPS mid-course guidance and allows the crew to release the weapon in poor visibility. The bomb will now fly itself to the pre-entered target coordinates, taking steering commands from an onboard GPS receiver. Once in the target area the WSO can take control as normal. Over Yugoslavia, some F-15Es returned to base with some spectacular video footage from their GBU-15 exploits; in one instance a man can be seen running from an SA-6 moments before the weapon impacts the target.

Above: By the time of the 1990s Balkans conflicts, precision-guided weapons were far more commonly used. This USAF F-16 carries a 2000lb (907kg) GBU-15 TV-guided bomb during tests over the Gulf of Mexico.

France, by January 1999 the US-led NATO force was still growing in size.

ALLIED FORCE IN ACTION

On the night of 24 March 1999 Operation Noble Anvil, the US component of Operation Allied Force, commenced. Following several strikes by B-52s armed with AGM-86C CALCMs, the 26 F-15Es in theatre concentrated on striking Serbian air defence targets, as they followed behind a 'wall' of F-15Cs flying offensive counter-air (OCA) sorties. SEAD was provided by USAF F-16CJs (the replacement for the now-retired F-4G), USN EA-6B Prowlers, as well as the Tornado ECR (Electronic Combat Reconnaissance) flown by the air arms of Germany and Italy. The RAF's

Tornados also fired ALARMs at air defence targets, while other RAF Tornados, Jaguars and Harriers attacked further ground targets.

The USAF's B-2 Spirit 'stealth bomber' also made its operational debut on the night of 24 March, when two examples dropped 32 2000lb (907kg) Joint Direct Attack Munitions (JDAMs) during a 31-hour, non-stop mission from Whiteman AFB, Missouri. Over the course of Operation Allied Force, 45 B-2 sorties delivered 656 JDAMs.

JDAM was born from the post-Operation Desert Storm debrief. It had been known all along that the laser-guided bomb's Achilles' heel was the fact that it required good weather in order that the target could be seen and marked with a laser. But the weather in Iraq had rarely cooperated and had hampered the Coalition's efforts to strike certain key targets. In 1992, the US military embarked on an 'adverse-weather precision-guided munition' programme that resulted in the appearance of the JDAM.

JDAM uses satellites to pinpoint its position, and is a modular upgrade

To the chagrin of many, the F-16CJ (pictured) replaced the F-4G 'Wild Weasel' shortly after the 1991 Gulf War. Its effectiveness was initially limited, but it has since undergone software upgrades that make it much more potent.

In the right hands, and using the right tactics, both Yugoslavian air and ground elements could cause NATO trouble. But the boot was on the other foot.

for unguided, low-drag, general-purpose bombs like the 500lb (227kg) Mk 82, 1000lb (454kg) Mk 83 and 2000lb (907kg) Mk 84 bombs. JDAM consists of a tail section with integrated aerodynamic control surfaces, a stabilizing strake kit that is attached to the bomb body, and a combined inertial guidance and GPS unit in the tail. Low-rate production of JDAM began in 1995, and weapons tests achieved circular error probable (CEP) results of 10.3m (34ft), which is to say that the bomb has a 50 per cent chance of impacting within 10.3m of the target. Considering the JDAM can fly as far as 24km (15 miles), this is a very impressive degree of accuracy.

Following the cessation of hostilities and the subsequent Dayton Peace Accords in 1995, the Federal Republic of Yugoslavia air force reduced its inventory. By 1998 it had a mixed force of jet combat aircraft on strength including 60 MiG-21s, 16 MiG-29s and 60 or more Orao attack aircraft. These were all integrated into a multi-layered air defence system that included mobile SAM systems, many of which were located in the mountains and were therefore very difficult for NATO to hit. In the right hands, and using the right tactics, both Yugoslavian air and ground elements could cause NATO trouble. It soon transpired though, that the boot was on the other foot.

As the first NATO strike package of the war ingressed towards its targets, an airfield in Montenegro and the early warning radars that were linking the adjoining Kosovo/Montenegro airspace, an escort of F-15s went with them. The Eagles were armed with the AIM-120 AMRAAM.

THE AMRAAM ADVANTAGE

At the very end of the 1991 Gulf War, the US had hurried the AIM-120 Advanced Medium-Range Air-to-Air Missile (AMRAAM) into service. The AMRAAM had superseded the AIM-7 Sparrow, paving the way for some dynamic and effective new tactics to be developed. Whereas the Sparrow is a semi-active radar-homing (SARH) missile that requires the shooter to keep a radar lock on the target until the missile impacts, the AMRAAM requires the launch aircraft to illuminate the target with its radar only until such a time as the missile's own onboard active radar seeker can acquire the target, at which point the shooter is free to leave the area. AMRAAM uses a secure datalink with the launch aircraft to report its position and to receive any updates from the launch aircraft's own radar.

NORTHROP GRUMMAN B-2 SPIRIT

Type: stealth bomber

Crew: 2

Powerplant: four 77kN (17,300lbf) General Electric turbofans

Maximum speed: 760km/h (470mph)

Service ceiling: 15,000m (50,000ft)

Weights: maximum take-off weight 152,634kg (336,500lb)

Armament: two internal bays for 22,700kg (50,000lb) of ordnance

Dimensions:	span	52.4m (172ft 7in)
	length	21m (69ft)
	height	5.2m (17ft)
	wing area	460m² (5000 sq ft)

The AMRAAM had already been proven for the first time in 1992, when an F-16 shot down a MiG-25 over the Northern NFZ in Iraq, and while F-15s downed two Yugoslavian MiG-29s with the missile on 24 March, it was on the night of 26 March that the AMRAAM proved its real potential. That evening an F-15 scored the first ever double AMRAAM 'kill'. The F-15 pilot, Capt. Jeff Hwang, fired two AIM-120s at two separate MiG-29s in very short order. His AN/APG-63 radar first provided

him with an EID that his targets were hostile, and then supported both the missiles in flight against the two separate targets until the missiles' seeker heads went active to guide them to the MiGs.

The event demonstrated just how far things had come in the field of air combat. The Vietnam air war had almost always demanded that a visual ID of the target be made before missiles were fired. By the time of Desert Storm in 1991, electronics

Above: While the F-117 'stealth fighter' had been the first to enter Iraqi airspace in 1991, the subsequent B-2 'stealth bomber' was the first to silently enter Yugoslavian airspace during Operation Allied Force in 1999.

could be used to ID a target, but often a visual confirmation was required, and when a Sparrow was fired from beyond visual range it had to be supported throughout its time of flight, which created the possibility that another enemy fighter could close to the merge unnoticed. Finally the AMRAAM now gave the likes of the Eagle a viable capability to engage multiple targets at the same time. It was a capability that pilots could only have dreamt of during Desert Storm.

Another 'first' accomplished during Operation Allied Force was the first successful combat use of the powered version of the GBU-15 glide bomb, the AGM-130. Used to successfully destroy two MiG-29s on the ground, the weapon features a GBU-15 with a rocket motor mounted on the underside to increase the bomb's range. Featuring a GPS mid-course guidance system, the weapon functions in a very similar manner to the GBU-15 but can be programmed with a low-altitude ingress, flying as close to the terrain as 61m (200ft).

COALITION LOSSES

It had not entirely gone NATO's way, however. In 1995 a USAF F-16 had been downed by an SA-6 over Bosnia, while on a routine patrol. A French Mirage 2000 had also been downed, so too had an Italian transport aircraft and a Sea Harrier. Most notable of all, however, was the loss of an F-117.

The modern Combined Air Operations Centre (CAOC) was developed throughout the 1990s and is based loosely on the Tactical Air Control Centre of the first Gulf War in 1991. As troubles flared in the Balkans in the 1990s, NATO established a Balkans CAOC at Vincenza, Italy, to support NATO operations against Serbian and Yugoslavian forces. Allied Force taught the US and its allies many lessons about centralized command, control and execution, and by the time Al-Qaeda's terrorists struck the US on 11 September 2001, the CAOC was considered a weapon system in its own right.

An F-15E drops a 2000lb (907kg) AGM-130 precision-guided weapon. The AGM-130 was used to great effect in the Balkans, destroying ground targets from stand-off distances.

The Global War on Terror

2001–Present

The Al-Qaeda terrorist organization was given sanctuary by the Taliban regime that governed the war-torn country of Afghanistan. For almost a decade during the 1980s the people of Afghanistan had staved off the attempts of the Soviet Union to take control of the country, and its Mujahideen guerrilla fighters had been covertly assisted by the US. Moscow eventually pulled out of the costly Afghan war, but in 1995 the radical Islamic Taliban took power and provided the Al-Qaeda movement with a location from which to operate in relative safety.

Under Operation Enduring Freedom (OEF), the US fronted yet another post-Cold War Coalition in the immediate aftermath of the 11 September 2001 terrorist attacks. The Combined Air Operations Centre (CAOC) for OEF was based at McDill Air Force Base (AFB), Florida, and in October 2001 it generated an Air Tasking Order (ATO) that saw the beginning of a bombing campaign against Afghanistan.

The B-2A Spirit earned a place in the record books for the longest non-stop combat missions ever, which lasted in excess of 40 hours. They carried weapons loads that included GBU-31 2000lb (907kg) Joint Direct Attack Munitions (JDAMs). With the transit time to Afghanistan from the Spirit's home base at

The USAF's B-1B Lancer, better known to its crews as the 'Bone', was an unlikely choice for close air support missions during the opening stages of Operation Enduring Freedom in 2003, but nonetheless performed the role well, offering an unrivalled payload.

The B-2 represents some of the most modern 'stealth' technology in a manned operational aircraft.

Whiteman AFB, Missouri, being so long, the B-2s often took off without having a target assigned to them. As they approached Afghanistan, targets were passed to them via E-3 Sentry AWACS (Airborne Warning And Control System). Targets ranged from terrorist training facilities and the Taliban's few radars and airfields, to command and control facilities.

The B-2 represents some of the

Joint Direct Attack Munitions were one weapon of choice during the campaign to oust the Taliban regime from power in Afghanistan.

most modern 'stealth' technology in a manned operational aircraft, and it is immediately apparent that whereas the F-117 Nighthawk's 'faceted' design bears the hallmarks of 1970s technology, the smooth, clean lines of the B-2 are the products of the extremely powerful computers and software that were available a decade later. It is the aircraft's 'flying wing' design itself that gives the B-2 its first level of radar avoidance, but it also features a reduced aural and infra-red (IR) signature from the exhausts, composite materials and coatings, a

radar absorbent structure, and triangular-shaped leading edges on undercarriage and bomb bay doors that do not reflect radar energy back to the transmitter. And, while the USAF's F-117 used only a laser designator to attack its targets, the B-2 has a very sophisticated AN/APQ-181 radar that can map the ground and sweep the sky, and do so with a very low probability of its emissions being intercepted by enemy electronic listening equipment.

COALITION AIR ASSETS

While the B-2 struck the most important Taliban targets early on, conventional forces formed the backbone of OEF. F-16 Fighting Falcons, F/A-18 Hornets, B-1B Lancers, B-52H Stratofortresses, F-15 Eagles and others all gathered in the

LOCKHEED MARTIN F-22A RAPTOR

Type: single-seat fighter

Powerplant: two 156kN (35,000lb) Pratt & Whitney F119-PW-100
Pitch Thrust vectoring turbofans

Maximum speed: 2132km/h (1325mph)

Service ceiling: 19,912m (65,000ft)

Weights: maximum take-off weight 36,288kg (80,000lb)

Armament: one 20mm (0.787 in) M61A2 Vulcan gun; internal bays
for about 910kg (2,000lb) of bombs and/or missiles

Dimensions: span   13.56m (44ft 6in)
           length   18.9m (62ft 1in)
           height   5.08m (16ft 8in)
           wing area   78.04m² (840sq ft)

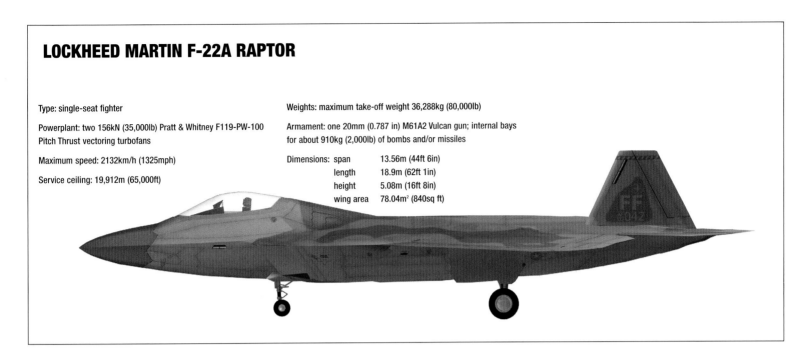

crowded Afghan airspace as the Taliban were driven to the mountains.

Both the AGM-130 and Enhanced GBU-15 stand-off weapons were used throughout the first weeks of the war to hit caves leading to underground facilities. It was the first time that the EGBU-15 had been used in anger, and it was one of just a number of 'firsts' achieved. The latest types of GBU-24, a 2000lb (907kg) laser-guided bomb (LGB), and the 'bunker-busting' 4500lb (2041kg) GBU-28 LGB were also both used for the destruction of reinforced targets and underground facilities. The GBU-28 in particular was targeted at Taliban command and control centres and cave entrances.

Also part of the so-called Global War On Terror was the March 2003 invasion of Iraq, Operation Iraqi Freedom. Iraq posed a much greater threat to the Coalition's air component since Saddam Hussein had consolidated his integrated air defence system (IADS) to form what became known as the Baghdad Super Missile Engagement Zone (MEZ). The Super MEZ was shaped like the head of Walt Disney's Mickey Mouse character, and was a dense array of surface-to-air missile (SAM) systems and AAA. The F-117 would once again penetrate the MEZ to attack Baghdad just as it had in January 1991, but taking out Iraq's IADS was now the

task of the F-16CJ 'Wild Weasel'.

The bulk of the F-16CJ's first Iraq sorties were force protection, operating inside pre-assigned 'kill boxes' into which strike aircraft were routed to attack fixed and mobile targets. Threats that came 'online' within these boxes were struck expeditiously, or scared off-air by the threat of a HARM in flight. These missions were supplemented by the less common force-projection sorties, which saw four-ship flights of F-16CJs fire two HARMs each towards the locations of known threat emitters. Disappointingly for the Coalition, the Super MEZ stayed off-line for the most part, and when it appeared that the 'Wild Weasels' were meeting with almost no resistance, they turned their attention from suppressing the IADS to physically destroying it.

The air war over Iraq in 2003 bore some resemblances to that of 1991, a key difference being that this time around the Iraqi Air Force (IrAF) remained on the ground almost throughout. But this time there were also new technologies emerging that were making the job of ousting Iraq's dictator even easier. The first was the RQ-1 Predator drone that had debuted in the Balkans in 1995, but which was

FROM FIGHTING FALCON TO 'WILD WEASEL'

The USAF's F-16CJ differs from other variants of the F-16 primarily because it features several items of SAM-killing equipment. The most obvious of these is the AN/ASQ-213 HARM Targeting System (HTS). The HTS is a small pod carried on the right side of the engine intake that is used to find, classify, range and display threat emitter systems to the pilot. In doing so, it allows the pilot to cue the AGM-88 High-speed Anti-Radiation Missile (HARM) to specific threat systems. Supplementing the HTS is the AN/ALR-56M radar warning receiver (RWR), the AN/ALQ-131(V)14 electronic countermeasures (ECM) pod, and underwing-mounted chaff dispensers to complement those already mounted on the rear fuselage adjacent to the horizontal stabilizers.

The Taliban in Aghanistan had few SAMs other than short-range, infra-red guided, man-portable weapons like the SA-7 and Stinger. This left the F-16CJ providing close air support and time-sensitive targeting support.

now able to stream live footage into the cockpits of some of the strike fighters over the battlefield. If a Predator unmanned aerial vehicle (UAV) located a target, rather than simply 'talking' the eyes of the pilot or weapons systems officer (WSO) onto it from the ground, the Predator could send footage to show exactly what it looked like. This was very useful against mobile targets when passing a set of fixed coordinates was ineffective.

The Predator 'pay-per-view' was just one part of a number of non-traditional methods of combat for which Operation Iraqi Freedom proved to be a testing ground. New targeting systems, such as the

AN/AAQ-28 Litening II pod were also introduced for the first time during Iraqi Freedom. The Litening II is externally similar to the LANTIRN targeting pod, but internally it offers a number of improved features, including an optical sensor, superior resolution, and a laser spot tracker, for example, that make it more potent. It allows those aircraft so equipped to snoop on the enemy at stand-off ranges, a mission known as Non-Traditional Intelligence, Surveillance and Reconnaissance, or NTISR.

NETWORK-CENTRIC WARFARE
But perhaps the most interesting of concepts developed and matured over Iraq from 2003 is that of network-centric warfare, where the strike aircraft and fighters are all linked to each other and AWACS, RC-135 Rivet Joint and the CAOC by datalinks. The Fighter Data

> If a Predator UAV located a target, rather than simply 'talking' the eyes of the pilot or weapons systems officer (WSO) onto it, the Predator could send footage to show exactly what it looked like.

Below: The General Atomics MQ-1 Predator drone had established itself in the Balkans in the late 1990s, but had become indispensable by the time it reconnoitred the battlefields of Afghanistan and Iraq.

Link (FDL), which allows the likes of the F-15 and F-16 to be sent target and threat data over the 'net' was just ready in time for Operation Enduring Freedom, but its first large-scale test in combat conditions came during Operation Iraqi Freedom (OIF).

Since then, OEF and OIF have continued unabated. In Iraq in particular the war zone has shifted firmly to an urban setting that requires specialist skills to be developed if the insurgency is to be countered. It is a form of conflict that actually brings the pilots participating in it back to the basics of air warfare, and limits the usefulness of some modern technology. It is, in effect, the least desirable form of war that today's pilot or WSO could hope to fight.

Conversely, the latest 'fifth-generation' fighters – the F-22A Raptor and F-35 Lightning II Joint Strike Fighter (JSF) – will combine network-centric information sharing with the latest in stealth characteristics and low probability of intercept active sensors. Essentially another term for

stealth, low observability (LO) was a key design requirement for both the F-22 and the F-35, and it is measured not just in terms of radar signature, but also by electronic emissions and heat, visual, and acoustic signatures.

Clearly, a large radar signature is undesirable since the objective is to

Above: F-15E Strike Eagles flew exhausting missions of up to 14 hours during Enduring Freedom. They employed a mix of JDAMs, LGBs, unguided general-purpose bombs and 20mm cannon to harass and destroy the enemy.

remain undetected by the enemy for as long as possible, but sophisticated airborne IR systems can detect a fighter-size target at a range of more

Replacement for the F-15 Eagle, the USAF's 'fifth-generation' Lockheed Martin F-22A Raptor combines exceptional air-to-air capabilities with a stealthy air-to-ground strike option.

> Essentially another term for stealth, low observability (LO) was a key design requirement for both the F-22 and the F-35.

Under a programme known as Have Glass, the USAF's F-16s received coatings of radar absorbent materials on a number of areas and received a gold-tinted canopy coating.

than 32km (20 miles), so the jet efflux from the exhaust, as well as the hot exhaust nozzle itself, must be either cooled or hidden as much as possible.

In many senses the future of 21st century combat aircraft, the Lockheed Martin F-35 JSF will provide a replacement for the USAF's A-10 and F-16, the US Navy/Marine Corps AV-8B and F/A-18 'legacy' Hornet, and will also be procured by at least eight other NATO air arms.

Likewise, the electronic emissions emanating from the aircraft, whether they be the radar altimeter, the radio or datalink, or the radar itself, must also be controlled; these emissions can be detected from great distances, and are therefore undesirable. In this case, the radar, radio and datalink 'hop' frequencies many thousands of times every second in a bid to ensure that the enemy's scanning equipment, tuned to

a particular range of frequencies, detects no more than a micro-burst of radiation and is therefore unable to determine the precise source or location of the transmissions.

Finally, the visual signature of these aircraft is also important; contrails at certain altitudes can act as a giant 'arrow' in the sky, so the exhaust that creates them can be treated with chemicals carried internally (as has been tested on the B-2), or the aircraft must be flown above the 'contrail level' at which this trail of distinctive condensation occurs.

For those aircraft not built from the ground up with LO technologies, a number of retrospective programmes have been run. Under a programme known as Have Glass, for

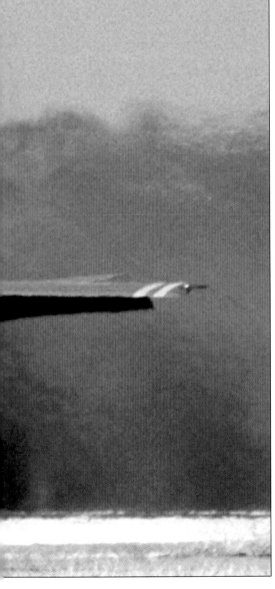

example, the USAF's F-16s received coatings of radar absorbent materials on a number of areas and introduced a gold-tinted canopy coating that helped reduce radar reflections from the cockpit. The B-1B received modified engine intakes that reduced radar energy bouncing back to the emitter, and the RAF has treated its Tornado fleet not only with a radar absorbent coating in specific areas, but also a paint that helps dissipate heat and thereby reduces the aircraft's overall IR signature.

LOOKING TO THE FUTURE

Assuming that the next major global conflict will be fought in a conventional manner between two professional military forces, the ability to gather and share information while remaining unseen by the enemy will almost certainly determine the outcome of the war. Sharing the information securely is the other key to winning, and US and Coalition fighter doctrine is increasingly becoming centred on the ability to impart the same 'picture' of the

The small fleet of F-117A Nighthawk 'stealth fighters' was retired by the US Air Force in 2008, while the B-2A Spirit will remain in service for some years as that air arm's major carrier of free-fall nuclear weaponry. At the same time, the needs of the Global War on Terror have seen the Spirit add increasingly flexible conventional weapons to its inventory.

battlespace to a broad number of 'players'. LO on its own is not enough – it certainly allows the fighter pilot to get into an advantageous position undetected, but every player has to enter the fight with a good degree of situational awareness: knowing where the enemy is and how many of his assets there are, and who is going to engage which target.

Of course, the old adage that even the best-laid plans fall apart when contact is first made with the enemy will always threaten to be a self-fulfilling prophecy. However, the increasingly sophisticated network-centric warfare capabilities of the leading air arms help to mitigate that possibility… or at the very least, reduce the chaos that ensues.

Index

Abyssinia (1935–36) 37
AEG:
    C.IV 21
    G.I 22
Aeritalia G.91 184, *184*, 186, 187, 188
Aermacchi MB.339 *258*
Aerodrome Albatros biplane 12
Aeronautica del Regio Esercito 36
Aérospatiale:
    Alouette III 186, 188, 189, 190, 191, 197
    Super Frelon 238, *243*, 244
Afghanistan 7, 307, 308–9, 310
Afrika Korps 74, 75, 85
AGM-45 Shrike missile 208–9, 247, 258, 263
AGM-62 Walleye missile 223
AGM-78 missile 209
AGM-88 high speed anti-radiation missile (HARM) 292, 293, 309
AGM-114 hellfire air-to-surface missiles *280*, 282
AGM-130 missile 305, *305*, 309
Agusta A109 259, *259*
Aichi D3A1 113, 114, 115, 117, 118, 119, 122, 133
AIM-4 missile *216*, 218–19
AIM-7 Sparrow missile 205, 206, 207, 208, 221, 223, 228, *270*, 287, 291, 292
AIM-9 Sidewinder missile 199, *207*, 214–15, 221, 223, 228, 241, 254, 255, 270, *270*, 287, 288
AIM-120 AMRAAM missile 302, *303*, 304, 305
Air Defence Great Britain (ADGB) 61
Air Launched Anti-Radiation Missiles (ALARMs) 293, 301
air tasking order (ATO) 275, 307
airborne forward air controllers (FACs) 167, 220
Airco:
    D.H.2 14, 15, *16*, 26
    D.H.4 *30*
    D.H.9 30, *31*
Airspeed Horsa 61, 64, 88
air-to-air missiles (AAM) 7, 199, 205, 206, 213, 214, 215, 241, 270, 273, 292
air-to-surface missiles (ASM) *209*, *280*
Akagi 113, 117, 118, 123, 125
Albatros:
    C.X 21
    C.XII 21
    D.I 16
    D.II 16
    D.III 17

D.V. *19*
Albion, HMS 177, 178
Algeria 182, 183–4, 186
Allied Expeditionary Air Force (AEAF) 61
Allied Force, Operation 299, 300, 301, 305
alpha strikes 216
Al-Qaeda 305, 307
AM.39 Exocet missile 255, 256
American Volunteer Group 120
Amiot 354 45
Andersen AFB, Guam 228
Angola 183, 186, *186*, 188–9, 190, 193, 197
anti-aircraft (AA) guns 24, 134
anti-aircraft artillery (AAA) 76, 206, 207, 211, 212, 216, 223, 226, 247, 260, 262, 266, 267, 283, 288, 289, 290, 294, 295, 309
anti-radiation missile 209, 263
anti-submarine warfare (ASW) 253
Anvil, Operation 194
Arado Ar 396 183
Ardent, HMS 256
Argentina 253, 254, 255, 256
Argus, HMS 71, 82
Ark Royal, HMS 72, 73, 82
Armée de l'Air 46, *180*, 184, 234
Armstrong Whitworth:
    Albemarle 60, 61
    Whitley 146, *146*, 150, *150*
atomic bombs 163–4, *163*
Audacity, HMS 67
Austro-Hungarian air arm 35
Avenger, HMS 67
Avia S.199 234
Aviatik:
    biplane 12
    D.I 35, *37*
Avro:
    Anson *65*
    Lancaster *149*, 150, 152, 155, 158, 175, 233
    Lincoln 175, 195, *195*
    Manchester 150, 147, *147*
    Shackleton 196
    Type 504 12
    Vulcan 254, 255, 258, *259*
AWACS 278, 284, 288, 290, 291, 292, 308, 310

BAe Sea Harrier 255, *257*, 258, 299, 305
balloon, hot-air *8–9*, 9, 29
Bangladesh 199
Barbarossa, Operation 92, 94
Bar-Lev Line 244
Battleaxe, Operation 76, 79

Beck, Lieutenant Paul 10
Beira Patrol 196–7
Bell:
    47G 184
    UH-1 'Huey' *200–1*, 202, 203, *203*, 225, *225*, 230, 231, 266, 283
    UH-60 Blackhawk *283*, *293*, 295
Berlin blockade 166
Biafra 192
Big Eye Task Force 213–14
Birmingham, USS 10, 11
Bismarck Sea, Battle of the 129
Bismarck Sea, USS 66, 67, 141
Black Buck, Operation 258
Blackburn:
    Buccaneer *190*, 191
    Skua 40, *41*
Blériot 12, 36
    Type XI 11, 12
Blitzkrieg 39, 46, *93*, 94
Bloch 152 45
Bock's Car 163
Boeing:
    AH-64 Apache 271, 278, *280*
    B-17 Flying Fortress *37*, 58, 88, 89, *89*, 117, 122, 124, 153, 156, *156*, 157, 158, 234, *234*
    B-24 Liberator 58, 66, 69, *69*, 88, 153, 161, *162*
    B-26 Invader 170, 184
    B-26 Marauder 124, 166, 167, 172, 178, 186, *192*, 193
    B-29 Superfortress *142*, 163, *163*, 166, 167, 170, 172
    B-52 Stratofortress 220, *222*, *223*, 225, 226, *228*, 229, 230, 231, 270, 280, 287, 300, 308
    KC-135 Stratotanker 221–2, 279
    RC-135 276, 278, 284, 290
Boelcke, Oswald 15, 17
Borneo 176
Bosnia-Herzegovina 298–9
Boulton Paul Defiant 45, 46, 49
Boxer, USS *175*
Brandenburg 35
Breguet 12, 13
Brereton, Major General Lewis H. 117
Brevity, Operation 76, 79
Brieftauben-Abteilungen (carrier pigeon detachments) 22, 23
Bristol:
    Beaufighter 53, 66, 78, 79, 81, 129, 174, 175, 234
    Belvedere 176, 177, *178*
    Blenheim 44, 54, 55, 78, 91, 92, 119, 146, 147
    Bulldog 91
    F.2B Fighter 17–18, *18*, 21
    Sycamore 179, 183, 195

British Air Forces France (BAFF) 44, 45, 46
British Expeditionary Force (BEF) 43–4, 45, 55
Brooke-Popham, Robert 115
Brown, Russell 168
Bulgarian air arm 11
bunker buster bombs 309
Bunker Hill, USS *140*
bush wars 7, 190
Bush, George W. 278

'cab rank' patrols 63, 183
Cape Eugano, Battle of 136, 140
Caproni 36
Cessna:
    O-2A 229, *229*
    337 196, 197
Chaco War (1932–35) 37
Chain Home radar stations 47
Challe, General Maurice 183–4, 186
Chastise, Operation 154, 155
Chennault, Brigadier General Claire I. 140
China 9, 166, 174, 201
Chiyoda 123, 134
Chromite, Operation 169
Churchill, Winston 31–2, 40, 46, 65, 160
CIA 277
circular error probable (CEP) 302
circus missions 55, 56
close air support (CAS) 166–7, 177, 188, 199, 240, 244, 263
Cold War 6–7, 163, 194, 236
College Eye 216, 218, 223
combat air patrol (CAP) 257, 264, 266, 275
Combat Tree 228, 230
Combined Air Operations Centre (CAOC) 305, 307, 310
Commando Hunt, Operation 220
Congo 192, 193–4
Consolidated:
    B-24 Liberator 69, 141
    PBY-5 Catalina 66, 69, 124
Convair F-102 Delta Dagger 254, 255
Conventional Air-Launched Cruise Missile (CALCM) 280
cookie bomb *151*
co-pilot/gunner (CPG) 277, 278
Coral Sea, Battle of the 122–3
Coral Sea, USS *137*
Cornwall, HMS 119
counter-insurgency (COIN) 173, 181, 188, 190, 194–5, 196, 253
Courageous, HMS 66
Coventry, HMS 256
Crete 72, 76–80, 93

Crissy, Lieutenant Myron 10
Crusader, Operation 79
Cunningham, Randy 227
Curtiss:
   A-1 10
   AB-3 11
   Golden Flyer 10
   P-40 Kittyhawk 84, 88, *88*, 89
   P-40 Tomahawk *84*
   P-40 Warhawk 117, 118, 127
Curtiss, Glenn H. 10
Cypriot Civil War 181
Cyprus 179–80, 181

Daguet, Operation 271
Dambusters raid 154
Dassault:
   Mirage F1 191
   Mirage III 191, 199, 237, 241,
      242, 244, 250, 254, 271, 272,
      273, *273*, *277*, 305
   Mirage IVA 234, 235, 236, 237,
      238, 244, 247, *248–9*
   Ouragan 234, 235, 236, *237*
Dayton Peace Accords 302
de Forest Chandler, Captain Charles
   11
de Gaulle, Charles 187
de Havilland:
   DHC-2 Beaver 195
   Dove 192, 194
   Mosquito 62, 63, 66, 152, 155,
      156, 160, 175
   Sea Venom 175, 179, 181
   Vampire 175, 194, 195, 196, 198,
      234, *235*
de Havilland, Geoffrey 16
Deliberate Force, Operation 299
Deny Flight, Operation 299
Deperdussin 12
Desert Air Force (DAF) 84, 85
Desert Shield, Operation 261, 270
Desert Storm, Operation *273*, 278,
   280, *297*, 301, 304
de Witt Milling, Lieutenant Thomas
   11
DFS 230 *80*
Dietz, Captain Tom 'Vegas' *295*
Doenitz, Admiral 69
Dornier:
   Do 17 39, 40, 47, 49, 78, 92, 94,
      95, *95*, 147, *152*
   Do 27 186, 187, 188
Dorsetshire, HMS 119
Douglas:
   A-4 Skyhawk 152, 208, 209, *211*,
      239, 245, *251*, 254, 261, 272, *288*
   AC-47 Spooky 220
   AD Skyraider 171, *171*, 173, 184,
      207
   C-47 Skytrain 56, 61, 88, *166*,
      172, 181, 183, 186, 188, 197,
      234, 235
   C-117 173, *173*
   DB-7 54

DC-3 Dakota 61, *61*, 64, 176, 195,
   197
F3D Skynight 174
SBD-3 Dauntless *86*, 122, *126*
TBD Devastator *122*, *124*
Dowding, Sir Hugh 46
Driscoll, William 227
dumb bombs *221*, *281*
Dunkirk 46
Dunning, Squadron Commander
   E.H. 17

Eagle, HMS 72, *81*, 82, 83
Eaker, Major General Ira 157
early air wars 8–37
Eastern Solomons, Battle of the
   127–9
Egypt 233, 234, 235, 236, 237, 238,
   239, 240, 241, 242, 244, 245, 246,
   248, 249–51, 258, 259
Egyptian Air Force (EAF) 234, 237,
   238, 241, 246, 250
electronic combat reconnaissance
   (ECR) 300
electronic countermeasures (ECM)
   206, 211, 220, 236, 237, 246, 309
electronic intelligence (ELINT) 206,
   207, 211, 212
electronic order of battle (EOB)
   276, 277
electronic warfare officer (EWO)
   208, 292
Ely, Eugene B. *10*, 10
Enduring Freedom, Operation
   (OEF) 307
English Electric:
   Canberra 175, 178, 180–1, 191,
      191, 194, 197, 199, 255
   Lightning 198
Enhanced ID (EID) 290
Enola Gay 163
Enterprise, USS 121, 124, *124*, 125,
   128, 132, *136*
Esmonde, Lieutenant Commander
   Eugene 56

Fairchild:
   AC-119 220
   C-119 Flying Boxcar 172
   C-123 Provider 225
Fairchild Republic A-10
   Thunderbolt II *268–9*, 270, 272,
      295, *299*, 314
Fairey:
   Albacore *81*
   Firefly 175, *176*
   Fulmar 72, 76, 119
   Swordfish 56, 66, 67, 71, 72, 81
Falklands War 7, 245, *252–3*, 253–8,
   254–5, *256*, *257*, *258*
Fall Gelb (Plan Yellow) 43
Fall Weiss (Plan White) 39
Fallschirmjäger 40–1, 43, 77, *78*, 79
Farman aircraft 12, 36
Felixstowe F.2 30, 31

Fiat:
   CR.32 94
   CR.42 52, 71, 73, 94
   G.50 52
Fighter Data Link (FDL) 310–11
Firedog, Operation 174
First Balkan War (1912–13) 11
First Indochina War 202
Fleet Air Arm 67, 71, 254
Fletcher, Rear Admiral Frank J. 122,
   124
Fleurus, Battle of (1794) 9
Fliegerabteilungen-Infanterie (FLAbt-Inf
   or infantry contact patrol
   detachments) 17
Focke-Wulf:
   Fw 190 56, 58, 59, 64, 88, 153,
      153, 154
   Fw 200 Condor 65, *66*
Focus, Operation 235–6
Fokker 14, 15
   C.X 92, *92*
   D.I 16
   Dr I 20, 21, *23*
   D.VII 21, *24*
   D.XXI 43, 91, *91*
   E.I *Eindecker* 14, *14*
Formidable, HMS 78
frei jagd (free chase) 47, 48, 54, 55,
   72, 84
Frente de Libertação de
   Moçambique (FRELIMO) 187–8
Fouga Magister 238, 240, *241*
Furious, HMS 17, 30, *81*

Garland, D. E. 45
Garros, Lieutenant Roland 13
GBU-15 precision-guided glide
   bombs 299, 300, *300*, 305, 309
General Aircraft Hamilcar 61
General Atomics MQ-1 Predator
   drone 310, 311, *311*
General Dynamics:
   F-111 273, 300
   EF-111 Raven 271, 275, 286
Gibson, Wing Command Guy 154,
   155
Glamorgan, HMS 256
Global War on Terror 6, 7, 307–15
Glorious, HMS 41
Gloster:
   Gauntlet 92
   Gladiator 41, 71, 73, *74*, 76, 77,
      92
   Javelin 178, 196
   Meteor 62, 63, 178, 195, 234
Gneisenau 147
Goebbels, Dr Josef 158
Gomorrah, Operation 157, 158
Gordian Knot, Operation 189
Göring, Reichmarschall Hermann
   48, 50, *50*, 51
Gotha 23, 24
   G.II 23
   G.III 25

G.IV 25
GPS (Global Positioning System) 6,
   282, 302, 305
Granby, Operation 270
Gray, Sergeant T. 45
Greece 71, 72, 73, 75, 77, 80, 181
Ground Moving Target (GMT) 298
Grumman:
   A-6 Intruder *216*, 227, *227*, 271,
      287
   E-2 Hawkeye 265, 266, *266*, 271,
      278
   F-14 Tomcat 271, 287
   F4F Wildcat (Martlet) 67, 69, *86*,
      114, 115
   F6F-3 Hellcat 128, 132, *132*, 134,
      135, *136*, 143
   F9F Panthers 168, 171, 174
   SB2 Helldiver 128, 134
Guadalcanal 126–8, 129

Hailstone, Operation 132
Halberstadt:
   CL.II 21
   CL.III 21
   D.II 16
Halsey, Vice Admiral William F. 121,
   139
Handley Page:
   Halifax 147, 150, 152, 155, *155*,
      233
   Hampden 146, 152
   Hastings 177, 178, 181
   O/100 25, *29*
   O/400 26, *32*
   V/1500 28
   Victor 255, *256*, 270
Hansa-Brandenburg W.29 29
Harris, Arthur 150, *150*, 151, 155,
   160
Have Glass 314–15
HAWK surface-to-air missile 120,
   241, 283
Hawker:
   Hunter 177, 178, *179*, 181, 196,
      199, 237, 240, 246
   Hurricane *43*, 44, 45, 46, 47, 49,
      52, 55, 56, 67, 71, 74, 75, 76,
      76, 77, 78, 79, 80, *81*, 82,
      86–7, 119, 120, 150
   Sea Fury 170, 198, *198*
   Sea Hawk 45, 181, 183, *183*, 199
   Tempest 63, 175
   Typhoon 58, 63
Hawker Siddeley Harrier 256, 271,
   295, 301
head-up display (HUD) *287*, 288,
   300
Heinkel:
   He 110 49
   He 111 39, 40, 45, 46, 48, 72, 78,
      94, 95, *95*
Henschel Hs 123 39
Hermes, HMS 119, 254
Hinton, Bruce H. 168

Hirohito, Emperor 143
Hiroshima 6, 142, 163
Hiryu 113, 115, 117, 118, 123, 126
Hispano-Suiza 16–17
Hitler, Adolf 39, 40, 41, 50, 51, 52, 59, 61, 72, 74, 77, 78–9, 81–2, 89, 91, 92, 93, 147, 151–2, 160
Hiyo 132, 134
Hornet, USS 118, 121, 124, 126, 127
Hosho 123
Hotchkiss machine-gun 13
Hudson, William G. 166
Husky, Operation 88
Hussein, Saddam 261, 271, 273, 296, 309
Hwang, Captain Jeff 304

IADS 274, 275, 278, 294, 309
IFF (Identification Friend or Foe) 218, 285, 290, 291–2
Igloo White 226
Illustrious, HMS 72
Ilyushin:
    DB-3 91–2
    IL-28 177, 181, 192
Immelmann, Max 15
Imperial Japanese Army Air Force (JAAF) 113, 117, 118, 119–20, 128, 135, 137, 141
Imperial Japanese Navy Air Force (JNAF) 113, 116, 128, 129, 133, 134
    21st Air Flotilla 113, 116–17
    22nd Air Flotilla 113, 115–16, 117, 119, 131, 132, 133
    23rd Air Flotilla 116, 118, 133
    24th Air Flotilla 127
    25th Air Flotilla 128
    26th Air Flotilla 128, 131, 132, 133
    61st Air Flotilla 133
imperial policing 35
Imphal, Battle of 141
Independent Force (IF) 26, 28
Indian Air Force (IAF) 197–8, 199
Indomitable, HMS 81
Indonesian Confrontation 176–80
Indo-Pakistan Wars 197–9, *197*, *198*
Infra-red (IR) signature 308
Invincible, HMS 254, 255
Iraq 7, 240, 247, 269, 270–98, 304
Iraq Air Force (IrAF) 273, 274, 275, 276, 277, 284, 287, 290, 295, 309
Iraqi Freedom, Operation 309, 310
Israel 233–51, 258, 259, 260, 261, 262
Israeli Defence Air Force (IDF/AF) 233, 234, 235, 236, 237, 238, 239, 240, 241, 242, *243*, 244, 245, 246, 247, 248, 249–50, 251, 258, 259, 260, 261, 262, 263, 264, 265, *265*, 266, 267
Italy 11, 36, 71, 72, 88–9, 95, 157

Jabara, James J. 171

Jagdgeschwader 50–1
Jagdstaffen (*Jasta*) (German fighter squadrons) 17, 18–19
jammers 208, 211–12, 215, 271
Japan 112–43
Johnson, Lyndon 202, 207, 212, 222
Joint Direct Attack Munitions (JDAM) 301, 302, 307, 308
Jordan 237, 239, 240, 241, 242, 249, 258
Junkers:
    J.I 21
    Ju 52 39, 40, 45, 77–8, *78*, *79*, 80, 86, 88
    Ju 55 77
    Ju 86 94
    Ju 87 39, 40, 46, 47, 48, 49, 72, 74, 75, 88, 92, 94
    Ju 88 46, 47, 49, 53, 67, 72, 74, 78, 82, 83, 92, 147
    Ju 90 88
Junyo 132

Kaga 113, 117, 123, 126
Kamikaze aircraft *140*, 141, 143
Kampfstaffen (battle squadrons) 22, 23, 54
Kashmir 197
Kelk, Captain Jon 292
Kenney, Major General George C. 129, 136
Kenya 194, 195–6
Kohima, Battle of 141
Korean War 7, 165–74
Kosovo 299
Kuwait 272, 288

Lamb, Dean I. 11
LANTIRN (Low Altitude Navigation and Targeting Infra-red for Night) 276, 288, 310
laser guided bomb (LGB) 223, 265, 309
Lebanon 7, 244, 258–67
Leigh Light 66
Leigh-Mallory, Air Vice Marshall 54
Lexington, USS 118, 122, 124, *124–5*
Leyte Gulf, Battle of 136
Linebacker, Operation 227, 228, 229, 230, 231
Lloyd, Air Vice Marshall 83
Lockheed:
    AC-130 Spectre 220
    C-130 Hercules 147, 177, 194, 199, *213*, 226, 270, 272
    C-5 Galaxy 272
    EC-121D Warning Star 213–14
    F-104 Starfighter 181, 197, 198
    F-117 Nighthawk 271, 279, 280, 282–3, *282*, 284, 288, 291, 292, 304, *304*, 305, 308, 309, *315*
    F-80 Shooting Star 166, 168, 170, 173, 174
    Hudson 65, 66
    P-2 Neptune 255

P-3 Orion 277
T-33 Shooting Star 199
U-2 206, 211, 271, *279*
Lockheed Martin:
    F-16 Fighting Falcon 7, 264, 266, 270–1, 272, *273*, 287, *300*, *301*, 304, 305, 308, 309, *310*, 311
    F-22A Raptor 309, *309*, 312
    F-35 Joint Strike Fighter 312, *314*
Locusta, Operation 272
LORAN (long-range navigation) 225–6
low observability (LO) 312, 314
Luftstreitkräfte (German air arm) 17
Luftwaffe 39, 40, 41, 43, 46, 48, 50, 54, 56, 58, 59, 65, 69, 72, 77, 78, 80, 82, 83, 84, 85, 89, 95, 145, 147, 151, 152, 154, 157, 161, 162
Lynx HAS.Mk 2 253

MacArthur, General Douglas 117, 130, 131, 168, *168*, 170, 171
Macchi:
    MC.200 71, *72*, 92
    MC.202 Folgore 79, 88
Maddox, USS 202
Malayan Emergency 174–6, 178
Malta 71, 80–4
Mandalay, Battle of 141
man-portable air defence system (MANPADS) 295
Marine Fliegerabteilung 28
Marine Luftschiffabteilung 28
Marita, Operation 92
Martin B-10 *37*
Masson, Didier 11
Mau Mau 195–6
Maynard, Commander F.H.M. 71
McCurdy, James 10
McDonnell Douglas:
    F/A-18 Hornet 175, 271, *303*, 308
    F-15 Strike Eagle 261, *262*, 265, *265*, 266, 275, *276*, 284, *287*, 288–9, 290, 291, 292, *295*, 298, 299, 300, 302, 304, *305*, 308, 311, *312*, *313*
    F-4 Phantom II 79, 203–4, 205, *205*, 211, 215, 213, *218*, 219, 220, 221, *221*, 223, 228, 229, 230, *232–3*, 239, 242, 245, 247, 248, 249, *249*, 250, 262, *263*, 264, 267, 271, 285, 293, 300, 301
McDonnell:
    F2H Banshee 170
    RF-101 Voodoo 211, 215
Merkur, Operation 77, 78, 93–4
Messerschmitt:
    Bf 109 43, 46, 47, 49, 52, *52*, *53*, 56, 58, 72, *75*, 76, 79, 82, 83, 84, 88, 95, 146, 147, 154
    Bf 110 39, 40, 43, 46, 47, 48, *48*, 52, 74, 75, *77*, 78, 146, 147
    Me 262 64, 65

Me 323 *85*, 88
Middle East, wars 1945–73 233–51
Midway, Battle of 121–5, *125*
Mikoyan-Gurevich:
    MiG-3 95
    MiG-15 168, 170, 171, 174, 234
    MiG-17 177, 187, 188, 189, 190, 192, 203, 205, 206, 216, 222–3, 227, *236*, 237, 240, 242, 244, 246, *250*
    MiG-19 177, 198, 216, 242, 244
    MiG-21 'Fishbed' 188, 189, 191, 199, 212–13, *214*, 215, 216, 223, 227, *236*, 239, 239, *241*, 242, 245, 246, 266, 273, 275, *275*, 290, 302
    MiG-23 266, 273
    MiG-25 273–4, 290
    MiG-29 273, 275, 290, 291, *291*, 292, 302, 304, 305
Mil:
    Mi-8 189, 190, 246
    Mi-24 296
Milosevic, Slobodan 299
Minh, Ho Chi 201, 202, 220, 224
Missile Engagement Zone (MEZ) 283, 292, 309
Mississippi, USS 11
Mitscher, Admiral Marc A. 132
Mitsubishi:
    A6M2 113, 114, 117, 118, *118*, 119, 122, 123, 132, 134
    G3M 114, 116, 117, 118, 119
    G4M 116, 117, 118, 119
    Ki-21 115, 117, *118*, 120
    Ki-27 116, 120
    Ki-43 116
    Ki-48 115
    Ki-49 117
Mobile Force 120–1, 134
Montgolfier brothers 9
Montgomery, General 62, 86, 87
Moonlight Sonata, Operation 173
Morane-Saulnier:
    MS.500 183
    Type L 13, 14
Movimento Popular de Libertação de Angola (MPLA) 186, 189, 190
Mozambique 183, 184, 189, 196, 197
Mussolini, Benito 71, 72, 92

Nagasaki 6, *163*
Nagumo, Vice Admiral Chuichi 113, 123
Nakajima:
    B5N2 113, 114, 115, 117, 118, 119, 122, 123
    B6N2 134
Namibia 189, 190, 193
Nasser, Colonel 180
National Security Agency (NSA) 218
Naval Air Squadron (NAS) 41, 56, 71
Niagara, Operation 226
Nieuport 12, 36

Nie.10 14
Nie.11 14
Nie.17 15
Nigeria 192
Nimitz, Admiral Chester W. 118
Nisshin 123
Nixon, Richard 231
Noble Anvil, Operation 300
Non-Cooperative Target
    Recognition (NCTR) 291
Non-Traditional Intelligence,
    Surveillance and Reconnaissance
    (NTISR) 310
North American:
    A-36 Invader 88
    B-25 Mitchell 121, 177, 178
    F-100 Super Sabre 179–80, 181,
        187, 208, 214, 214, 220
    F-51 Mustang 166, 167, 174
    F-82 Twin Mustang 166
    F-86 Sabre 168, 170, 171, 172,
        173, 174, 184, 194, 197, 197,
        199
    P-51 Mustang 60, 60, 63, 160,
        160, 161, 161, 177, 234, 235
    T-6 Harvard 194, 195, 197, 234
    T-28 Trojan (Fennec) 181, 181,
        183, 194
North Atlantic Convoys:
    PQ-16 67
    PQ-17 67
North Atlantic Treaty Organization
    (NATO) 299–300, 302, 305, 314
North Korea 165–74
North Vietnamese Air Force (NVAF)
    203, 206, 212, 216, 218, 221, 223,
    227, 230
Northrop F-5 88
Northrop Grumman B-2 Spirit 301,
    301, 307–8, 314, 315

Ocean, HMS 183
offensive counter-air (OCA) 300
Overlord, Operation 59, 61
Ozawa, Admiral Jisaburo 134

Pakistani Air Force (PAF) 198, 199
Palestine 233, 240, 262
Palestinian Liberation Organization
    (PLO) 258, 267
Panavia Tornado 270, 272, 287,
    293–4, 295, 300, 301
Parmalee, Philip O. 10
Pathfinder Force (PFF) 153
Paulhan, Louis 10
Paveway 223
e for Galilee, Operation 266,
    275

112–13, 113, 114, 115,

on Army of
) 191
    on 11
    of the 132

Piazza, Capitano Carlo 11
Pilot Night Vision Sensor (PNVS)
    277, 279
Piper:
    Comanche 194
    Tomahawk 79, 80
Polikarpov:
    I-15 91
    I-16 92, 95
    Po-2 172
Portugal 183, 184, 186
Portuguese Air Force (FAP) 187,
    189
precision-guided munitions (PGM)
    223
Prince of Wales, HMS 115, 116
Princeton, USS 137
Prinz Eugen 147
Provide Comfort, Operation 296
pulse repetition frequency (PRF)
    285
Puma helicopter 191
PZL:
    P.11c 39, 39, 40, 40
    P.24 94
    P.37 Los 39

Quénault, Caporal 13
Quick Reaction Capability (QRC)
    211, 215, 216, 218

RAAF (Royal Army Air Force) 74,
    118, 129, 136, 167, 169, 174, 177
radar
    AI Mk III 52
    AN/APG-63 266, 285, 287, 290,
        291, 304
    AN/APQ-181 308
    ASV (Airborne Surface Vessel) 69
    ASV Mk II 66
    Bar Lock 213
    Chain Home radar stations 47
    E-8 JSTARS (Joint Surveillance
        Target Radar System) 296, 298
    Early warning chain 56
    Fan song 208, 209, 211
    Fire can 206, 209, 211
    Flat Face 213
    Ground Controlled Interception
        (GCI) 53, 203, 206, 213, 215,
        223, 227, 266, 274, 276, 285
    MSQ-77 Combat Skyspot 225,
        226
    Pin Song 206
Radar homing and warning
    (RHAW) 208, 209
Radar warning receiver (RWR) 260,
    292
radar intercept officers (RIOs) 227
Rader, Phillip 11
RAF (Royal Air Force) 12, 18, 24,
    31, 41, 43, 45, 50, 53, 55, 56,
    61, 73, 75, 115, 145, 157, 160,
    161, 162, 174, 177, 255, 270,
    294, 301

Advanced Air Striking Force
    (AASF) 44, 46
Bomber Command 45, 46, 47,
    48, 67, 145, 146, 147, 150,
    151, 152, 153, 154, 156, 160,
    162
Coastal Command 65, 66, 69
Fighter Command 45, 48, 51, 56
Mediterranean Command 71
Squadrons
    No. 8 194
    No. 20 179
    No. 29 194
    No. 46 41
    No. 41 49
    No. 44 152
    No. 60 120
    No. 66 54, 178
    No. 67 120
    No. 72 49
    No. 73 49
    No. 79 49
    No. 97 152
    No. 139 55
    No. 141 49
    No. 213 86
    No. 417 82
    No. 605 49
    No. 616 49, 62
    No. 617 154, 154
    No. 800 176
    No. 827 176
Ramrod, Operation 56
Ranger, USS 86
Regia Aeronautica 71, 81
Reisenflugzeugabteilungen (Rfa) 501
    24
Reisenflugzeugabteilungen (Rfa) 502
    24
remotely piloted vehicles (RPV)
    263–4
Republic:
    F-84 Thunderjet 168, 170, 173,
        174, 174, 179, 181, 183, 186,
        234
    F-105 Thunderchief 204, 205,
        208, 209, 211, 213, 215, 216,
        220, 230, 292
    P-38 Lightning 60, 88, 130,
        161
    P-39 Airacobra 127
    P-47 Thunderbolt 58, 131, 157,
        157, 161
Republic of Korea Air Force
    (RoKAF) 167
Repulse, HMS 115, 116
Reynolds, L. R. 45
Rhodesia 196, 197
Richthofen, Manfred Freiherr von
    18, 19, 20
Ridgway, General Matthew 171
Roadstead, Operation 56
Rockwell B-1 Lancer 306–7, 308, 315
Rommel, General Erwin 74, 75, 80,
    81, 84, 85, 86

Royal Aircraft Factory:
    B.E.2 12
    S.E.5a 21, 29
Royal Australian Air Force (RAAF)
    115
Royal Engineers, Air Battalion 10
Royal Air Force see RAF
Royal Flying Corps (RFC) 11, 15, 16,
    18, 24, 26
    No 8. Squadron 14
    No 24 Squadron 14
    27 Group 26
    41st Wing 25, 26
    83rd Wing 26
    87th Wing 26
Royal Naval Air Service (RNAS) 11,
    15, 16, 18, 24, 26, 28, 30, 31, 33
Royal Navy 54, 66, 72, 78, 178, 196,
    253, 299
Royal New Zealand Air Force
    (RNZAF) 174, 177
Rumpler C.V. 21
Russian Civil War (1918–21) 37
Russo-Polish War (1919–20) 37
Ryujo 117, 118, 127, 132

SA-2 'Guideline' surface-to-air
    missile 206, 207, 208, 208, 211,
    212, 213, 227, 239, 259, 295
SA-6 missile 259–60, 265, 300, 305
Safraan, Operation 191
Samar, Battle of 136, 139
Santa Cruz, Battle of 130
Saratoga, USS 118, 141
Savoia-Marchetti SM.79 70–1, 71, 72
Sceptic, Operation 191
Scharnhorst 147
Schramme, Jean 194
Schwarzlose machine-guns 37
Scud missile 284, 288, 289, 298
Scalion, Operation 52
Second Indochina War 202
semi-active radar-bombing (SARH)
    302
SEPECAT Jaguar GR.Mk 1 270, 271,
    295, 301
Sheffield, HMS 256
Shoho 118, 122
Shokaku 117, 118, 119, 122, 127, 134
Short:
    seaplane 11
    Stirling 147, 147, 148, 152
    Sunderland 40, 66, 175
    Type 184 33, 33
short take-off and landing (STOL)
    176, 177, 179
Sibuyan Sea, Battle of the 136–7
Sicily 78, 80, 82, 84, 88, 157
Siemens-Schuckert D.III 21
Sikorsky:
    AH-3 11
    CH-53 Super Stallion 231, 246,
        260–1, 297
    EH-60 Quick Look 278

HO3S Dragonfly 167–8, *175*
Ilya Muromets 21, *25*, 31
S-58 238
Sims, USS 122
Sir Galahad, HMS 256
Sir Tristram, HMS 256
Six-Day War (1967) 235–9, 242, 246, 258
smart weapons 285
SOKO G-4 Super Galeb 299
Sopwith:
    1½-Strutter 15
    Camel 18, *22*, 30
    Pup 14, *17*, 22
    Tabloid 24
    Triplane 16, 17, 21, 23
Soryu 113, 115, 117, 118, 123, 126
South African Air Force (SAAF) 74, 167, *189*, 191, 192
South Korea 165–74
South West Africa Peoples Organization (SWAPO) 190
Soviet Union 52, 56, 166, 201, 206, 246, 274
SPAD:
    S.VII 16, 17, 18
    S.XIII 18
Spanish Civil War (1936–39) 37
Special Air Service (SAS) 253
Spruance, Rear Admiral Raymond 124
SRO-2 transponders 216, 218
Stalin, Josef 91
stealth:
    aircraft 279, 280, 301, 315, *315*
    weapons 285
St Lo, USS 136, 136
Strangle, Operation 171–3
Sud Aviation Vautour 236, 237, *239, 246*
Suez Canal 85, 180–3, *180*, 234–5, 237, 242, *242*, 244, 246, 247, 250
Super, Operation *189*
Surigao Strait, Battle of the 136, 137, 139
Sukhoi:
    S-55 184
    Su-7 191, *191*, 199, 239, 242, 244, *244*, 245, 246
    Su-20 273
    Su-22 192
    Su-23 273
    Su-24 273
    Su-27 *7*
Supermarine:
    Seafire 175, *176*

Spitfire 45, *45*, 46, 47, 52, 54, 55, 56, 58, 63, *81*, 82–3, 84, 86, 88, 89, 149, 150, 156–7, 174, *175*, 197, 233, 234
suppression of enemy air defence (SEAD) 293, 295
surface-to-air missiles (SAMs) 187, 188, 189, 192, 206, 207, 208–9, *208*, 216, 227, 230, 244, 245, 247, 248, 250, 251, 258–60, 262, 263, 264, 265, 275, 276, 279, 283, *292*, 295, 302, 310
Syria 234, 235, 237, 238, 241, 245, 247, 248, 249, 250, 258, 260, 265, 266, 267

Tactical Air Control Centre (TAAC) 275, 297–8
Taiho 134
Taliban 307, 308, 309, 310
Target Acquisition and Designation Sight (TADS) 277, 278–9
Target Identification System Electro Optical (TISEO) 228, 229
Taube monoplane 12
Thud (F*209*, 215
Tibbets, Colonel Paul *142*
Tobruk 75, 80, 85
Tonkin Incident 202–3, 212
Torch, Operation 86, 87
TOW anti-armour missiles 267
Transall C-160 181, 191
transporter-erector launchers (TELs) 259, 264
Treaty of Versailles 39
Trenchard, Colonel Hugh 24
Triumph, HMS 175, *176*
Tshombe, Moise 194
Tupolev Tu-16 177, 240, 246, 247, *247*, 273
Turkey 11, 33, 179, 181

U-boats 65, 66, *68*, 69, 81, 82, 147
União National para a Independência (UNITA) 189, 192, 193
Union (balloon) 9
United Arab Emirates 272
United Nations (UN) 166, 167, 168, 170, 172, 173–4, 179, 183, 193, 194, 197, 233, 241, 251, 296, 298–9
United States Air Force (USAF) 62, 153, 158, 166, 167, 168, *169*, 166–7, 168, 170, 171, 173, 174, 194, 200–31, 269–315

Far East Air Force (FEAF) 113, 117, 136
United States Army 19, 141
United States Army Air Force (USAAF) 58, 61, 87, 88, 114, 118, *121*, 124, 127, 129, 130, 136, 140–1, 143, 153, 156, 157, 162, 163
United States Civil War (1861–65) 9
United States Marine Corps (USMC) 11, 114, 126, 127, 141, 143, 166, 167, 168, 170, 172, 174, 203, 212, 226, 271, 272, 295, *297*, 314
United States Navy (USN) 10, 11, 113, 118, 114, *115*, 123, 126, 130, 133, 139, 141, 143, 167, 168, 171, 203, 205, 206, *210*, 211, 212, 214, 221, 222–3, 227, 251, 272, 277

Valley Forge, USS 171
Vickers:
    F.B.5 'Gunbus' *12*, 13
    Valettas 176, 181
    Valiant 180
    Wellington 66, 73, 146, 150, 151, *151*, 152
Viet Cong (VC) 224
Vietnam War 7, 200–31, 263, 275, 285, 290, 295, 304
Victorious, HMS *81*
Voisin 12, 13
von Rosen, Count Carl Gustav 192
Vought:
    A-7 Corsair II 271, 287, 293
    F4U Corsair 128, *141*, 143, 167, 172, 173, *175*, 181, 183, *183*, 184, 227
    F-8 Crusader 205, 213, 215
V-weapons (WWII) 59, 60, 61, *160*

Waco Hadrian 59, 61, 88
War of Attrition 241, 242, 243–4, 251, 258–9, 263
Wasp, HMS 83
Wavell, Sir Archibald 73
weapons systems officer (WSO) 266, 276, 285, 288, 300, 310, 311
Westland:
    Wasp HAS Mk 1 253
    Wessex
        HAS.Mk 3 253
        HU.Mk 5 *178*
'Wild Weasel' 208–9, *208, 209*, 216, 229, 231, 239, 242, 275, 292, 309

Wilhelm II, Kaiser 22
World War I 6, 10–11, 12, 13–37, *12, 13, 16, 17, 18–19, 20, 21, 22, 23, 24, 25, 26, 27, 28, 29, 30, 31, 32, 33, 34, 35, 36, 37*
World War II 21, 28, 35–6, *38*, 197, 201, 233
    African and the Mediterranean *70*, 71–89
    Augsberg Raid 152
    Baedecker Blitz 152
    Battle of Berlin 160
    Battle of Britain 46–54, *47, 50–1*, 147
    Battle of the Ruhr 155–6
    D-Day 60–1, 63
    Dieppe Landings *54*, 56, 58
    Operation Baseplate 64
    Operation Market Garden 69, 62
    Operation Overlord *59*, 61
    Operation Ramrod 56
    Operation Roadstead 56
    Operation Sealion 52
    Strategic Bombing 145–63
    The Eastern Front 91–111
    The Pacific 6, 112–43
    War in the West 39–69
Wright brothers 10
Wright Type B biplane 10, 11

Yakovlev:
    Yak-9 166
    Yak-18 172
Yamamoto, Admiral 123
Yamato 143
Yom Kippur War 245–51, 263
Yorktown, USS 118, 122, 124, 126, *127*, 132
Yugoslavia 298–302

Zaire 186, 194
Zambia 191, 195, 196, 197
Zeppelin:
    Z.I.X. 24
Zeppelin-Staaken:
    R.IV 26, *26*
    R.VI 24, 28
Zimbabwe 197
Zuiho 127, 133
Zuikoku 117, 119, 122
Zumbach, Jan 192

Picture Credits

All artworks courtesy of Art-Tech/Aerospace
All photographs courtesy of Art-Tech/Aerospace except for the following:

Art-Tech/MARS: 22, 28, 32, 34, 62, 70–71, 73, 77, 78, 80–82, 86, 114, 120–123, 147–149, 159, 160, 162, 163t, 166, 180, 185, 203, 207, 209–211, 213, 215, 221, 224, 226, 267
Cody Images: 125, 127–129, 134, 150, 177, 187, 189b, 192, 195–197, 200–201, 202, 222, 223, 225, 227, 230, 231, 234, 243, 254, 256, 259, 262–264
Corbis: 186 (Francoise de Mulder), 188 (Patrick Chauvel/Sygma), 236, 242 (David Rubinger), 268–269

(Aero Graphics Inc.), 284
Getty Images: 194, 260–261
Rex Features: 257
Ukrainian State Archive: 96, 97, 99
US Department of Defense: 8–9, 27, 44 126, 130, 135–137, 140–142, 144–1 204, 205, 212, 214, 220, 271–275, 285–314